FIFTH AVENUE

FIFTH

AVENUE

by
THEODORE JAMES Jr.

with Photographs by Elizabeth Baker

 WALKER AND COMPANY · NEW YORK

PHOTOGRAPHS BY ELIZABETH BAKER appear as the frontispiece and on pages 2, 6, 50-51, 53, 96-97, 98, 110, 112, 113, 114, 115, 117, 186, 187, 188, 189, 194-195, 196-197, 199, 200, 201, 202, 203, 208, 209, 210-211, 244-245, 248-249, 250, 251, 252, 253, 256, 257, 275, 282, 284, 285, 286, 287, 288, 289, 290-291, 292, 293, 294, 295, 296-297, 298, 299, 300, 301, 302, 303

PHOTOGRAPHS REPRODUCED THROUGH THE COURTESY OF THE MUSEUM OF THE CITY OF NEW YORK appear on pages 10-11, 14-15, 20-21, 22-23, 25, 56-57, 60-61, 62-63, 64-65, 66-67, 68-69, 90-91, 99, 104-105, 122-123, 144-145, 146, 147, 150-151, 160-161, 192-193, 204-205, 258, 274, 276-277, 278-279, 280-281

PHOTOGRAPHS FROM THE J. CLARENCE DAVIES COLLECTION, REPRODUCED THROUGH THE COURTESY OF THE MUSEUM OF THE CITY OF NEW YORK, appear on pages 16-17, 48-49, 92-93, 94-95, 108-109, 148-149, 206-207

PHOTOGRAPHS BY BYRON FOR THE BYRON COLLECTION, REPRODUCED THROUGH THE COURTESY OF THE MUSEUM OF THE CITY OF NEW YORK, appear on pages 102-103, 116, 152-153, 190-191, 212-213, 259

PHOTOGRAPHS FROM THE EDWARD W. C. ARNOLD COLLECTION (LENT BY THE METRO-POLITAN MUSEUM OF ART), REPRODUCED THROUGH THE COURTESY OF THE MUSUEM OF THE CITY OF NEW YORK, appear on pages 8-9, 18-19, and 58-59

PHOTOGRAPHS REPRODUCED THROUGH THE COURTESY OF THE NEW YORK HISTORICAL SOCIETY, NEW YORK CITY, appear on pages 12-13, 54-55, 70-71, 72-73, 100-101, 106-107, 111, 118-119, 120-121, 154-155, 156, 157, 158-159, 184, 246-247

THE PHOTOGRAPH REPRODUCED THROUGH THE COURTESY OF GENE MOORE, appears on page 283

Copyright ©1971 by Theodore James, Jr.

First published in the United States of America in 1971 by the Walker Publishing Company, Inc.

Published simultaneously in Canada by Fitzhenry & Whiteside, Limited, Toronto.

ISBN: 0-8027-0361-5

Library of Congress Catalog Card Number: 76-161109

Designed by Carl Weiss

Printed in the United States of America.

For
my MOTHER
and
FATHER

CONTENTS

ACKNOWLEDGMENTS

I would first like to express my gratitude to my dear friend James Fox who, one day over the asparagus, suggested that I write this book and to Helen d'Alessandro, now Mrs. Anthony Hecht, my editor, whose patience, understanding, and encouragement have been so important to me. I would also like to express special thanks to my loyal friend Betsy Baker, whose photographs have added so much to this volume.

In addition, I am grateful to Marise Campbell Blair, Pauline Bogardus Werth, Florence Somers, Sue Lyman, Jerome Zerbe, Wilette Ockenden, and Ed Cee for sharing many hours of delightful reminiscences with me.

Thanks are also due the following, who have contributed interest, time, encouragement or assistance: Louis Herndon Werth, Anne Richards, Sue Cunningham Blair, Stanley Korab, Elizabeth Peer, David Bickimer, Richard Kagan, John and Brenda Scranton, Andrew Stasiuk, Susan Madden, William Johns, Anne Hopkins, Robert Brower, Robin Moles, Peter and Martine Baschnonga, Tom and Elaine August, Ellen Kerney, Herman Wertz, David and Alice Brown, Duncan Hoxworth, Barbara Miller, Richard and Nancy Mullan, Barbara Bikle, Charles Naylor, Gerald and Diana Raibourn, Dorothy Pitman, Jill Krementz, Ted and Ima Ziebko, Susanne Stack, Lee and Sally Abell, Kenna Hudson, James K. Page, Jane Litzenberg, and Alicia Tysciewicz. Special thanks are also due my basset hound William Ackerwood Findlay and my nephew Jay Christopher James, who kept me company during the long period of researching and writing this book.

I would also like to express my appreciation to Mr. Albert Baragwanath and Charlotte La Rue of the Museum of the City of New York, and Mr. John Preston of the University Club. Thanks also to the staffs at the following for their assistance: Metropolitan Museum of Art, the Frick Collection, the New York Public Library, the Salmagundi Club, the Church of the Ascension, St. Thomas Church, Grace Episcopal Church, Marble Collegiate Church, the First Presbyterian Church, St. Patrick's Cathedral, Temple Emanu-El, the Solomon R. Guggenheim Museum, the Jewish Museum, the New York Historical Society, and the Union Club. Special thanks are due the ladies of the Madison, New Jersey, public library who provided substantial assistance in leading me to obscure material.

Thanks are also due the public relations staffs of Lord and Taylor, Tiffany and Co., Cartier, Inc., Saks Fifth Avenue, Bonwit Teller, Bergdorf Goodman Co., B. Altman and Company, Arnold Constable, Franklin Simon, the St. Regis Hotel, the Gotham Hotel, the Hotel Pierre, the Sherry-Netherland Hotel, the Plaza Hotel, and Rockefeller Center.

INTRODUCTION

For more than a century, Fifth Avenue has been known throughout the world as America's Avenue of Avenues, one of the most elegant and dazzling boulevards on earth. While gaining this renown, it has served four different purposes: it has mirrored the history of New York geographically, economically, and politically; it has been a showcase of architectural taste in New York; it has been the center of the social history of the city and to a great extent of the country; and finally, it has reflected the history of the country itself.

In its first age, which lasted from 1824 until 1850, the Avenue was an extension of "Little Old New York," the area that today extends from the Battery north to Houston Street. During this period, it was lined with the residences of families descended from prerevolutionary Dutch and English settlers in the Hudson Valley. Following that, it became the thoroughfare of the newly arrived merchant class, with Belmonts, Astors, Vanderbilts, and Goulds taking up residence. The Golden Age, from 1890 until World War I, saw the building of ostentatious palaces up and down the Avenue by hundreds of American multimillionaires. During the fourth age, the Avenue became a retailer's showcase for all the best that America has produced in consumer goods.

During all its history, the Avenue has served as the grand processional thoroughfare of the country and the focal point for the city's enthusiasm for new styles, fads, causes, personalities, and newsworthy events. Such activity survives on the Avenue to this day, although more recently it has also become a forum for social and political demonstrations. This cult of the new has unquestionably helped to make New York the dynamic place that it is. At the same time, disregard for traditional manners and mores has caused the demise of many cherished institutions and the loss of much of the city's physical and spiritual heritage.

Finally, Fifth Avenue has always symbolized the American Dream, or that aspect of it concerned with money and success. From its first age when the fine residences of old families were built, to its present as a shopper's paradise, Fifth Avenue has always represented the best that money can buy. Money and ambition have ruled the Avenue's progress, a factor that now threatens its existence.

This volume is necessarily selective. When one considers that Fifth Avenue stretches more than seven miles in length from Greenwich Village to Harlem, that it has been in existence for more than 150 years, that thousands of buildings have come and gone along its route, and that tens of thousands of personalities have peopled its history, the reasons are obvious. Much has been omitted, primarily in areas that have already been covered extensively in other works. The author hopes, however, that after you have browsed through this volume, your feeling for New York and Fifth Avenue will be enhanced, and that, as you promenade up and down America's Avenue of Avenues, you will relive some of the romance of its fabulous past.

Chapter One

THE WASHINGTON SQUARE AREA AND "LITTLE OLD NEW YORK"

CHRONOLOGY

1820   New York becomes the largest city in the United States with a population of 152,056, exceeding that of Philadelphia.

1822   Washington Square is opened as a park.

1824   Fifth Avenue is opened as far north as 13th Street.

1825   Erie Canal is opened, and the course of the city's history is changed profoundly.

        The Barber of Seville, the first performance of grand opera in New York, is given at the Park Theatre.

1826   Lord and Taylor is founded.

        All property qualifications are removed from voters in the city.

1827   *Journal of Commerce* is established.

1830   New York City population is 242,278.

        A regular stage line is established on Broadway from Bowling Green to Bleeker Street.

        Five Points area is condemned as being a "focus of social and housing problems and source of cholera." ·

1831   New York University established.

1832   *New York Morning Post* established by Horace Greeley.

        New York and Harlem Railroad begins operating with horse cars from Prince Street to Murray Hill.

        Cholera plague sweeps city, driving half the population out of town.

1833   First opera house built on Church Street.

        New York Sun founded by Benjamin Day.

1834   Brooklyn is incorporated as a city.

        New York and Harlem Railroad extended to Harlem, and first steam trains appear.

1835   Great Fire breaks out in Hanover and Pearl Streets, destroying nearly seven hundred buildings, and property to the value of $17 million.

1836   James Gordon Bennett establishes the *New York Herald.*

Union Club is founded in New York.

1837   Panic causes ninety-eight business failures; $60 million is lost.

First vaudeville show held at Niblo's Garden, on the east side of Broadway, between Prince and Houston streets.

Professor Samuel F. B. Morse of New York University invents a practical electric telegraph and transmission code.

1838   The first Tombs Prison is completed.

1840   New York City population is 391,114.

Edgar Allan Poe comes to live in the Fordham Cottage, still standing on the Grand Concourse and Kingsbridge Road in the Bronx.

1841   Horace Greeley founds the *New York Tribune,* and Isaac Van Arden, the *Brooklyn Eagle.*

St. John's College founded in the Bronx, much later, in 1904, to become Fordham University.

First steam fire engine is tried in New York.

1842   Croton water system is completed and opened with celebration in New York.

Astor Library founded by John Jacob Astor.

Charles Dickens visits New York.

New York Philharmonic Society is organized.

Tom Thumb exhibited for the first time by P. T. Barnum.

1845   A municipal police system is adopted.

1846   Present Trinity Church is consecrated.

Elias Howe patents the sewing machine, and his invention spurs the growth of the garment industry in New York.

1847   First free evening schools are opened.

Gas streetlights extended to 18th Street on Fifth Avenue.

1848   Immigration of Germans spurred by revolution in Germany.

1849   New York Free Academy founded.

Astor place Riot occurs with much bloodshed, as a result of the quarrel between William C. Macready, an English actor, and Edwin Forrest, an American actor. Opposing factions divided along class lines.

In 1820, New York became the largest city in the United States with a population of 152,056, exceeding for the first time that of Philadelphia, but its Avenue of Avenues —the Fifth Avenue—was yet but a mark on an official map.

Washington Square Park, the area where the legendary street begins, was a potter's field and a place of execution with brant goose, black duck, and yellowleg splashing in the marshes and fox, rabbit, and partridge finding cover in the thickets. North of the park along what is now Fifth Avenue lay farmland.

The social elite, descendants of the early Dutch and English settlers of the Hudson Valley, lived on Stuyvesant Square, Lafayette Street, and the presently nonexistent St. John's Square. Lower Second Avenue too was lined with elegant residences, while Wall Street and the Battery were promenades for fashionable ladies and gentlemen.

The southern boundary of what is today Greenwich Village was still largely fields and pastureland, with blackberries growing wild along the length of Bleecker Street. To the north the countryside was dotted with farms and an occasional dusty country lane. Where Greenwich Street ended at the Hudson River, fishermen could be seen pulling in their nets at the end of the day.

The existing streets were narrow and crooked, having followed earlier footpaths, and the Bowery was still a dusty country lane lined with little cottages and farms. The Boston Post Road meandered north to what is now Madison Square, where it turned and continued on through Harlem and eventually reached Boston.

Had you walked down a typical street of the period, you would have seen rows of Dutch-shuttered brick houses with the characteristic stoop leading to the front door. Inside the lady of the house entertained her friends at tea in the afternoon and at elaborate dinners in the evening. One or two servants, either black or recently arrived Irish women, assisted with the chores. Candles lighted the tables at dinner; oil lamps, the rest of the house. The ladies seated around the table wore bell-shaped skirts and spencer jackets, boleros with tight sleeves that were left open in the front. These jackets customarily were made of dark-colored velvet edged in fur or swansdown. Their heelless slippers, made of kid or fabric, were cut low and tied to the feet with ribbons. Their hair was piled high and ornamented with lace, velvet ribbons, or jeweled bibelot.

The men were dressed in the fashion of Beau Brummell, with a frock coat or cutaway and pantaloons over black boots. Colors were somber, and even then the clothes were imported from England.

During the morning, the streets were beehives of activity. Dressed in a cotton frock and wearing a cloak, the mistress of the house went to the markets or to the wagons of peddlers to shop for the food for the day. The markets abounded with wild boar, wild turkey, wild duck, wild geese, venison, partridge, and squab. Fresh fruits and vegetables were available only in season. A tomato, or love apple, would not have been found anywhere; that it was not poisonous had yet to be discovered. Cries of chimney sweeps, milkmen, fishmongers, and peddlers filled the air. Hot corn girls walked the streets barefoot shouting, "Hot corn! Hot corn! Here's your lily white corn!" Others sold fresh mint, strawberries, blackberries, radishes, and hot yams.

"THE FIFTH AVENUE" WAS PLANNED MORE THAN A DECADE BEFORE ITS OPENING

The bustling streets testified to the vitality of the city, and to accommodate the swelling population, the New York City Council Commission had as early as 1811 marked out the route of "The Fifth Avenue"—its designation on the street map—as part of the general plan to open the city to the north.

But first the potter's field at the foot of the Avenue must be cleared. The gallows were torn down, the ducks were shooed away, the swamps were filled, the coffins of the dead were disinterred. Then marble pillars surmounted with scroll ironwork and lanterns were erected at the gateways on the south side of the new park. The iron railing to surround the square was imported from England, but shipped in parts so the city fathers could avoid paying the duty on manufactured goods.

Washington Square Park was completed by 1824, and in August of that year, the city took title to "The Fifth Avenue" as far north as 13th Street. Opened in November, Fifth Avenue was an impressive one hundred feet in width—the roadbed sixty feet and each sidewalk twenty feet.

FIFTH AVENUE IMPRESSED THE FIRST OF THOUSANDS OF CELEBRITIES EVEN BEFORE IT WAS OPENED

In August, 1824, the Marquis de Lafayette, accompanied by his son George Washington Lafayette, revisited America on the invitation of the United States Government. As his ship entered New York Harbor, it was surrounded by an armada of American ships, and Mayor General Jacob Morton boarded to greet the marquis and his son. Lafayette was so profoundly moved by the warm welcome that he burst into tears.

Two days later, the visitors were given a tour of the northern reaches of the city. The growth of Manhattan and its ripening traditions filled the marquis with admiration. As he viewed the proposed Fifth Avenue and the prospective street improvements about Madison Square, he inquired facetiously, "Do you expect that Broadway and the Fifth Avenue will reach Albany?"

CANNON FIRE MARKED THE OPENING OF A NEW ERA FOR NEW YORK CITY

It was Buffalo, however, not Albany that was the immediate goal for New Yorkers. On October 26, 1825, the Erie Canal was opened. The waterway, 363 miles long, four feet deep, twenty-eight feet wide at the bottom, and forty feet wide at the surface, stretched from Buffalo to New York. Built by the brawn of Irish immigrants, it was considered one of the greatest engineering feats in the history of mankind. The news of the opening was announced by the discharging of a series of cannons that stretched along the entire route of the waterway. The sound of the first cannon at Buffalo signaled the second to fire and so on down the line, with the message arriving in New York in eighty-one minutes. The course of the city's history was profoundly changed.

Lewis Mumford expressed it succinctly: "New York City became the mouth of the continent, thanks to the Erie Canal." It assured New York's growth to a major metropolis and the city almost immediately became the nation's financial and commercial capital while solidifying its position as the country's leading port and immigration center. Because Buffalo was situated on Lake Erie, the canal also opened up the Middle West and the Great Lakes country for trade and settlement. Before the canal, transporting goods from Buffalo to New York overland took three weeks and cost $120 a ton. On the canal, raw materials from the hinterlands and finished goods from Europe and the eastern seaboard went back and forth in eight days at a rate of $6 a ton, significantly spurring the growth of the city and the nation.

Statistically, that year Manhattan merchants gained control of more than 50 percent of the country's imports and one-third of its export trade. In 1825, more than five hundred new businesses were started in the city. Twelve new banks and thirteen new marine insurance firms were founded. Banking capital in the city rose from $3 million in 1800 to $25 million and more in 1825. The city's population was now close to two hundred thousand, double that of 1800, and in spite of the fact that more than three thousand new houses were built in 1825, an acute housing shortage persisted. The owners of shops and stores doubled their rents. In the Lower Manhattan commercial district, old buildings were torn down and new ones were constructed, a constant shifting that made the entire area almost impassable.

That year several families of substantial means and social position, including the Parishes, Roberts, Rhinelanders, and Minturns, erected houses on the north side of Washington Square. These families, like those who lived on Stuyvesant Square, Lafayette Street, and Second Avenue, were well-to-do, but by no means rich. The new merchant class was beginning to replace the old guard in social leadership, but the age of immense wealth in the city was yet to arrive.

At the other end of the social structure, newcomers from Ireland, Scotland, and Germany accounted for 11 percent of the city's population. Both the old landed families and the *arriviste* merchant class were concerned with the changing aspect of the city's ethnic character. The Roman Catholic Irish, in particular, were welcomed in the city only as a source of cheap labor. Lacking money, education, and skills, they were able to find shelter only in the Five Points district. This incredibly squalid slum lay northeast of the present New York County Courthouse and centered at the intersection of Anthony, Orange, Cross, Little Water, and Mulberry streets. Today Anthony is Worth Street, Orange is Baxter Street, Cross is Park Street, Little Water has vanished, and only Mulberry Street keeps its original name. Few American historians or writers of the period had a good word to say of the Irish. It took James Bryce, a British historian, to set things straight: "There is a disposition in the United States to use the immigrants, and especially the Irish, much as a cat is used in the kitchen to account for broken plates and food which disappears. . . . New York was not an Eden before the Irish came."

IN 1830, FIFTH AVENUE WITNESSED ITS FIRST PARADE AS THOUSANDS OF PEOPLE GATHERED TO SALUTE THE SUCCESS OF THE FRENCH REVOLUTION OF 1830

New Yorkers turned out for the first of the thousands of official parades that have since passed along the Avenue when the population, seized with acute Francomania, honored the

The Washington Memorial Arch (1889-92) was first erected in wood in 1876 for the centennial celebration. Designed by McKim, Mead and White, it was so popular with New Yorkers that Polish pianist Jan Paderewski gave a benefit concert to help finance the permanent arch. The Washington statue on the west face was sculpted by Alexander Calder's father, Alexander Stirling Calder.

Washington Square, the parade ground for the Seventh Regiment of the New York State National

Guard, during the early days of the nineteenth century. From a painting by Major Otto Boetticher.

The Brevoort House at Fifth Avenue and Ninth Street, in the early 1850s.

The Croton Reservoir at Fifth Avenue and 42nd Street, later the site of the

New York Public Library. The horse trolley is traveling west on 42nd Street.

Julia Gardiner as the
"Rose of Long Island."

I'll Purchase at
Bogert & Mecamly's
N⁰ 86 9th Avenue.
Their Goods
are Beautiful &
Astonishingly Cheap.

The Hotel Brevoort at the northeast corner of Fifth Avenue and Eighth Street

around the turn of the century. This building stood as recently as 1952.

F. PALMER. lith.

The William H. Coventry Waddell villa on the northwest

corner of Fifth Avenue and 37th Street in 1844.

St. Luke's Hospital on the west side of Fifth Avenue between

54th and 55th streets. It occupied this site from 1854 to 1896.

The August Belmont residence, Fifth Avenue at the corner of 18th Street. Notice the bill-boards on the walls of the building. This photograph was taken just before the structure was razed during the 1870s. To the rear of the house, facing 18th Street, is the art gallery.

The Edison United Manufacturing Company, 65 Fifth Avenue, decorated for the Washington Centennial in 1889. The first electrically lighted Christmas tree in history appeared in a window of this house.

THE EDISON UNITED MANUFACTURING CO.

THE
EDISON
UNITED
MANUFACTURING
CO.

French Revolution of 1830. Sixteen divisions long, the parade reached from Canal Street to Washington Square, where speeches and exercises were scheduled. When the front division of the marchers reached the square, the last division, two and one-half miles to the rear, had not yet started.

In his diary, Philip Hone, a former mayor, described Washington Square on that day: "The crowd on the parade ground was tremendously great, and the tumult and pressure along the stage were such as to preclude the possibility of hearing. Indeed, for a short time the danger of a riot was great. The military sentinels on the stage, who had been forced to use violent measures to prevent the people from ascending, had been driven from their posts, and it required all the address of Mr. Swarthout, the Marshal, and myself to keep tolerable order during the exercise. When they were finished and the persons engaged in them had left the stage, it was taken possession of by boys and others who nearly demolished it."

Students, faculty, and the president of Columbia College, the citizens of France who resided in New York and its environs, the fire department some fifteen hundred strong, the printers who distributed copies of the speech read in the square, the butchers on horseback with leg-of-mutton sleeves, and a working steamboat on a float all participated. At the head of the procession were Frenchmen in the uniforms of the National Horse Guard of France, who rode majestically on prancing chargers. They were followed by former President James Monroe who had come to town to participate in the revels.

That year also marked another milestone for Fifth Avenue: title to the area from 13th Street to 24th Street was taken by the city in May. The next acquisition came in 1837-38, when the city took title as far north as 129th Street. It was not until after the Civil War that the city extended its ownership to the area from 130th Street to the Harlem River. In 1833 and 1844 the city gave property owners permission to extend fifteen feet from their property lines to provide for stoop and garden areas. This permission survived until 1908, when all stoops, gardens, and sidewalk cafés were ordered destroyed or moved back to within the original private property lines.

BY THE EARLY 1830S, THE AREA SURROUNDING LOWER FIFTH AVENUE HAD BEGUN TO EXPAND RAPIDLY

One reason for the development of the Greenwich Village area was the great cholera plague of 1832, which ravaged Lower Manhattan. At the height of the epidemic almost one hundred deaths a day were reported. Thirty-five hundred persons perished, and more than one hundred thousand people deserted the downtown area. Many built new houses farther to the north in what is now the village.

Many of these lovely houses were made of Holland brick. Holland brick, as such, was not imported from Holland for building purposes, but as ballast by American sailing vessels because it was cheap. The bricks were either sold on arrival or dumped on the shore of the Hudson River. Good bricks were made in this country, but the ballast bricks could always be bought cheaply or picked up for nothing.

1834 WAS THE YEAR THAT ESTABLISHED FIFTH AVENUE AS AN OUTPOST OF SOCIETY

Henry Brevoort, Jr., still referred to as Uncle Brevie in some rarefied Hudson Valley Dutch circles, started to build his "country" mansion on his father's property at the northwest corner of Fifth Avenue and Ninth Street in 1834. It was a bold move that proved to be a clever one. Because Mr. and Mrs. Brevoort were socially prominent, their decision to build on Fifth caused nothing short of a run on their real estate all the way to 20th Street. One by one the lots were sold, and the social sheep ensconced themselves as Brevoort neighbors.

Designed by Ithiel Town and A. J. Davis, who also designed the Subtreasury Building on Wall Street, the distinguished Georgian mansion was freestanding, with a garden entrance on one side and a curved window bay on the other. Greek key motif ornamented the cornice. Its stately gray brick-paneled facade, with two simple Ionic columns on each side of the door, probably served as the model for the ubiquitous row houses of nineteenth-century New York City.

In 1838, the Brevoorts held a grand opening for some five hundred friends, the first occasion when New York's first families gathered en masse in splendor on Fifth Avenue.

Philip Hone described the opening of the mansion: "Mrs. Brevoort opened her splendid house on Saturday evening to a large party. I went with my daughter Catharine. It was a grand affair; there is not a house in the city so well calculated to entertain such an assemblage. Five large rooms open on one floor, and a spacious hall besides, with a noble staircase. This is the first time all this had been shown to the bon-ton, and the capriciousness of the master and mistress is so great that it may remain a sealed book for half a dozen years, unless the present freak should continue. This was a musical party, and even I, who in instrumental music am no great dab, was delighted by the violin of Signor Rapetti, and the piano by Mynheer Schaftenberg."

Amusingly enough, Hone makes no mention of Mrs. Brevoort's ace in the hole. As guests made their way into the spectacular house, they were led up the imposing staircase to view the bathroom and more specifically the tub. Despite the fact that things French were decidedly suspect, Mrs. Brevoort had installed a tub that filled and emptied with faucet and drain. Made of porcelain and enclosed in a box of Santo Domingo mahogany, the tub was decorated with garlands of delicate pink rosettes entwined with lavender forget-me-nots.

Two years later, the Brevoorts held the most elaborate extravaganza the city had yet seen, the Brevoort costume ball of February, 1840. For weeks beforehand, "nothing else was talked about," wrote Hone. "The ladies' heads are turned nearly off their shoulders; the whiskers of the dandies assume a more ferocious curl in anticipation of the effect they are to produce; and even my peaceable domicile is turned topsy-turvy by the 'note of preparation' which is heard. My daughters are all going in character, and I am preparing to play the harlequin in my old days. If Cardinal Wolsey don't astonish the fold with his magnificence, then I have spent in vain my money in the purchase of scarlet merino and other trappings to decorate the burly person of the haughty churchman."

On Friday, February 28, the house on Ninth Street was ablaze with light. At nine thirty in the evening the carriages started to arrive, and by ten most of the rooms in the house were filled with guests. Because the invitations had specified costume, everyone came as somebody else. The ladies wore dresses made especially for the occasion, many superbly decorated with gold, silver, and jewels, sparing neither expense nor effort to dazzle their peers. Among the guests was a Mr. Atree, a reporter and one of the editors of the six-year-old *New York Herald,* appearing as a knight in shining armor. This was perhaps the first time that a private party had been covered by the press in New York. After threats from publisher James Gordon Bennett, the Brevoorts succumbed and permitted press coverage. The event was significant in that a new function of the press was unleashed, that of assuring that the public would be informed about private parties.

The ball was memorable, although marred by an incident that rocked New York society to its foundations. Included on the guest list was Matilda Barclay, whose father was then British consul. She appeared in domino and mask as Lalla Rookh; and Captain Burgwyne, a dashing cavalier from the South, was dressed as harlequin. The couple were very much in love, but their families strongly objected to the alliance. At four in the morning, without changing their costumes, they met in one of the salons and quietly slipped out the side door. A waiting carriage took them directly to a clergyman before whom they were married. When the news broke the following day, Fifth Avenue was aghast. The scandal gathered momentum for several weeks, until finally a law was passed banning masked balls, with a fine of $100 for anyone who ignored it. For fourteen years the city stoically dispensed with the delights of costume balls.

The superb Georgian house of the Brevoorts stood until 1925 when it was demolished to make way for the present Fifth Avenue Hotel, a building quite banal architecturally.

In March, 1970, Henry Brevoort, Jr., came into the news once again, but this time because of a bizarre tragedy. On 11th Street, just west of Fifth Avenue, he had built four houses as wedding presents for his children. Weatherman, a radical left organization, turned one of these lovely old homes into a bomb factory, and a crudely manufactured bomb exploded, killing several members of the group. The house burned to the ground, but the adjoining houses were saved.

IN 1842, CHARLES DICKENS PAID HIS FIRST VISIT TO NEW YORK

Quite probably the Brevoort costume ball of 1840 was superseded in the memories of Fifth Avenue residents only by the "Boz" ball of 1842. It was staged as part of the extravagant welcome extended to Charles Dickens and his wife on their first visit to New York. For weeks the city was thrown into a Boz mania, which the *Journal of Commerce* ridiculed in these words:

> They'll tope thee, Boz, They'll soap thee, Boz—
>   Already they begin!
> They'll dine thee, Boz, They'll wine thee, Boz,
>   They'll stuff thee to the chin!
> They'll smother thee with victuals, Boz,
>   With fish and flesh and chickens.
> Our authorlings will bore thee, Boz,
>   And hail thee "Cousin Dickens."
> While ladies, spite their better half,
>   Blue, yellow, foul and fair,
> Will coax thee for thy autograph,
>   And likewise locks of hair.
> Beware, Boz! Take care, Boz!

> Of forming false conclusions;
> Because a certain sort of folks
>   Do mete thee such obtrusions;
> For they are not the people, Boz,
>   These templars of the cork,
> Nor more than a church steeple, Boz,
>   Is Boston or New York.

The committee organizing the Boz ball, which was attended by New York's elite, decided that only eight hundred tickets would be issued. This number was immediately sold, and many members of the committee lacked tickets for themselves and their friends. The final number was twenty-two hundred tickets, and, needless to say, the crush the night of the party was overwhelming. The ballroom had been decorated with Pickwickian motifs, murals of scenes from Dickens's novels, and wreaths bearing the titles of his works. During the evening, a series of *tableaux vivants* were exhibited, including groups of characters in poignant episodes from *Pickwick, Nicholas Nickleby, Oliver Twist,* and others. Dickens and his wife were presented at nine o'clock to a crowd that by that hour numbered many more than twenty-two hundred.

The hospitality accorded Dickens was evidently appreciated, but did little to counteract his impressions of the squalor and poverty of most of the city, which he recorded in his *American Notes.* These highly critical comments were deeply resented in America and helped to fan the flames of anti-British sentiment. Fences with England were not mended until the young prince of Wales made his triumphant visit to New York in 1860.

LATER IN 1842, THE CROTON RESERVOIR WAS FORMALLY OPENED FAR IN THE NORTHERN WILDS AT 42ND STREET AND FIFTH AVENUE

On July 4, 1842, the hysteria of celebration once again seized the city, as the Croton River, diverted into the great Croton Aqueduct, gushed gloriously into the Croton Reservoir. The project had been discussed for years before construction began, and the great fire of 1835, and the lack of water to extinguish it, actually spurred action. The starting point of the aqueduct lay some forty miles north of Manhattan, and its construction involved tunneling through solid rock and crossing valleys with embankments. A bridge 1,450 feet long and 114 feet high was built at the Harlem River, and two reservoirs were constructed, one south of 86th Street, the other on the west side of Fifth Avenue between 40th and 42nd streets, the site of the present New York Public Library and Bryant Park.

The massive structure on Fifth Avenue that contained the water resembled a gigantic ancient Egyptian temple. At the top was a charming promenade where New Yorkers gathered at all hours for relaxation. During the day, Long Island, the hills of Westchester, and the magnificent Palisades were in view. At night, one could see the reflection of the moon in the waters of the Hudson. For nearly half a century, this promenade was the destination of afternoon traffic uptown from Lower Fifth Avenue, St. John's Park, and Stuyvesant Square.

Across the street, on the southeast corner of 40th Street and Fifth Avenue, was Croton Cottage, opened on July 1, 1853, where ice cream and other refreshments were sold. To the rear of the little cottage on a two-acre plot was the Maze Garden, a labyrinth modeled after the one at Hampton Court in England.

On the day of the opening celebration, a gigantic parade marched through the city. As it passed, fountains were turned on, gushing forth Croton water. At City Hall Park, an ingeniously constructed fountain had been built with the main jet spouting water sixty feet into the air. A shifting plate device enabled the water to assume seven different shapes. On a float in the parade, the same printing press used by Benjamin Franklin turned out leaflets that bore George P. Morris's poem saluting the water. The poem was sung by large choruses at both City Hall Park and the Fifth Avenue Reservoir. The closing lines were:

Water leaps as if delighted,
While her conquered foes retire!
Pale contagion flies affrighted
With the baffled demon Fire!
Water spouts a glad hosannah!
Bubbles up the earth to bless!
Cheers it like the precious manna
In the barren wilderness.

Round the aqueducts of story,
As the mists of Lethe throng,
Croton's waves, in all their glory,

Troop in melody along.
Ever sparkling, bright, and single
Will this rock-ribbed stream appear,
When posterity shall mingle
Like the gathered waters here.

One of the high points of the celebration was the appearance of four daredevils. After traveling the entire length of the eight-foot-high aqueduct in a tiny boat named the *Croton Maid,* they popped out of the pipe and into the Fifth Avenue Reservoir to the cheers of thousands of on-lookers.

The arrival of the water served another purpose as it became a vehicle for temperance propaganda. Dozens of "dry" groups marched in the parade. Their influence extended to the grand banquet that evening where no alcohol was served —only Croton water. Philip Hone visited the Fifth Avenue and Yorkville reservoirs that day and wrote in his diary: "They are at present about half full, and the clear, sweet, soft water (clear it is, and soft and sweet, for to be in the fashion I drank a tumbler of it and found it all these) is flowing in copiously and has already formed two pretty, limpid, placid Mediterranean seas, of wholesome temperance beverage, well calculated to cool the palates and quench the thirst of the New Yorkers, and to diminish the losses of the fire insurance companies." He concluded: "Nothing struck me with more pleasure than the perfect order and propriety which prevailed among the immense masses of male and female spectators on the route of the procession; not a drunken person was to be seen. The moral as well as the physical influence of water pervaded everything."

George Templeton Strong, another diarist, limited his comments to, "The Croton Water is slowly flowing towards the city, which at last will stand a chance of being cleaned—if water CAN clean it."

The availability of Croton water may well have inspired a medical craze of the period called hydropathy, based on the use of a great deal of water both internally and externally. In the city, as well as in the country, health resorts were established that regularly drew the Fifth Avenue crowd. Patients were implored to give up all stimulants, eat plenty of plain food, take plenty of exercise in the fresh air, and use great quantities of water. Not surprisingly, it was a short-lived fad.

IN 1843, JAMES LENOX, WHOSE SUPERB COLLECTION OF RARE BOOKS AND MANUSCRIPTS EVENTUALLY BECAME PART OF THE NUCLEUS OF THE NEW YORK PUBLIC LIBRARY COLLECTION, BUILT HIS MANSION ON THE NORTHEAST CORNER OF 12TH STREET AND FIFTH AVENUE

The James Lenox house was ninety feet in width and built of a light-colored stone with a crenellated roof. Next door, he built a smaller home of the same material for his unmarried sister. Lenox cherished his privacy. He was almost painfully formal and, in fact, when he ventured next door to visit his sister, he dressed in his best clothing complete with high silk hat, gloves, and imposing cane.

Two years after he moved into the house he began to collect books. Henry Stevens, Lenox's foreign book agent, was one of the few people who often visited the house. He has left an interesting memoir on the formation of the Lenox Library and how Lenox utilized his house for storage: "The great bulk of his book collection was piled away in spare rooms of his large house 'til they were filled to the ceiling, from the further end back to the door, which was then locked and the room for the present done with. He was extremely nervous and fidgety about the safety of his treasures when out of his own keeping, and uniformly declined applications to see his library. He even refused, among a good many others, Mr. Prescott, the historian, author of *The Conquest of Peru*. But, at the same time, he politely informed that distinguished writer that any particular book or manuscript he possessed which Mr. Prescott might name would be forwarded for his use, *if possible.*"

When he did lend books, he deposited them at the Astor Library on Lafayette Street, and requested that they be returned there, thus avoiding any personal contact with the borrower.

Among his treasures was George Washington's Farewell Address, now in the collection of the New York Public Library. The document was believed to have been destroyed in the fire in the capitol in Albany, but Lenox announced that, in fact, it was in his private collection. Once owned by David C. Claypoole of Philadelphia, Lenox had offered $2,200 for the manuscript at an 1848 auction, outbidding the Library of Congress.

In 1875, Lenox, who had paranoiacally guarded his collection for years, suddenly donated to the city his entire houseful of books, plus $300,000 to build the Lenox Library at 75th Street and Fifth Avenue. The books were carefully packed and boxed. Teams of horse-drawn vans pulled up before the great house and dragged the precious cargo the three miles north to the library. Eventually, the Lenox Collection in the old Lenox Library at 75th Street, and the Astor and Tilden collections in the Astor Library, became the basis for the first collection of books and manuscripts of the New York Public Library at 42nd Street.

1841 SAW THE CONSTRUCTION OF THE FIRST CHURCH ON FIFTH AVENUE, THE CHURCH OF THE ASCENSION.

After the fire that destroyed their church on Canal Street, a controversy over where to rebuild raged within the congregation of the Church of the Ascension. Conservative parishioners insisted on rebuilding on the old site, but the vestry argued that, as the city was rapidly expanding northward, the new church should be built farther north. Two locations were discussed: one on Second Avenue, at the time the city's center of fashion; the other, on Fifth Avenue. The decision was finally made by the devil, as dice were rolled to determine the location. He chose Fifth, and the wisdom of the choice, taken by whatever means, is evident today.

The new church was built on the northwest corner of 10th Street and the Avenue and was surrounded by lush meadows. A boardwalk across the vacant lots on Fifth Avenue gave access to the church from Broadway. Henry Brevoort's country mansion was one of the few homes in the area.

The church, designed by Richard Upjohn, was opened in November, 1841, and was described as "a remarkably chaste and beautiful edifice of the Gothic Style, the proportions faultless, with the interior finished in a style of appropriate solemnity and grace." Upjohn, however, was not happy, for he was at odds with the rector over the chancel. Upjohn wanted a deep chancel similar to the ones in English Gothic churches, whereas Eastman, who was low church, favored a shallow chancel so that there "would be no room for high church doings." The rector won.

After a fire in 1863, redecoration of the church began. By the 1880s, a new chancel designed by Stanford White had been built. White commissioned John La Farge to execute the painting of the Ascension that fills the west wall of the chancel at the present time.

On June 25, 1844, the Church of the Ascension was the scene of a unique historical event. President John Tyler, then elderly, married young Miss Julia Gardiner, the only time a president of the United States has married while holding office. Because the president had fallen out of favor with New York's power structure, much vicious tongue wagging took place when the secret nuptials became known. Young Julia of the Gardiner's Island Gardiners had already caused gossip about town because of the Rose of Long Island incident of 1839-1840.

The incident centered around a cheap throwaway advertisement promoting a second-rate dry-goods and clothing establishment named Bogert and Mecamly. The picture showed a young lady nonchalantly standing in front of the store, carrying on her arm a small sign shaped like a lady's handbag, which boldly proclaimed: "I'll purchase at Bogert and Mecamly's, No. 86 Ninth Avenue. Their Goods are Beautiful and Astonishingly Cheap." She was outrageously overdressed and wore a sunbonnet graced with immense ostrich feathers. Beside her stood an unidentified older man dressed in a fop's top hat and light coat, wielding a flamboyant hand-wrought cane. The advertisement was captioned "Rose of Long Island," and was New York City's first commercial endorsement by a "lady of quality."

Several months later the incident gained widespread notoriety when a poem entitled "Julia—the Rose of Long Island," a sixty-eight-line effort by one "Romeo Ringdove," appeared on the front page of the Brooklyn Daily News. The Gardiners were understandably embarrassed, but that no lawsuit was forthcoming seems to prove that Julia indeed posed for the picture. The family, of course, shopped at Stewart's, the first-class

mercantile store, and the fact that Julia had been pictured in the company of an older man who was dressed as a dandy was the ultimate humiliation.

A month after "Romeo Ringdove" phrased his love for the Rose of Long Island, Julia and her sisters were packed off to Europe on the grand tour. After her travels, she visited Washington where she met John Tyler.

On Tuesday morning, June 25, 1844, the Tyler party arrived by train from Washington and quietly slipped into the Howard Hotel. The comings and goings of the couple were cloaked in secrecy and, in fact, the president had even persuaded the owner of the hotel to lock up his servants overnight so that word of his presence would not leak out. The following day at two, a hot Wednesday afternoon, the marriage took place with only the immediate family and a few friends and cabinet members present.

When the news was blazoned in the newspapers, the effect was electric. The New York Herald referred maliciously to the rumor that Tyler was about to withdraw from the 1844 presidential campaign and throw his influence behind James K. Polk in exchange for the ambassadorship to the Court of St. James's. The paper wrote of Julia: "In her form and personal appearance, she is beautiful; and we should be proud to have her appear at the Court of Queen Victoria."

George Templeton Strong, in his diary entry of June 26, 1844, reported: "I've just heard a rumor that infatuated old John Tyler was married today to one of those large, fleshy Miss Gardiners of Gardiner's Island. Poor, unfortunate deluded old jackass; it's positively painful to think of his situation and the trials that lie before him."

Philip Hone was somewhat kinder, saying: "No sooner was Tyler shaking off the cares of public life and bidding adieu for a brief period to the palace of which he accidentally became an unworthy occupant, flew on the wings of love (the old fool) to the arms of his expectant bride in New York, where the hymeneal altar was prepared for the happy couple. His arrival here on Tuesday evening was sudden, unexpected and unheralded. The illustrious bridegroom is said to be fifty-five years of age, and looks ten years older, and the bride is a dashing girl of twenty-two."

Alexander Gardiner, Julia's brother, wrote in

a letter to their sister Marjorie: "The city continues full of the surprise and the ladies will not recover in some weeks. At the corners of the streets, in the public places and in every drawing room it is the engrossing theme. The whole affair is considered one of the most brilliant *coup de main* ever acted; and I cannot but wonder myself, that we succeeded so well, in preserving at once the President's dignity, and our own feelings, from all avoidable sacrifice."

WITHIN A FEW YEARS, SEVERAL MORE CHURCHES WERE BUILT ALONG FIFTH AVENUE

The second church to grace Fifth Avenue, and one that also still stands, was the First Presbyterian Church on the west side of the Avenue between 11th and 12th streets, which was dedicated on January 11, 1846. The tower is copied from that of Magdalen College, Oxford. Before ground was broken, George Templeton Strong, whose church loyalties and religious affiliation lay one block to the south, began to carp about it in his diary. In July, 1844, he wrote: "Isaac Green Pearson is the architect of Phillips new schism shop on the Fifth Avenue, and from what I can hear of the plan, it's going to prove an abortion, and just such a travesty of a Gothic Church as one might expect from a bankrupt Unitarian amateur builder of meeting houses."

A year later he wrote: "Phillips show grows uglier and uglier, and when its tower is finished it will resemble a corpulent Chinese gander with its neck rigid, stout and tall, and its square-built rump and broad expanse of back, sturdy, squat, and not easily shaken. A deeply engaged tower in such a dumpy body as this, and a tower of such height and breadth won't improve, as if risen."

During the nineteenth century, the church graveyard and surrounding lawns became a playground for the local children. Frederick Van Wyck in his *Recollections of an Old New Yorker,* wrote: "The First Presbyterian church had no sanitation, only two little privvies back of the church. We boys used to climb on top of them

and jump to the fence of 12 West 12th Street, now the Parsonage. We would then walk the fences till we reached our house, 22, or the carpenter shop, 30, and come out as innocent as lambs, particularly if a cop was looking for the bad boys whose baseball had broken a pane of glass, or put a tick-tack on some old lady's window to annoy her."

Furthermore, the church provided sanctuary for other boys wishing to elude the police. "The railings on the north and south sides of the First Presbyterian Church may look like handsomely wrought iron, but they aren't. They are wood ingeniously painted to resemble sterner stuff. Many small boys have discovered this oddity and have used it to their advantage by removing a rail and slipping through to gain sanctuary from pursuing police."

Today if you enter the First Presbyterian you will notice an enormous crack in the aisle of the nave that runs the entire length of the church. During the nineteenth century, a popular minister, the Reverend Harry Emerson Fosdick, delivered fiery sermons on the issues of the day. One Sunday when he was preaching to his usual full congregation, the weight of the crowds in the galleries placed so great a stress on the superstructure that, with a resounding "crack," the floor suddenly split from end to end. Panic was averted and no one was injured, but the breach remains in the floor to this day.

Other churches were built farther north along Fifth Avenue. The South Dutch Reformed Church was constructed in 1850 on the southeast corner of 21st Street, and the Fifth Avenue Presbyterian Church was built at 19th Street and Fifth. In 1854, the Marble Collegiate Church, which also is still standing, was dedicated at 29th Street and Fifth Avenue, when the Avenue was still a dirt road. Recently, the Nixon-Eisenhower wedding took place in this church.

A few years after its dedication, the Marble Collegiate Church figured in a most un-Christian incident. When the actor George Holland died, a friend of his asked the minister at the church if the funeral could be held there. The minister replied that actors were not respectable enough for their funerals to be held in his church, and he added, "But, there's that little church around the corner." Hence, the Church of the Transfiguration, just east of Fifth Avenue on 29th Street, received its nickname. In time it became the favorite church of writers, playwrights, and people of the theater in New York.

A poem was written about the incident at the time.

> When from the stage of real life
> George Holland made his exit
> To rest until the final "call"—
> The trumpet "Resurrexit."
> He left no blot upon his name
> No wrong had he done to man,
> But laid, with his good life aside
> His well-played part of "Tureman."
>
> Upon his tomb write "Honest Man"
> And cry with "Rip" blind mourner
> "All honor to the little Church
> The Church around the corner!"
> Stern, bitter word of strong rebuke
> Might we speak to that Pastor
> But leave him—as he should have left
> The dead man—to his Master.
> We will not judge as he hath judged
> Nor wit with him—the scorner!
> But say "God bless the little Church
> The Church around the corner!"

In the years that followed, Edwin Booth and O. Henry were both buried from this church. Many blacks were sheltered within it during the Draft Riots of 1863.

IN MAY, 1849, MANY FIFTH AVENUE CITIZENS BECAME INVOLVED IN A CONTROVERSY THAT LED TO THE ASTOR PLACE OPERA HOUSE RIOT

For many years, professional jealousy had raged between Edwin Forrest, the American tragedian, and William C. Macready, the English actor. The press had fueled it, and chauvinistic emotions had been stirred. Sides were chosen also on class lines, with many newly arrived, anti-British, Irish immigrants siding with the American Forrest, while New York's elite sided with the Briton.

On May 7, the "Bowery Boys," Forrest's claque, succeeded in completely disrupting Macready's performance of *Macbeth* at the Astor Place Opera House, not only by the traditional hissing and egg-throwing, but by slinging chairs and tearing apart the whole theater. After this fracas, Macready announced that he would cancel his engagement and return to England. Many of the elite of Fifth Avenue, under the leadership of Washington Irving, implored the great actor to continue his performances, hoping that ultimately reason would prevail.

The actor agreed, and on May 10 he appeared again. In the meantime, the British crew of Cunard's *America* arrived in town and demonstrated in front of the theater in favor of their countryman. They carried not only placards in their hands, but pistols at their sides. The mayor ordered out the militia. Uncontrolled rioting broke out both inside and outside the theater when the curtain went up, and before the disturbance could be quelled, twenty-three people lay dead in the streets.

This slaughter caused deep resentment among the immigrant groups in New York, and eventually was one of the causes of the Draft Riots of 1863.

BY 1850, LOWER FIFTH AVENUE HAD BECOME THE SOCIAL CENTER OF NEW YORK

At 1 Fifth Avenue, a large three-story brick Victorian building was erected during the 1850s. It housed a famous private school, Miss Lucy Green's, and among its pupils was Jennie Jerome, who later became Lady Randolph Churchill, mother of Sir Winston. Bayard Taylor, Elihu Root, and Lyman Abbott were all visiting tutors at the school. After Miss Green's moved away, Sara Teasdale, the poet, came to New York from St. Louis, lived at Number 1, and wrote much of her poetry there. During the 1920s the house was torn down, and an apartment building was erected on the site. After it opened, Number 1, a "great pile of stones," was referred to as Dracula, because of two "eyes" that shone balefully in its cupola at night.

In 1855, John Taylor Johnston completed his mansion at the southeast corner of Fifth Avenue and Eighth Street. This home was the first marble dwelling house in a city of brownstones. A traditional stopping place on the tour circuit, visitors from out of town stared in wonder at the luxurious residence.

Behind the hose was a stable that Johnston converted into an art gallery in 1860. A few years later, he adapted a second stable for the same purpose. The latter was the first gallery of any importance, public or private, in the city of New York and was also the first art gallery open to the public. Admission was by card on Thursdays. All applicants received these cards either directly from Johnston or through several of his friends. The Johnston gallery unquestionably created a demand for a larger and more public institution in the city and led to the establishment of the Metropolitan Museum of Art in 1870, with Johnston as its first president.

Among the more important pictures in the Johnston Collection were Frederick E. Church's *Niagara,* now in the Corcoran Gallery in Washington; *Slave Ship* by Turner, in the Boston Museum of Fine Arts; and Winslow Homer's *Prisoners from the Front,* still owned by the Metropolitan. His collection was dispersed by his heirs in 1877.

Other persons who moved into the neighborhood at the time were Lispenard Stewart, Isaac M. Singer, who introduced the sewing machine to America, and General David Sickles, later to be one of the heroes of the battle of Gettysburg.

At Number 17, on the corner of 12th Street and Fifth Avenue, resided Henry Bergh, founder of ASPCA, a man whose life work is all but forgotten. Today it is difficult to imagine how important the horse was to the domestic economy of the city during the last century. All vehicles were horse drawn. One could transport no goods or go any distance without the aid of a horse. In fact, during an epidemic of an epizootic disease in horses, the city was virtually paralyzed, much as it was during the transit strike of January, 1966.

During Bergh's crusade for humane treatment of horses, a poem by an unknown author entitled "Bergh on the Line" appeared in the newspapers:

> Two and twenty street cars standing in a row,
> Horses in, drivers there—why do they not go?
> Cross and sulky men—folk grumbling up the street,
> Cross and sulky women, looking at their feet,
> Or asking the policemen with an angry sign,
> "What's the matter?" "Well, madam,
>   Bergh is on the line."
>
> "What a nuisance!" and with scorn
>   Beauty walks away.
> Says a little foreigner, "Who's dis Bergh,
>   Sar, pray?
> Some great general, no doubt?"
>   "Yes, he's had some fights
> Hard-won fights for horses, Sir,
>   and for horses' rights."
> "But I understand not it." "That's your care,
>   not mine.
> Move forward, Sir—crowd enough:
>   Bergh is on the line."
> Grumbling, praising, on all went;
>   but I heard one say,
> "Gentlemen, we're proud to walk

> in the snow today—
> Proud to think our mother-land
>   has so great a heart
> She can stoop, with love and law, to take
>   a wronged beast's part;
> For the good time coming, Sir,
>   'tis a gracious sign
> We may well afford a cheer for Bergh
>   upon the line!"

At 47 Fifth Avenue, there still stands a house that was typical of the 1850s. Originally the property of Ira Hawley, it is now the home of the one-hundred-year-old Salmagundi Club, the country's oldest artists' club. This private all-male club moved into the building in 1917, its membership list including John La Farge, Louis C. Tiffany, and Stanford White. The lounge on the first floor, open to the public, is typical of the interiors of the 1850s. A double Palladian screen divides the room into front and rear parlors. Four Corinthian columns and their corresponding pilasters support elliptical three-point arches between the columns. An elaborate Greek Revival cornice, a paneled ceiling, and molded dado are other features of this period room. In the front parlor is a carved marble fireplace decorated with graceful female figures costumed in the manner of the mid-nineteenth century, holding baskets of flowers. Pictures from the club's collection line the walls. The name of the club derives from a series of essays written by Washington and William Irving and James Kirke Paulding, who poked fun at the ridiculously formal manners of their contemporaries. The essays were called Salmagundi, which means a hash made of minced veal, pickled herrings, anchovies, and onions served with lemon juice and oil.

IN 1854, THE BREVOORT, THE FIRST HOTEL TO BE ERECTED ON FIFTH AVENUE, WAS OPENED

The Brevoort Hotel, fashioned out of three already existing brownstones on the northeast corner of the Avenue and Eithth Street, was the last word in elegance for almost a century. In its early days, the Brevoort had the distinction of housing most of the titled and well-connected Englishmen who visited New York. One story said the hotel became an English haven because of a rumor that circulated in London: Indians roamed Broadway, and the Brevoort was the best insurance against scalping. At the same time, a legend prevailed that the prince of Wales, later King Edward VII, had been feted in the dining room, and that he had passed the word around in England. The truth probably lies in the fact that many captains of ocean liners steered their passengers to the Brevoort in exchange for free accommodations.

Among its early guests, the hotel entertained the Dowager Queen Emma of the Sandwich Islands, Jerome Bonaparte, the marquis of Queensberry, and Abraham Lincoln, James A. Garfield, and Chester A. Arthur. Anna Held dazzled everyone in the lobby whenever she entered. Jenny Lind was entertained at the Brevoort. A large dinner was given for Annie Oakley when she appeared in Buffalo Bill's Wild West Show at Stanford White's Madison Square Garden on Madison Square.

Major George Anderson of the Grand Army of the Republic registered at the Brevoort on his way to Fort Sumter and again on his return to New York after the fort had fallen. On his second visit, he carried with him the flag that had been fired upon at the fort in the opening shots of the Civil War.

Year in and year out the carriages of the rich and famous pulled up to the coach block. But perhaps the most spectacular was the tandem of the great strong man Eugene Sandow. He was wont to charge down Fifth Avenue in his vehicle, drawn by three spirited white steeds, to pull to a halt in front of the Brevoort where he raced into the bar for a drink, and then to drive to Madison Square Garden where he appeared on the stage lifting the same three white horses above his head.

The fabled musicians Edward and Jean de Reszke often stayed at the Brevoort, and Luisa Tetrazzini was overheard practicing in her room by Oscar Hammerstein, who gave her a contract and made her the leading diva of the Metropolitan Opera. Among the celebrities who supped in the dining rooms were Richard and Robert Hard-

ing Davis, Charles Dana Gibson, Mark Twain, Edith Wharton, Maxim Gorky, Emma Goldman, Jan Paderewski, and Count Leo Tolstoy.

With the growth of Greenwich Village as an art center, the Brevoort assumed a new position in the history of Fifth Avenue. In the early 1900s the basement around the corner on Eighth Street was transformed into a tiny Paris café with marble-topped tables imported from France. Such luminaries as Edna St. Vincent Millay, Isadora Duncan, Mable Dodge, Lincoln Steffens, Theodore Dreiser, and Eugene O'Neill could be found at late hours quaffing demitasse. Lee Simonson, Helen Westley, Phillip Moeller, and Lawrence Langner, among others, shaped the nucleus of the Theater Guild in the Brevoort café. Jo Davidson and Leon Dabo drew sketches on tablecloths. Feodor Chaliapin used to sit down to a half pound of caviar, a dozen or two oysters, steak, and guinea hen.

Raymond Orteig, a Frenchman, was the manager of the hotel. He was devoted to the new science of aviation and in 1927 offered a $25,000 prize to the first man to cross the Atlantic Ocean in an airplane. When Charles Lindbergh did just that, Orteig feted him at a memorable luncheon and presented the award. The canceled check, together with the United States flag that Lindbergh dropped over Paris, is cherished by the Orteig family to this day.

A most charming story persists about the Brevoort. One day, shortly after World War I, a lovely young woman, her hair piled up on the top of her head, strolled into the lobby. With a determined expression on her face, she made her way to the men's barbershop. Faltering for only a moment, she opened the door and walked in. The barbers and their clients sat aghast as she removed her hat and started to take the pins from her hair. She sat down in the barber's chair, her long tresses flowing halfway down her back, and demanded, "Cut it off! Cut it to here!" And the flabbergasted barber complied. That young woman was Irene Castle whose haircut started the craze for bobbed hair.

The Brevoort was finally demolished in 1954 and replaced by an undistinguished apartment building, the first floor of which now houses one of a chain of schnitzel restaurants.

JUST NORTH OF THE BREVOORT HOTEL ON THE SOUTHEAST CORNER OF NINTH STREET AT 21 FIFTH AVENUE STOOD THE MARK TWAIN HOUSE

This Gothic Revival structure was built during the 1850s as the residence of James Renwick. His son, James Renwick, Jr., was the architect for St. Patrick's Cathedral and Grace Episcopal Church. Washington Irving was a close friend of the family, and, in fact, a room was set aside for him on the second floor.

In 1904, Mark Twain, who had lived in the neighborhood for many years, moved into the house. He had long been a fixture in the area, strolling up and down the Avenue in his well-known white suits and white shoes. While he lived at Number 21, he was often seen sitting on his front porch, talking to his cronies.

From 1904 to 1908, Robert Louis Stevenson stopped at the old Hotel St. Stephen at University Place and 10th Street. He and Twain became close friends and often visited in Washington Square. A drawing of the two literary giants at their favorite bench can be seen at the National Arts Club on Gramercy Square.

While residing at Number 21, Twain wrote "Tsar's Soliloquy," "The War Prayer," and a speech for his seventieth birthday. A. B. Paine was in residence at the time, working with the old man on his biography. Twain moved out in 1908, and the building, after much effort had been made to save it, vanished under the wrecker's ball in 1954 along with the Brevoort Hotel.

ALSO BUILT AROUND 1850, THE BISHOP MANSION STOOD AT 65 FIFTH AVENUE, ON THE EAST SIDE BETWEEN 13TH AND 14TH STREETS

This house became significant during the 1880s when Thomas Alva Edison rented it to promote commercial use of his inventions. He started by placing electric chandeliers in the larger rooms and then installed electric lights in every room of the elegant house. Edison also had the first outdoor electric sign ever used placed on the facade of the building, and during the first Christmas of occupancy, the inventor displayed an electrically lighted Christmas tree in the front window.

James Gordon Bennett was one of the first to see the display and immediately ordered the offices of the *New York Herald* to be lighted electrically. Hundreds of other people paraded through the house nightly to view the new illumination and perhaps to catch a glimpse of the inventor, who wandered among them dressed in a seedy black Prince Albert coat, dark trousers, a stiff-bosomed white shirt with a white silk handkerchief wrapped around his neck, and a sombrerolike hat clapped on his head.

The company that the inventor formed in this house was the forerunner of today's Consolidated Edison.

The Edison family can claim another first on Fifth Avenue. In 1906, Mrs. Thomas A. Edison bought a house built around 1850 at the north-west corner of Eighth Street and Fifth Avenue. The house was never occupied by the family but leased to carefully selected tenants. Two years before World War I, Charles Edison converted the ground floor into the Thimble Theater, the first off-Broadway theater in New York. Hundreds of young singers and musicians made their debuts and those who were critical successes were allowed to immortalize themselves on Edison's recently invented recording machine.

FAR NORTH OF THE DEVELOPING LOWER FIFTH AVENUE AREA, WILLIAM COVENTRY WADDELL BUILT HIS "SUBURBAN" GOTHIC FANTASY IN 1845

Designed by A. J. Davis, a one-time partner of Ithiel Town, the yellow gray stucco villa, located on the west side of the Avenue between 37th and 38th streets, cost the owner $9,150. Martha Lamb reported in the *History of New York,* an early chronicle of the city, that after Waddell had selected the site, he and his wife ventured north along the dirt road that was then Fifth Avenue, sat under an apple tree looking down upon the city in the distance, and discussed the deal with the property owner. When the house was completed, its grounds contained lovely paths and gardens and a field reserved for wheat. A barrel of flour was made annually from the harvest. Within the house a winding staircase led from the broad marble hall to a tower from which one could view both the East and Hudson rivers.

The Waddell house soon became one of the social centers of the city. A party held there was described in a newspaper of the period: "We noticed present a greater array of city fashionables than we have seen gathered before this season; the hostess and the flowers (the beautiful conservatory was thrown open), the bay windows, the winding stairways through the towers, the oriels, the corbels, the tapestries, the supper, the music and the ball, the gathering of beauty, and the concourse of gallant knights could not be surpassed."

It was at that party that the traditional New York City policeman's uniform was introduced. James W. Gerard, then a resident of Gramercy Park, appeared in the costume that he had designed as a proposed uniform for New York's finest. Shortly after the party, it was adopted by the Common Council. Although the blue coat, brass buttons, helmet, and club in which he appeared have been somewhat modified since, the basic uniform remains as Gerard designed it.

In 1856, Waddell suffered financial reverses and moved elsewhere. His house was demolished to make way for the relentless northward march of brownstones.

THE ARSENAL WAS BUILT AT 64TH STREET AND FIFTH AVENUE IN 1848

The building that today houses the New York Commissioner of Parks and his staff was originally the central cache for the state's military explosives. In 1857, it became city property and housed the city's first zoo in the basement.

Chapter Two

THE SECOND AGE OF FIFTH AVENUE: THE 1850S

CHRONOLOGY

1850   New York City population is 696,115.

First elevator in city installed at 201-203 Cherry Street.

P. T. Barnum brings Jenny Lind to New York.

Exiled Giuseppe Garibaldi arrives in Staten Island to work as a candlemaker prior to returning to Italy and victory.

1851   Hudson River Railroad is opened from New York to Albany.

Louis Kossuth, the Hungarian patriot, is welcomed to New York.

Henry J. Raymond founds the *New York Times*.

1852   William Marcy ("Boss") Tweed enters politics as alderman of the Seventh Ward.

William M. Thackeray visits New York.

Police adopt uniforms: blue coats with brass buttons and gray trousers.

1853   World's Fair held at Crystal Palace.

Uncle Tom's Cabin runs for two hundred performances at the Chatham Theater in Chatham Square.

1854   Academy of Music is opened on 14th Street and Irving Place.

1855   Castle Garden becomes station for immigrants.

First "model tenement" built by the Association for Improving the Condition of the Poor. Restricted to "colored persons," the upper floors contained rooms for concerts, lectures, and meetings.

1856   Central Park site purchased.

1857   Wall Street panic.

1858   Olmsted and Vaux win competition for Central Park development.

1859 Crystal Palace destroyed by fire.

R. H. Macy's Department Store founded.

Celebration of the first laying of the transatlantic cable by Cyrus W. Field.

Voters register for the first time in New York.

"Dixie" sung for the first time, from the stage of Bryant's Minstrels at 472 Broadway.

Cooper Union opens first building at Astor Place and Fourth Avenue.

Acquisition of land for Prospect Park in Brooklyn.

By 1850, the city's population approached seven hundred thousand, almost double that of 1840. The growth was spurred by the continuing immigration of Irish people, and the great German influx, prompted by the revolution of 1848 in Germany. Fifth Avenue was lined with mansions as far north as 23rd Street, and its fame as America's Avenue of Avenues had spread to Europe. The rest of the city stretched north to 34th Street, and a row of brownstone houses had already appeared on 42nd Street. North of there, the city was still largely rural, with the exception of the village of Yorkville, where more than one hundred homes had been constructed to house the thriving community. Steam trains had been introduced, and gas lights were installed as far north as 18th Street. The New York Philharmonic, as well as the New York City Police Department, had been organized.

The aura of "Little Old New York" still lingered in the area around Washington Square, but the second age of the Avenue had arrived, as new money began to change the aspect of society. August Belmont instituted the age of ostentation when he built his palace at the corner of 18th Street and Fifth Avenue.

Although the residents on Fifth Avenue went to the theater, the opera, and symphony concerts, most of the entertaining still took place at home. Dinner parties became more elaborate, with the list of courses on some occasions numbering nine or ten. The ladies dressed in bloomers, full Turkish pantaloons, and crinolines, and for afternoon strolls, wore straw hats with ribbons. The gentlemen wore Prince Albert frock coats and extremely tight trousers. Bowler hats and derbies made their appearance. During this era, sports clothes first appeared. These were in light colors of washable linen or cotton. Evenings at home were often spent before the "optique," the children particularly enjoying these "magic lantern" shows. Adults were concerned with spiritualism, and (of all things!) hashish enjoyed great popularity among the rich. Characteristic zeal and enthusiasm prevailed as the Avenue welcomed a continuing procession of foreign dignitaries and opened its first World's Fair.

DURING THE 1850S, THE FIFTH AVENUE BEGAN TO BE MENTIONED IN GUIDEBOOKS AND FOREIGN DIARIES, ALWAYS IN THE MOST SUPERLATIVE TERMS

In 1853, *The Stranger's Hand-book for the City of New York; or What to See and How to See It* described Fifth Avenue as "the most magnificent street on this continent if not yet the finest in the world. The imposing dwellings of the city's leading residents have caused Fifth Avenue to supersede Broadway in the interest of the visiting public."

A year or so later, Lord Acton, in his *American Diaries,* confirmed the fact that Fifth Avenue had become the most elegant street in the city.

"The 'great people' of the city no longer live on Broadway but on Fifth Avenue. Here impressive structures of brown sandstone, of a richly decorated style of architecture, lend quietude and splendor to this New World Belgravia."

Another Londoner, William Chambers, in *Things as They Are in America,* wrote of "their plate glass windows, silvered door handles, plates, and bellpulls, and 'superb' furnishings and interiors." He described one mansion: ". . . the spacious entrance hall was laid with tesselated wood; one of the apartments was panelled in the old baronial fashion; and in a magnificent dining room, the marble chimney-piece cost as much as $1500."

There were some people, however, who did not think life on Fifth Avenue was quite up to snuff. Fanny Kemble Butler, an English actress who had been well received in the city at the time, wrote:

This is one of the first houses here, so I conclude that I am to consider what I see as a tolerable sample of the ways and manner of being, doing, and suffering of the best society in New York. There were about twenty people. The women were in a sort of French demi-toilette, with bare necks and long sleeves, heads fizzled out after the very last petit-courtier, and thread-net handkerchiefs and capes, the whole of which, to my English eye, appeared a strange marrying of incongruities. The women, here like those of most warm climates, ripen early and decay proportionately soon. They are generally speaking, pretty, with good complexions and an air of freshness and brilliancy, but this, I am told, is very evanescent; and whereas in England a woman is in the bloom of health and beauty from twenty-five to thirty, here they scarcely reach the first period without being faded and old looking. They marry young, and this is another reason why age comes prematurely upon them. There was a fair young thing at dinner to-day who did not look above seventeen, and she was a wife. As for their figures, like those of French women, they are too well dressed for one to judge what they are really like; they are, for the most part, short and slight, with remarkably pretty feet and ankles; but there's too much pelerine and petticoat and de quoi of every sort to guess anything more. The climate of this country is the scapegoat upon which all the ill-looks and ill health of the ladies is laid; but while they are brought up as effeminately as they are, take as little exercise, live in rooms like ovens during the winter, and marry as early as they do, it will appear evident that many causes combine with an extremely variable climate to sallow their complexions and destroy their constitutions.

In contrast to the elegance of Fifth Avenue to 23rd Street, the area farther uptown was still the home of farmers and squatters. The *New York Times* on December 9, 1851, included the following item: "A few days ago a man by the name of Cornelius Sullivan was arrested by the 19th Ward police, charged with violating the law by persisting in skinning dead horses in 40th and 42nd Streets, just off of the Fifth Avenue, to the great annoyance of the residents in that section of the city. He was sentenced to six months in prison as a caution to men who are in the habit of skinning dead horses or other animals in that area."

AS LATE AS 1848, THE NORTHEAST CORNER OF 14TH STREET WAS STILL OCCUPIED BY A WORKING FARM

The old Springler market-garden farm, twenty-two acres in size, was originally a part of the Elias Brevoort farm, passing to the Springler family in 1788. For years the old house retained its charming bucolic atmosphere, with vegetable gardens and fruit trees on the grounds and cows and chickens wandering in the front yard. It was said to be the most expensive piece of pastureland known to agriculture. Springler, when told that keeping loose chickens in the front yard was rather low class in light of the newly attained elegance of the neighborhood, was said to have commented: "There's nothing wrong with chickens. They provide eggs for breakfast, soup for lunch, meat for dinner and pillows to sleep on at night. If they want to walk around in my front yard, it's quite all right with me." The house was finally demolished about 1850, and the Van Beuren house, built by Mrs. Mary S. Van Beuren, Springler's granddaughter and principal heir, was put up in its place.

IN 1850, ON THE NORTHEAST CORNER OF 18TH STREET, AUGUST BELMONT BUILT HIS SPECTACULAR HOUSE

With the opening of the Belmont house, Fifth Avenue entered a new phase of its history. No longer was it strictly the home of the New York families of the older society. It became a status symbol for the socially aspiring new millionaires. In the following decades the names of Astor, Vanderbilt, Rockefeller, Gould, Carnegie, Frick, Clark, Ryan, Whitney, Yerkes, and Stewart all figured prominently in the history of the Avenue.

As yet, the Astors still lived on Astor Place in Colonnade Row. Commodore Vanderbilt, despite his immense wealth, had no desire to climb socially and led a quiet life. It was the cultured and erudite Belmont who almost singlehandedly transformed New York society from provinciality into international urbanity.

Belmont, shortly after his marriage to a Gentile girl, Caroline Slidell Perry, daughter of Commodore Matthew Calbraith Perry, moved with his bride into the impressive mansion. Commodore Perry had successfully opened the ports of Japan to the commerce of the world. Prior to his arrival, the Land of the Rising Sun had been known as the Hermit Kingdom and had had little trade with foreign nations. Perry arranged a treaty guaranteeing protection for shipwrecked United States seamen, granting United States vessels the right to buy coal, and opening the ports of Shimoda and Hakodate to United States trade. In acknowledgment of his service, the United States Government presented the Commodore with a silver plate service of great elegance and value. It was used in the Belmont house on great occasions, as was the commodore —as a butler! Needless to say, eyebrows arched and shocked gasps were scarcely stifled when the parvenu Belmont sent the old man down to the wine cellar to fetch some bottles of fine Madiera, adding, "Try not to shake them on the stairs!"

The novelist Edith Wharton in *The Age of Innocence* wrote at length of the Belmonts and their annual ball: "Mrs. Julius Beaufort [Mrs. Belmont], on the night of her annual ball, never failed to appear at the Opera: indeed, she always gave her ball on an Opera night in order to emphasize her complete superiority to household cares, and her possession of a staff of servants competent to organize every detail of the entertainment in her absence."

The ballroom itself claimed the novelist's attention: "The Beauforts' house was one of the few in New York that possessed a ball room . . . and at a time when it was beginning to be thought Provincial to put a 'crash' over the drawing-room floor and move the furniture upstairs, the possession of a ball room that was used for no other purpose, and left for three-hundred-and-sixty-four days of the year to shuttered darkness, with its gilt chairs stacked in a corner and its chandelier in a bag; this undoubted superiority was felt to compensate for whatever was regrettable in the Beaufort past."

Of the dinners held at the house, Edith Wharton wrote: "[Beaufort] carried everything before him and all New York into his drawing rooms, and for over twenty years now people had said they were going to the Beauforts' with the same tone of security as if they had said they were going to Mrs. Manson Mingott's and with the added satisfaction of knowing they would get hot canvas-back ducks and vintage wines, instead of tepid Veuve Cliquot without a year and warmed-up croquettes from Philadelphia."

She shed this light on customs of the era: "The Beaufort house was one that New Yorkers were proud to show to foreigners, especially on the night of the annual ball. The Beauforts had been among the first people in New York to own their own red velvet carpet and have it rolled down the steps by their own footmen, under their own awning, instead of hiring it with the supper and the ball-room chairs. They had also inaugurated the

The Crystal Palace's most spectacular hour. The structure, which stood behind the

reservoir at 42nd Street and Fifth Avenue, burned to the ground on October 5, 1858.

Central Park as it looks today in the early spring.

The gates at the entrance to the Central Park rose garden at Fifth Avenue and 105th Street, formerly the gates of the Cornelius Vanderbilt mansion which stood on the site of the present Bergdorf-Goodman department store.

A Fifth Avenue belle supervising the packing of her Saratoga trunk in 1879.

Corporal Thompson's Madison Cottage at the intersection

of Broadway, Fifth Avenue, and 23rd Street in 1852.

The grand ball for the prince of Wales at the Academy of Music, October 12, 1860.

The Colored Orphan Asylum, on the west side of Fifth Avenue between 43rd

and 45th streets. Lithograph from *Valentine's Manual*, 1868.

The destruction of the Colored Orphan Asylum at Fifth Avenue

between 43rd and 45th streets during the Draft Riots of 1863.

The Croton Cottage or Old Country Inn, on the corner of Fifth Avenue

and 40th Street, was destroyed during the Draft Riots of 1863.

The entrance hall of A. T. Stewart's marble palace, Fifth Avenue and 34th

Street, where the widow Stewart would wander aimlessly through the night.

Tyson's Meat Market and Ye Olde Willow Cottage, Fifth

Avenue at 44th Street. This picture was taken in 1905.

The view north from Fifth Avenue and 51st Street. In the right foreground is one of the

William H. Vanderbilt twin houses, with the William K. Vanderbilt house to the north.

custom of letting the ladies take their cloaks off in the hall, instead of shuffling up to the hostess's bedroom and recurling their hair with the aid of the gas-burner; Beaufort was understood to have said that he supposed all his wife's friends had maids who saw to it that they were properly coiffed when they left home."

Shortly after Commodore Perry returned from Japan in 1854, a great reception was held at the house in honor of the first visiting Japanese envoys. It was a nine-day wonder, as New York's elite scrambled to secure invitations to the Belmont reception, and great crowds gathered outside the house the evening of the party to see what real Japanese looked like. The Japanese were followed all over the city by crowds for the duration of their visit.

Belmont's substantial collection of pictures was hung in a gallery in the house, which was the first to use a skylight for natural illumination.

It included works by Madrazo, Meyer, Rosa Bonheur, Meissonier, Munkacsy, Vibert, and several nudes by Bouguereau. It is interesting to note that today the pictures of most of these once-fashionable artists barely bring at auction the original cost of the canvas.

Belmont was never one to be put down. Even before he moved into his 18th Street mansion, his neighbor across the street, James Lenox, disapproved of virtually all that he did. When Belmont learned that Lenox outspokenly had said that he thought the nude Bouguereaus were scandalous, Belmont purposely hung the most erotic of them in the front hallway where it was on view to Lenox directly across the street every time that Belmont's door was open. According to the late Lucius Beebe, Lenox had become obsessive about Belmont's extravagance, and hearing from his butler that Belmont spent at least $20,000 a year on wine alone, the old man collapsed of a heart attack and died on the spot.

IN 1850, FIFTH AVENUE'S CITIZENS WERE SEIZED WITH A MANIA THAT TOOK SEVERAL YEARS TO RUN ITS COURSE

Spiritualism, a craze that developed after the notorious "Rochester knockings" of 1849, and the subsequent performance of two sisters named Fox who had managed to conjure up some unearthly sounds at a public demonstration, invaded the parlors of nearly every major house on the Avenue.

Spirit circles emerged, mediums flourished, the most renowned and powerful men in the country became involved, publications such as the *Spiritual Telegraph* appeared, and a member of Congress proposed that the government appropriate money for an investigation. James Russell Lowell, having serious doubts about the entire matter, said of a Judge Wells ". . . he is such a powerful medium that he has to drive back the furniture from following him when he goes out, as one might a pack of too affectionate dogs."

In 1855, George Templeton Strong wrote: "Professor Hare's lecture last Friday night somewhat talked of. As reported it seemed sad stuff . . . What would I have said six years ago to anybody who predicted that before the enlightened nineteenth century was ended, hundreds of thousands of people in this country would believe themselves able to communicate daily with the ghosts of their grandfathers? . . . that ex-judges of the Supreme Court, senators, clergymen, professors of physical sciences, should be lecturing and writing books on the new treasure of all this, and that others among the steadiest and most conservative of my acquaintances should acknowledge that they look on the subject with distrust and dread, as a visible manifestation of diabolic agency?"

According to one story, Cornelius Vanderbilt himself had consulted a seer and in her presence mentioned that he had respected the late Jim Fisk's tips on the stock market. When the medium conjured up the presence of his late wife, Sophia, the commodore refused to speak with her. "Business before pleasure," he commanded. "Let me speak with Jim Fisk."

By 1860, the craze had run its course. At a lecture in Chickering Hall at 18th Street and Fifth Avenue, a discourse on the subject became such a ludicrous farce that the audience got its money's worth in laughter rather than in practical instruction. The incident marked the demise of spiritualism as a fashionable diversion.

DURING THE FIRST HALF OF THE DECADE, A STEADY STREAM OF FOREIGN NOTABLES PASSED THROUGH THE CITY; WITH ONE GLARING EXCEPTION, ALL WERE ENTERTAINED IN FIFTH AVENUE HOMES

The first to arrive, in September of 1850 was Jenny Lind, the "Swedish Nightingale," imported by the noted impresario, P. T. Barnum. Thousands of New Yorkers awaited her arrival at the wharf, and when she disembarked, bouquets of flowers and baskets of fruit were showered upon her. The fashion crowd—dressmakers, milliners, and furriers—were out in full force, offering to clothe her from head to toe gratuitously. A chorus of 250 people gathered nearby to sing a welcome, which Philip Hone described as being "a blast . . . loud and dread."

The following day, a prize was awarded to Bayard Taylor of Fifth Avenue. A contest had been arranged by Barnum, in which amateur songwriters were to submit a song for Jenny Lind to sing at her first concert. The prize was $200, plus the diva's rendition of Taylor's "Welcome to America."

Her concerts, needless to say, were completely sold out. Wherever she went, crowds followed her, ultimately compelling her to leave her hotel in order to escape the hysterical fans. In a gracious token of her appreciation of her reception she changed her contract with Barnum. Instead of $1,000 a night originally stipulated, she took one-half of the net profits. Her share for the opening performance amounted to the enormous sum of $12,500, which she distributed among the charitable and benevolent organizations of the city. The gesture endeared her to everyone from the fire department to the ladies of Fifth Avenue. To quote Hone on her visit, "New York is conquered; a hostile army or fleet could not effect a conquest so complete."

The following year, in 1851, Louis Kossuth, one of the principal figures in the Hungarian revolution of 1848, came to the United States to raise money. In April, 1849, Kossuth had become president of the newly proclaimed Hungarian republic, independent of Austria. He resigned the post in August, when Russian troops came to the aid of Austria, and spent the rest of his life in exile. Americans were naturally sympathetic to the democratic movement and the city accorded an unprecedented welcome to the Hungarian.

Hungarian national colors and flags virtually covered the city. Everyone wore Kossuth hats, and an immense parade proceeded up Fifth Avenue, witnessed by more than a million people. Kossuth was entertained at dozens of banquets, several given in the mansions along Fifth Avenue.

The same day, again under the aegis of the unpredictable P. T. Barnum, the notorious Lola Montez reached New York. Lola, an Irish girl whose success as a dancer was attributable more to her beauty than to her talents, had already generated her share of publicity. Everyone knew she was the mistress of mad King Ludwig of Bavaria, who had conferred upon her the title of countess of Lansfeld, and that she had virtually ruled the country until her banishment during the 1848 revolution. After fleeing from Bavaria, she had made her mark in Paris. The provocative announcement by Barnum of her arrival in this country caused a great deal of indignation among the ladies and even more eager anticipation among the men.

From the start, her visit was surrounded with stormy controversy. She made the crossing on the same boat as Kossuth, a fact that ruffled her feathers, because despite her beauty and reputation, she knew the Hungarian patriot would steal the show upon arrival in New York. He did. Then there was the messy business between Barnum and Lola's French agent, with the result that both threatened to sue her. In addition, there was the gossip. It was said that Lola held wild orgies in her quarters every night and that her bed was large enough to hold three people comfortably. The fact that the star smoked, and, according to the stories, five hundred cigarettes a day, added more to her lurid reputation. Mezzotints of her appeared in New York shops, the most popular entitled "A Belle of the Boulevards," which portrayed her as a ranking Paris poule de luxe. The New York Herald ran a series titled "Three Evenings with Lola Montez" that was supposed to describe soirees in her Paris salon.

This notoriety, and the fact that Kossuth had upstaged her, forced Lola to retreat to a large house on Waverly Place. Night after night, the curious and the young bucks of the Lower Fifth Avenue area stood beneath her window begging her to appear. She would come to the window to acknowledge their presence, but she apparently never invited them to her quarters.

Finally, Kossuth departed on his tour of the rest of the country. The New York Herald said: "Lola Montez, lacking only the sanctification of the Church and a pair of wings to make her a complete angel—Lola Montez—the bright eyed, the piquant, witty, handsome, and sparkling Lola—will, with the departure of Kossuth, come out, like the moon emerging from a total eclipse in a clear sky, and the more brilliant from the late obscuration." The New York Herald was correct. A few days later, on Christmas Day, Lola emerged to take what was hers. New Yorkers were informed that she would present one performance, on December 29, of a ballet especially written for her. A public auction of seats was held, and tickets were sold for from four to five times the usual price.

Twenty-seven hundred men and thirty women came to see her dancing feet and her noncostumes. The next day the New York Herald said: "As a danseuse, she is decidedly inferior to Cerrito, Madame Augusta, and others, but there is a nameless grace of nature about her person and movements, which with her history, gives her an attraction that a better artist could not command, but which is not destined to be very lasting."

The notice was prophetic, as Lola left town shortly thereafter. Ultimately she died in poverty in California.

The following November, the parade of visitors resumed. In the wake of the Swedish soprano, the fiery Middle European patriot, and the Irish sex siren, came a British literary lion, the author of Vanity Fair, William M. Thackeray, accompanied by his artist protégé, Eyre Crowe. From the day that his ship pulled into the harbor at Halifax, Nova Scotia, the newspapers were filled with news of his visit. After a quiet reception and favorable reviews in Boston, the author made his way to New York where controversy raged in the press. James Gordon Bennett campaigned to discredit him as a snob, but Henry James, Sr., in the *New York Tribune* wrote cordially: "The merchant clerks of New York aspire to the culture of scholars and gentlemen, and import from abroad—not the latest teacher of double entry, but the most thoughtful critic of manners and society, the subtlest humorist, and the most effective, because the most genial satirist the age has known."

Thackeray's first lecture was delivered on November 19 and was, with the rest of the series, a sellout. More than two thousand New Yorkers heard him speak. William Cullen Bryant wrote in the *New York Evening Post:* "Few expected to see so large a man; he is gigantic, six feet four at least; few expected to see so old a person, his hair appears to have kept its silvery record over fifty years; and there was a notion in the minds of many that there must be something dashing and 'fast' in his appearance, whereas his costume was perfectly plain; the expression of his face, grave and earnest; his address perfectly unaffected and such as we might expect to meet with in a well bred man somewhat advanced in years." The *New York Times,* however, was quite irreverent: "We were never more thoroughly impressed with the extreme utility of *pockets,* than after witnessing the infinite service to which he put them. If, on commencing his lecture, he had suddenly discovered that they had vanished from his coat-skirts—one in and the other out—one in his coat and the other in his vest—one upon the desk, and the other pocketed—these various movements constituted the *gamut* of his gesticulation."

Of his lectures the *New York Herald* said: "[Thackeray] lectured on some of the most objectionable writers in all English literature to an audience that included women and children. These lectures have already created a market for these works (of unmitigated filth and grossness) and they are scattering their insidious poison in thousands of families, sapping the virtue of thousands of young hearts."

But Thackeray was not to be undone or outdone. Under a pseudonym, he wrote a hilarious article for *Fraser's Magazine* entitled "Mr. Thackeray in the United States." About his writing practices he said: "One of his most singular habits is that of making rough sketches for caricatures on his fingernails. The phosphoric ink he originally used has destroyed his entire nails, so his fingers are now tipped with horn, on which he draws his portraits." His moral character was summed up in these words: "Mr. Thackeray has a passion for daguerrotypes, of which he has a collection of many thousands. Most of these he took unobserved from the outer gallery of St. Paul's." His autosatirical comments on his personality included this story: "He is disputatious and loquacious to a degree in company; and at a dinner at the Bishop of Oxford's the discussion with Mr. Macaulay, respecting the death of Mausolus, the husband of Zenobia, occupied the disputants for thirteen hours ere either rose to retire. Mr. Macaulay was found exhausted under the table."

Shortly after his first lecture Thackeray was besieged with invitations to the great houses of Fifth Avenue. He wrote home to his daughters, "I go to dinner before the lecture, to parties afterwards, and receiving visitors or writing notes all day, and the pace of London is nothing to the racketing life of New York."

He wrote of his impressions of New York in letters saying, "the jolly manner answers here very well, which I have from Nature or Art possibly." Of the ladies he said, they are "as lean as greyhounds and all dressed like the most stunning French actresses." Comparing New York to Boston and Philadelphia, he said: "New York society is the simplest and least pretentious; it sufficeth that a man should keep a fine house, give parties, and have a daughter to get all the world to him. I went to a ball lately at the house of one of the veriest order of counter-jumpers. I mean not pretending to be anything but the commonest man, making money out of a dry-goods store (and a great deal of money too); covering his walls with gilding and damask and his table with foie-gras, canvas-back ducks and the best wines. And the Society all came—the very best society.

The houses are got up in a style of extraordinary uncomfortable splendor—every house is new—so new that none of 'em are even papered as yet; and the drawing rooms blaze with gold and yellow damask; and on the bare walls you see little two-penny pictures and coloured prints." He closed his letter by saying: "The nouveau riche have not got the sentiment of the Fine Arts yet, which is the last to come generally in a civilization."

Thackeray's exposure to New York was not restricted to the Fifth Avenue glitter circuit. One evening, a Mr. Baxter invited him to dinner at his modest home on Second Avenue. The author accepted promptly and with enthusiasm. It was at that dinner that he met Sally, the eighteen-year-old daughter of the unpretentious gentleman. He soon became quite attached to the family and was welcomed as a regular member of the household. At dinner a place was always set for him at the hostess's right, and a bottle of his favorite claret was placed there. From the start, he found Sally enchanting and said that she was "exactly my idea of Beatrix Esmond," the heroine of one of his novels. He listened to her tales of dances and beaux and feigned melodramatic jealousy. As time passed, he became more and more infatuated with the girl and the rather touching relationship continued through the years. Sally eventually married, and Thackeray became a lifelong friend of the young couple.

Many years later, on the wall of his sitting room in London, hung a print that he had bought because it resembled Sally when he first met her. Among the superb Queen Anne furniture and the old masters, the inexpensive Currier and Ives lithograph, *The Belle of the West,* must have seemed quite out of place, but it was a poignant reminder of the joy, the frivolity, the sentiment, and the love he had found in New York.

WHILE THE PARADE OF CELEBRITIES PASSED THROUGH THE CITY, SEVERAL MAJOR AND MINOR CRISES OCCUPIED THE MINDS OF THE DENIZENS OF THE AVENUE

The week-long oyster panic of 1854 began with a rumor: Oysters—whether raw, broiled, boiled, or roasted—caused cholera. Housewives boycotted them. Delmonico's refused to serve them. Gourmets denied themselves. Finally, Bishop Brown heartily consumed a plateful at a party and issued the following edict: "If any gentleman can prove he died of the oysters, I'll pay his expenses to the cemetery. There is no serious increase of cholera cases, and probably no foundation for distrust of osyters". The bishop lived and the oyster panic died.

In October, 1854, a disaster at sea affected many prominent Fifth Avenue families. On the morning of the eleventh, people were awakened by newsboys shouting, "Four hundred lives lost at sea!" Many families, including Allens, Pearsons, Browns, and Woodruffs learned from lists in the extra editions of their papers that their loved ones had perished in the sinking of the *Arctic.*

In 1857, public order again became a problem. Since the Astor Place Riot of 1849, more than half a million immigrants had settled in New York, mostly on the Lower East Side. The newcomers were primarily either German or Irish in origin, and there was contention between the two groups. The Five Points area along the Bowery was reputed to be so lawless that a well-dressed citizen could not pass safely in the neighborhood even at high noon. On the Fourth of July, fighting broke out between the Germans and the Irish, and when the authorities intervened, the two groups united to battle the New York City militia. Several persons were killed and many were injured before the disturbance was quelled.

ON JULY 14, 1853, ON LAND IMMEDIATELY WEST OF THE CROTON RESERVOIR AT FIFTH AVENUE AND 42ND STREET, PRESIDENT FRANKLIN PIERCE OPENED THE FIRST WORLD'S FAIR TO TAKE PLACE IN THE UNITED STATES

The Crystal Palace, an imitation of its prototype in London, constructed of glass and iron and presumably fireproof, housed the international exhibition of the arts and industries of many nations.

The day of the opening the structure was a beehive of activity as laborers worked among the crowds of spectators to finish the building and merchants from abroad supervised the unpacking of large cases and crates of every size and description. One hundred and fifty exhibitors entered the show, and more than seven thousand people attended on opening night.

New York's merchants, with characteristic commercial enterprise, opened dozens of shops in the area bearing the name *Crystal*. There was a Crystal Cake Shop, Crystal Dairy, Crystal Orangerie, Crystal Fruit Stall, and Crystal Stables, and one dilapidated old building was named the Crystal Hall of Pleasure.

World fairs have not changed much over the past century. To be found at the Crystal Palace were statues of George Washington, Daniel Webster, Napoleon, and various gypsies as well as porcelain pigs, a painting of naked whites being cooked by cannibals, wild boars' heads in bronze, dying herons in stone, bits of machinery, newly found gold nuggets from California, and bad copies of good paintings. But perhaps the most unusual exhibition involved the most unfortunate gentleman "it was ever our lot to encounter," to quote the *New York Times*. He inhabited a glass case belonging to an exhibition of trusses, artificial limbs, and suspenders. There was not a single part of the poor man's body that did not require relief. He had a patent left leg, and his right leg was covered in a bandage for the cure of varicose veins. The trusses he wore were in alarming numbers. His arms were in splints, and his suspenders were something approximating a straitjacket. "He was a lamentable instance of human infirmity and, although made of wax, much to be pitied," according to the *Times*.

Immediately after the palace opened, it assumed symbolic significance. During the mid-nineteenth century, virtually everything that happened in the city was covered extensively from the pulpit, and most of the more spectacular sermons were reprinted in the newspapers. One clergyman, a Mr. Chapin, preached a sermon on the "moral implications" of the Crystal Palace on the next Sunday. He said: "We look upon those forms of beauty and implements of utility, and ask, for what means all this?—why is man to toil and achieve?—there must be something beyond all this—can Man be satisfied with this mere outward splendor? Would all the riches displayed beneath that dome of glass enable him to walk through the temptations of life, and prepare him the better to meet Death? What is it, if there be not a great object to be attained beyond all this toil and struggle? Cast our eye around that glorious array, and if you look at it in its moral significance, it teaches us that there is a great end in life beyond merely toiling and achieving conquests of Matter. . . . And it tells us that Man can break through material limits, and, by the grace of the Divine Spirit in his soul, press forward to higher activities, and a closer assimilation to God himself."

Or, in short, as far as the church was concerned, the Crystal Palace brought all those who viewed its exhibition nearer to God.

William Wallace, a poet of the period invariably called upon to immortalize in verse all that happened in the city, wrote an ode, which also took on an exultant tone:

> No signal-fires are shown,
> No blood-red banners are unfurled,
> No haughter trumps are blown,
> No glittering armies shake the world,
> And yet the Nations meet;
> They meet, with placid brows, and hateless eyes,
> From distant realms, and Oceans shadowy foam,
> As meet the stars in evening's stormless skies,
> Beneath one mighty dome—
> As meet the rivers, and, in meeting make
> One peaceful and majestic sea,
> Whose crystal deeps, through far expanses, take
> The aspect of Eternity.

Whether or not man was reconciled to God is debatable. An event in the Crystal Palace did precipitate America's reconciliation with Queen Victoria. On August 16, 1858, after the successful laying of Cyrus W. Field's Atlantic cable, President Buchanan received a message via the cable from the British sovereign. New York was overcome with excitement. In the morning scores of guns and cannons fired salutes, at noon hundreds of bells rang out over all the city, and in the evening the sky was illuminated by fireworks—so

many, in fact, that City Hall caught fire. That night, Field was feted in the grand manner in the Crystal Palace. The party was jubilant. The following day, however, much to everybody's chagrin, the cable failed, not to be repaired until after the Civil War.

The most spectacular day for the Crystal Palace came five years later. At about five o'clock in the afternoon on October 5, 1858, fifteen hundred people were milling around viewing the international exhibitions. One of the three giant steam calliopes had just finished playing "Pop! Goes the Weasle." Suddenly, from a small room in the basement, a burst of flames appeared. Fire rushed up the staircase, igniting a thirty-one-star gas illuminator, swept through a room filled with paints and varnishes, and climbed an exhibit of bedding to the side of the main dome. In an instant, the entire dome was encircled with fire. The heat caused the iron girders to snap like glass, and in precisely thirteen minutes, the entire palace collapsed.

The light from the fire drew crowds larger than the palace had seen since its opening. The fire department arrived, but nothing remained to be saved. Miraculously, not one life was lost. As there were no turnstiles to block the exits and the sides of the building were made of glass, patrons could escape by hurling bricks through the glass walls. The loss was staggering, and the fire put an end to "fireproof" iron and glass structures in this country.

Another showplace, the Latting Observatory, just north of the palace, suffered a similar fate. The invention of the elevator had made possible the construction of this timber and iron structure, which rose 350 feet into the air. A steam elevator carried the passengers to the top for a panoramic view of the city. Despite the fact that $100,000 had been invested in the project, it failed because the reservoir at Fifth Avenue and 42nd Street, with its high walls, provided a space where visitors could stroll and stare out over the city without cost. The Latting Observatory burned down in 1856.

AS FIFTH AVENUE CONTINUED TO STRETCH NORTHWARD, MANY OF NEW YORK'S EXCLUSIVE CLUBS AND PROMINENT CITIZENS MOVED UP-TOWN

Organized in 1864, the Manhattan Club, home of "Swallow-tail Democracy," moved into the Parker mansion at the southeast corner of Fifth and 15th Street, where it remained until 1890 when it moved into the A. T. Stewart mansion at 34th Street and Fifth. Colonel Henry Watterson, one of its most picturesque members, said of it: "With the Union Club and the Union League its contemporaries, and Century its senior, the Manhattan Club links the life of old New York with that of the wonderous great Metropolis." Its first president was John Van Buren, son of President Van Buren.

The Lotos Club, founded several years later, occupied the southwest corner of 21st Street. Known for almost one hundred years as the Godfather of the Arts, it originally confined its membership to men of eminence in the professions or the arts. As time passed, membership was broadened "to let in such businessmen as were lovers of literature and art".

The name of the club derives from Tennyson's poem "The Lotos-Eaters," which contains lines the founders thought epitomized their aspirations for the club: "In the afternoon they came unto a land, in which it seemed always afternoon."

The dinner honoring Sir Henry Morton Stanley for his successful search for Dr. David Livingstone in Africa was held at the Lotos Club. Others honored at dinners or receptions have included Offenbach, Strauss, Saint-Saëns, Paderewski, Caruso, Joan Sutherland, Van Cliburn, the de Reszkes, Martinelli, Lily Pons, and Lawrence Tibbett.

At the dinner to fete Mary Garden in 1922, Chauncey Depew stared all evening at her strapless evening gown, the first ever seen this side of the Atlantic. He finally asked the diva what held it up, only to be told, "Nothing but your extreme age." The club is currently located in a landmark building on East 66th Street that dates to the turn of the century.

The Union League Club, located south of 23rd Street on Fifth, was established in 1863 to provide a focus for pro-Lincoln sentiment in New York. Its original members included William Cullen Bryant, Frederick Law Olmsted, William T. Blodgett, Joseph H. Choate, John Taylor Johnston, and the Reverend Henry W. Bellows. It was in the Union League Club that John Jay first proposed the establishment of the Metropolitan Museum of Art. At a meeting on November 23, 1869, Jay said, "The Union League Club might properly institute the best means for promoting this great object of a major art museum."

The Union Club, the first of its kind in the city, was founded in 1836, with Number 1 Bond Street as its first home. In 1854, the land at the northwest corner of 21st Street was secured. The following year the club moved into its new Fifth Avenue building, the first in New York erected exclusively for club purposes.

Washington Irving was primarily responsible for the formation of the Saint Nicholas Society. In 1832, when he returned to this country after living in Europe for seventeen years, his many friends gave a large dinner in his honor at the City Hotel. Three hundred persons were present to welcome him home. Responding to the tributes and toasts, he called attention to the fact that "there did not exist such a thing as a society of old New Yorkers, some of whom I have written about sometime since." The Saint Nicholas Society, organized in 1835, restricted its membership to descendants of prerevolutionary settlers of the city. The club was housed for a time at the southwest corner of 45th Street and Fifth Avenue.

In 1855, Marshall O. Roberts built a mansion on the southeast corner of 18th Street and the Avenue in which he displayed his *Washington Crossing the Delaware,* now the property of the Metropolitan Museum of Art. During the period, Peter Marie, Samuel F. B. Morse, W. Loring Andrews, and Edward Clark also took up residence on Fifth Avenue.

IN 1856, JOHN GOTTLEIB WENDEL BUILT A SEVERELY SIMPLE FOUR-STORY BRICK HOUSE AT THE NORTH-WEST CORNER OF FIFTH AVENUE AND 39TH STREET, FAR BEYOND THE FASHIONABLE DISTRICT

John Wendel's fortune was tied up with that of John Jacob Astor, for his grandfather was Astor's first partner in the fur business. Wendel and the three sisters who lived with him were quiet, antisocial, and always surrounded by mystery. As recently as 1934, strollers along the Avenue gazed through the high fence that surrounded the house and viewed the runway that Ella Wendel had built as a playground for her treasured

dog Toto. All during the early days of the twentieth century, real estate interests unsuccessfully tried to induce the remaining Wendel sisters to sell the property. When Ella died, the house was assessed at $5,000, and the entire property assessed at $1,897,000. Today it is the site of Kress's five-and-ten-cent store. A plaque on the door of the building commemorates this peculiar family.

THE FORESIGHT OF A SMALL GROUP OF MEN IN 1856 PROVIDED FIFTH AVENUE AND THE ENTIRE CITY WITH A GREENSWARD THAT TODAY IS ONE OF THE FEW OASES IN MANHATTAN— CENTRAL PARK

As Fifth Avenue and the city spread northward, it became apparent to civic-minded persons that park space was sparse indeed. In 1850, London's 1,442 acres of park provided recreation areas of 500 acres for every one hundred thousand people, whereas in New York the meager 100 acres afforded only 16 acres per one hundred thousand. Andrew J. Downing, an American landscape gardener, was the first to point out this discrepancy. Mayor Kingland ordered a three-man committee to investigate the situation. At the time, the area between Park Avenue and the East River from 66th Street to 75th Street had been set aside as parkland. The mayor thought, however, this area far too small for a city that soon would house three-quarters of a million people. The present area of Central Park was suggested.

At that time, the area consisted of outcroppings of rock, barren landscape, quarries, and a shantytown of five thousand squatters. These people, primarily Irish and German immigrants, lived in huts, ate garbage, and kept more than one hundred thousand animals on their appropriated property. Horses, pigs, goats, cows, chickens, ducks, dogs, and cats freely roamed the area. Many streams crisscrossed the land, most ending in swamps whose miasmas polluted the air. The reeking enclave hardly seemed destined to become the lovely place it is today.

Many objected that the location was simply too far away. With the exception of a few hardy souls who had built farther uptown, 34th Street was the northern limit of the city at the time. Fortunately, the city's public officials realized that unless action were taken immediately this open space would soon be lost. Park commissioners were appointed, and with pistols at their sides to protect themselves against the squatters, they marched through the area north of what is today 59th Street. The park was laid out, 760 acres in size. Some 376 acres of ground that lay in private hands had been purchased at a cost of $5.5 million.

Thirty-three renderings were entered in the competition for the design of the park. The plan by Frederick Law Olmsted and Calvert Vaux was selected. Olmsted had adopted an informal plan modeled on the gardens of France and Italy. The construction of the park provided many immigrants with work during the depression of 1857, and the formal opening took place twenty years later in 1876.

Chapter Three

THE MADISON SQUARE ERA IN THE 1860S

CHRONOLOGY

1860   New York City population is 1,174,779.

Abraham Lincoln, candidate for president of the United States, makes his famous speech at Cooper Union.

Commissioners are appointed to lay out streets north of 155th Street.

1861   Fort Sumter is captured by the Confederates, and the Seventh Regiment of New York departs for the front under Colonel M. Lefferts.

A seat on the Stock Exchange is sold for the first time at auction for $460.

1862   The first hansom cab appears on the streets of New York.

John Ericsson's *Monitor,* later famous because of its engagement with the *Merrimac* during the Civil War, is launched at Greenpoint, Brooklyn.

Delmonico's opens at 14th Street.

1863   The Subtreasury occupies the building at Wall and Nassau streets.

The Draft Riots occur in New York.

1864   A metropolitan fair held in New York nets more than $1 million for the United States Sanitary Commission.

1865   The volunteer fire department is replaced by a professional metropolitan fire district.

Telegraph communication is opened between New York and San Francisco.

The funeral cortege of Lincoln passes through the city.

1866   The Free Academy becomes the College of the City of New York.

1867   "Stock tickers" are introduced.

Plan for West Side development, including Riverside Drive, is adopted by the city.

Prospect Park opens in Brooklyn.

1868 Sorosis, the first women's club in New York, is founded.

New York Athletic Club is organized.

The Beach Pneumatic Transit Company is given the right to build a subway from 14th Street to Nassau Street, but the attempt is abandoned.

The first experimental elevated railroad is erected from the Battery to Cortlandt Street on Greenwich Street.

Plans for consolidation into five boroughs are proposed by Andrew H. Green of Brooklyn.

1869 Broadway is laid out as a boulevard north of 59th Street.

First apartment house built by Rutherford Stuyvesant at 142 East 18th Street; Richard Morris Hunt is the architect.

The panic of Black Friday occurs when Jay Gould and Jim Fisk attempt to corner the gold market.

In 1860, the nation hovered on the brink of Civil War, and in New York sympathy for the Southern cause was not lacking. Merchants of the city controlled the cotton trade and the power structure stood to gain by the status quo. An illegal slave trade thrived, and traders met regularly at Sweet's Restaurant on Fulton Street.

In this year before the storm, the center of Manhattan stood at Madison Square. Lower Fifth Avenue continued to be a prosperous residential area and mansions were being constructed in the forties and even as far north as the fifties. Other avenues of the city paralleled the expansion on Fifth with more modest constructions, and the city fathers, considering the population of 1,174,779, had laid out the streets as far north as 155th Street.

Society was dominated by the "robber barons" as Astors, Vanderbilts, Goulds, and Fisks built houses along the Avenue. Fortunes made in rent gouging, opium smuggling, prostitution, and the slave trade became respectable.

Entertaining was still done primarily in private homes. Ladies dressed in crinolines, with full skirts and tightly corseted waists. Black net over flesh-colored stockings set off high shoes or boots. A poem of the period summarizes the fashion:

Now crinoline is all the rage with ladies of whatever age,
A petticoat made like a cage—oh, what a ridiculous
 fashion!
'Tis formed of hoops and bars of steel, or tubes of air which
 lighter feel,
And worn by girls to look genteel—or if they've figures
 to conceal.
It makes the dresses stick far out, a dozen yards or so
 about,
And pleases both the thin and stout—oh, what a ridiculous
 fashion!

MADISON SQUARE BECAME THE CENTER OF ELEGANT NEW YORK IN THE 1860S

Originally a potter's field, the area that became Madison Square subsequently was used as a parade ground. During the first few decades of the ninettenth century, a law still on the books required that every male sixteen years of age and over serve a specified period each year in the militia. In accordance with the law, the first of May was designated as Training Day, and each year, every eligible male appeared in uniform on the parade ground, which at that time stretched from Union Square on 14th Street to 34th Street. As the years passed, the uniforms from the revolutionary war and the War of 1812 became shabby and dirty, and the young men began to appear in every conceivable substitute. Eventually, the drill itself took on a festive atmosphere and, in fact, became merely an excuse for the men to get drunk. Finally, it was abolished, and by 1837, the parade ground was reduced to the present dimensions of Madison Square.

The square, named after President Madison, was formally opened in 1847. Prior to this date, a first in the annals of sports history took place in the square when organized baseball made its bow. The game was invented during the 1830s and was originally known as the New York game. The first code of rules was drawn up in 1845 by the Knickerbocker Baseball Club, whose principal participants were the Gotham, Eagle, and Empire clubs of New York and the Excelsior, Putnam, Atlantic, and Eckford clubs of Brooklyn. The first game was played in Madison Square.

By 1860, Fifth Avenue around Madison Square was lined with substantial mansions. Along the famous Ladies' Mile, stretching south down Broadway, were all the exclusive shops of the period. William Allen Butler in his poem "Miss Flora McFlimsey of Madison Square" satirized the fashionable young ladies of gentle birth:

Research in some of the upper ten districts
Reveal the most painful and startling statistics
Of which let me mention only a few
In one single house on the Fifth Avenue
Three young ladies were found, all below 22
Who have been three whole weeks without anything new
In the way of flounced silks, and, thus left in the lurch
Are unable to go to ball, concert or church.

During the 1860s a plague descended on the city, threatening the many tall poplars and sycamores that lined the streets in the Lower Fifth Avenue area. Armies of caterpillars infested the trees and stripped them of their leaves. Unaware of the principles of ecology, someone advanced the unfortunate idea of importing English sparrows from Britain to devour the caterpillars. As usual, the city responded with great enthusiasm. The birds readily adopted the houses built for them in Madison Square Park, devoured the caterpillars, and having accomplished that, proceeded to drive the finches, warblers, orioles, bluebirds, and every other native species from the city. Today, along with the pigeons, sparrows rule the roost in New York.

The statuary in and around the square was placed there between 1854 and 1898. The Worth Monument, erected in 1854, commemorates Major William J. Worth, a hero of the war with Mexico. He died in San Antonio in June, 1849, and a month later the Common Council appointed a committee to make arrangements to bring his body to the city for burial. His remains were temporarily interred in Greenwood Cemetery, and were moved in 1854 to the location between Broadway and Fifth Avenue, south of 25th Street, where they are today. This interment was the last allowed on city property.

In the years that followed, statues of Roscoe Conkling by J. Q. A. Ward, of Chester A. Arthur by George Bissell, and of William H. Seward by Randolph Rogers were all placed in the square. The Seward statue was made partially of a left-over Lincoln statue and was dedicated in 1876. It is a figure of colossal proportions with the legs and arms too long for the head. Evidently money ran out, so an earlier version of Lincoln was decapitated, and Seward's head was placed on top. To this day Seward holds a copy of the Emancipation Proclamation in his hand.

The Farragut statue by Augustus Saint-Gaudens, with a base by Stanford White, was dedicated on March 26, 1881. The city celebrated with a parade and an unveiling ceremony, and thousands of people gathered to witness the event.

Shortly after the Farragut unveiling the first electric light bulb to be publicly exhibited was placed in Madison Square. High atop a pole in the square, the gigantic light was visible up and down the Avenue and as far away as the Orange Mountains in New Jersey. The ladies were not particularly pleased with the invention; they found it unflattering to their complexions.

FIFTH AVENUE ALONG MADISON SQUARE CONTINUED TO PROSPER AND A SITE IN THIS AREA BECAME THE LOCATION OF THE FIFTH AVENUE HOTEL

The site on which the Fifth Avenue Hotel was built had a long and interesting history. In 1670, an unusual bequest was made by the governor of the province, Sir Edmond Andros. He granted thirty acres of land from 21st Street to 26th Street, bounded by Broadway on the east and Seventh Avenue on the west, to a free black man named Solomon Peters. This land remained in Peters's family until 1716, when his descendants sold the acreage to two whites, John Horn and Cornelius Webber.

The farmhouse on the property eventually passed to John Horn II in 1815. The house stood in the center of Fifth Avenue just south of 23rd

Street until November, 1839, when the city took possession of the land and moved the house to the northwest corner of 23rd Street and Fifth. There it was converted into a roadhouse, with Corporal Thompson as proprietor. A favorite meeting place of riders and drivers during the 1840s, Madison Cottage posted the following list of house rules:

Four pence a night for Bed
Six pence with Supper
No more than five sleep to one bed
No boots to be worn in bed
Organ Grinders to sleep in the Wash house
No dogs allowed upstairs
No beer allowed in the Kitchen
No Razor Grinders or Tinkers taken in.

The historian Abram Payton described the tavern as "the last stopping place for codgers, old and young." Many old New Yorkers, including Schermerhorns and Whitneys, frequently ended their day's activities with some liquid refreshment and a visit with the corporal at Madison Cottage.

Eventually, the cottage was torn down to make way for Franconi's Hippodrome. This mammoth structure, a circus, was two stories high and seven hundred feet in circumference. The roof was made of wood and canvas, and spanned the entire enclosure without supporting pillars. The immense oval central ring was two hundred feet wide and three hundred feet long. The hippodrome seated more than ten thousand people, with standing room for another three thousand spectators.

Spectacles presented in the hippodrome included pageants, gladiatorial contests, circuses, and chariot races. Before the opening night performance, ostriches and dozens of reindeer marched down Fifth Avenue in what was probably the most bizarre parade ever staged there.

Although the hippodrome was initially a spectacular success, the novelty soon wore off, and in 1859, after several years of failing business, the structure was torn down to make way for the Fifth Avenue Hotel. One of the city's most elegant institutions, it occupied the site from 1859 to 1909.

The opening of the hotel had been anticipated for several years, and with somewhat dubious enthusiasm. Martha Lamb noted in her *History of New York:* ". . . the world wondered, as it seemed quite too far from the heart of the city for popular patronage." When the building was finished, the *New York Times* commented: "That immense structure of white marble which has lighted up Madison Square and 23rd Street with its snowy front has at last been christened the Fifth Avenue Hotel, and is to be opened to the travelling public today. It is worthy to bear the name of the magnificent street on which it is placed and it may be taken, for the present at least, as the best specimen we can offer of the possibilities of hotel luxury, so far as mere externals go."

The hotel was constructed on the site by Abram Eno and leased to Paran Stevens of Boston, a man of notable credentials in the hotel business. It was the last word in elegance, with a gleaming marble facade and pillars with Corinthian capitals. The grand entrance hall was more than 160 feet in length, 27 feet in width, and 15 feet in height. The floors were of marble laid in alternate blocks of dark red and white. Barely one year after it opened, a foreign visitor assured its reputation as New York's finest hotel.

1860 WAS THE YEAR THE PRINCE OF WALES CAME TO NEW YORK ON AN OFFICIAL VISIT AND STAYED AT THE NEW FIFTH AVENUE HOTEL

The city showed no reticence in welcoming the nineteen-year-old future monarch. The climaxes of the visit were to be a grand ball at the Academy of Music on 14th Street and a spectacular

The New York Coaching Club proceeds down Fifth Avenue during the 1870s.

A bird's eye view of Central Park during the winter of 1865.

The first wing of the Metropolitan Museum of Art.

The Metropolitan Museum of Art as it looks today.

A refreshment stand at Fifth Avenue above 59th Street, near the entrance to Central Park, about 1870.

The Statue of Liberty's torch, displayed at Madison
Square in 1882 to raise money for the pedestal.

A view of Delmonico's restaurant on the southwest

corner of Fifth Avenue and 26th Street about 1890.

Mark Twain's seventieth birthday dinner at Delmonico's on December 5, 1905.

LEFT TO RIGHT: KATE DOUGLAS WIGGIN RIGGS, MARK TWAIN, THE REV-
EREND JOSEPH H. TWITCHELL, BLISS CARMAN, RUTH MCENERY STUART,
MARY E. WILKINS FREEMAN, HENRY MILES ALDEN, AND HENRY H. ROGERS.

A view of Fifth Avenue from 26th Street to Madison

Square about 1895. Delmonico's restaurant is to the right.

The New York Coaching Club and one of its public coaches, *The Peacock,* which ran from Dobbs Ferry and Hastings to Manhattan. The coach stands before the Holland House, a restaurant of the period located at the corner of Fifth Avenue and 30th Street.

Fifth Avenue four years after the death of Madame Restell. Notice

the plethora of perambulators. From a German edition of *Puck*.

The entrance to the University Club at Fifth Avenue and
54th Street, designed by McKim, Mead and White in 1899.

St. Patrick's Cathedral, shortly after its consecration.

Detail from the roof of the St. Regis Hotel, built in
1902 and designed by Trowbridge and Livingston.

The towers of St. Patrick's Cathedral today.

The statue of Abundance by Karl Bitter which stands before the Plaza Hotel.

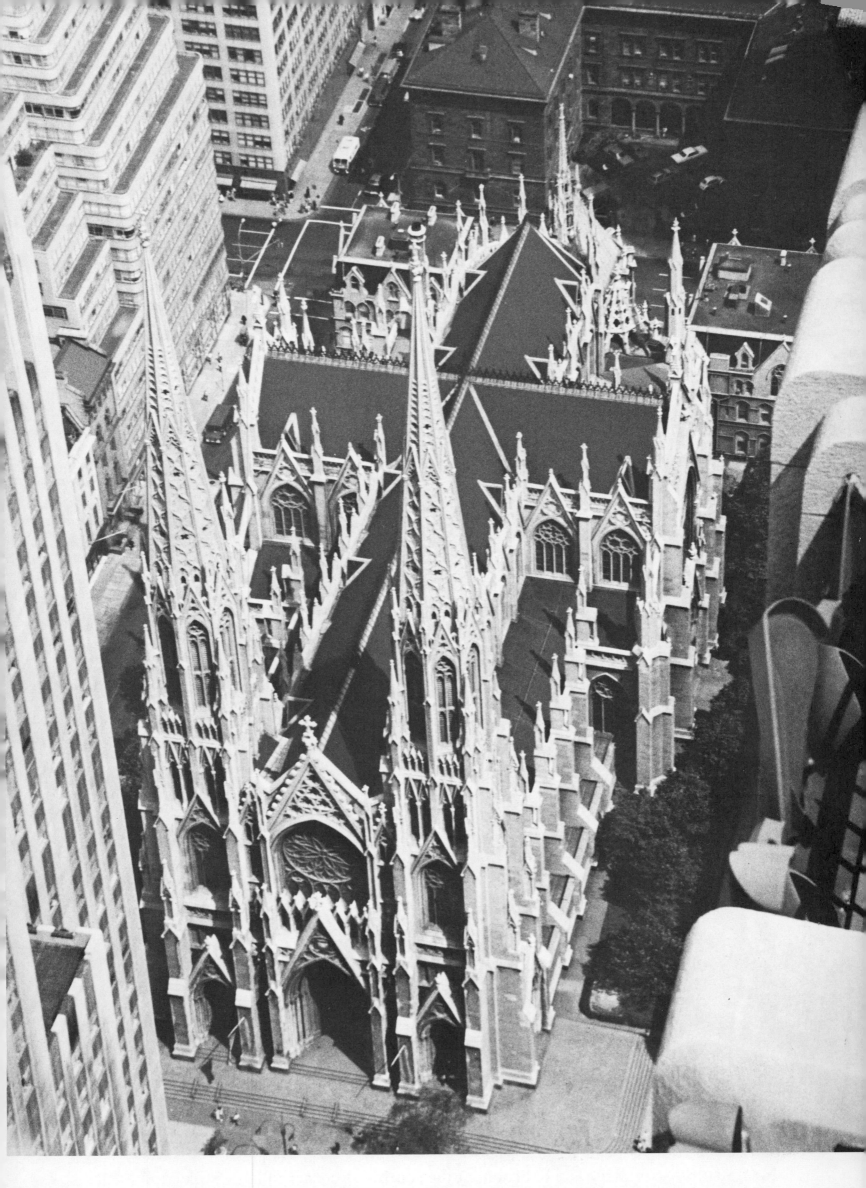

A view of St. Patrick's Cathedral from the top of Rockefeller Center.

Mrs. Astor's art gallery and ballroom at the southwest corner of 34th Street and Fifth Avenue. It was here that the Four Hundred gathered annually for Mrs. Astor's ball.

The tower of the Sherry-Netherland Hotel at Fifth Avenue and 59th Street. In the background is the General Motors building.

The Central Park Reservoir viewed from Park Avenue and 95th Street about 1880.

Chickering Hall on the northwest corner of Fifth Avenue and 18th Street about 1885. It was here that Oscar Wilde spoke to his New York public. Many important concerts, lectures, and recitals were presented in this building.

The residence of Mrs. William Astor at the southwest corner of Fifth

Avenue and 34th Street in the shade of the Waldorf Hotel in 1893.

torchlight procession on Fifth Avenue.

Naturally, every socially prominent citizen in town participated in planning the festivities, and for weeks discussion centered on points of etiquette involved in feting the man who would one day be the king of England. Members of the reception committee argued the order of dress. Would white vests and black cravats be appropriate or vice versa? "Are silk vests considered provincial in Paris?" asked George Templeton Strong. What kind of gloves were worn at the Tuileries the last time Governor Fish was there?

About a week before the arrival of the prince, the controversies became so heated that Strong in his diary, tiring of the entire business, commented: "Much occupied with devers [sic] matters growing out of the expected advent of our 'sweet young Prince.' 'Long may he wave,' but I wish he were at home again with his royal mamma, and I hope the community won't utterly disgrace itself before he goes away."

Early on October 11, a bland, soupy autumn day, people began to station themselves along the prince's route to the Fifth Avenue Hotel. By noon, all other activity in the city had come to a standstill. The crowds waited through the afternoon, and dusk had fallen before the prince finally proceeded uptown to the hotel. His entire route was jammed with people and in every window ladies sat waving their handkerchiefs. Once ensconced in his quarters at the hotel, the prince was subjected to yet another demonstration as hordes of shrieking women stormed his dressing room and bottled the water with which he had washed his royal hands.

On the night of the twelfth, the entrance to the Academy of Music on 14th Street was jammed with people eager for a close look at the prince. The royal party made its way down Fifth Avenue to the academy and arrived at around 9:30 P.M. The house blazed with lights and was decorated with thousands of bouquets of flowers. As the prince entered, the orchestra played "God Save the Queen," followed by "Hail Columbia."

After making his way through the receiving committee, the prince was presented to many of the thousands of persons invited to the ball. The spectacle must have been ludicrous: greetings included handshakes, back slaps, bows, deep curtsies, and even a devout genuflection from one bewildered matron. Suddenly, a thunderous noise interrupted the gaiety. Heads whirled just in time to see two sections of the temporary flooring that had been constructed for the ball give way. Many present tumbled into the cavernous holes along with the flooring but miraculously escaped injury.

The scheduled promenade was canceled, and the young prince, followed by his entourage, made his way to the supper rooms. In a pavilion offstage, a tent was surmounted by the triple plumes of the prince's crest. The tables were decorated with set pieces made of sugar paste and isinglass depicting Victoria and Albert. The royal party ate from a blue-and-gold dinner service made especially for the occasion, and drank from glasses to match. Pieces of this service can now be found in many private and public collections throughout this country. The buffet offered consommé de volaille, galantine of turkey and suckling pig, grouse, pheasant becasses et becassines, and ended with a medley of dessert.

In the meantime, the holes in the floor were roped off and a score of carpenters and policemen appeared. Within fifteen minutes, under the supervision of Sexton Isaac Hull Brown of Grace Church, the damage was repaired and by midnight the dancing commenced. The prince made his way onto the floor and thousands followed, oblivious to danger. A number of grande dames, with small restraint, thrust their daughters on the young man, who managed to elude their forays with firm tact and dignity. When the evening was over, it was judged a success by all who attended.

The following evening, New York City's firemen, carrying flaming torches, paraded up Fifth Avenue from 17th Street to the Fifth Avenue Hotel in honor of the prince, who saluted them from a balcony outside his suite. Roman candles, fireworks, thundering cannons, and calcium lights illuminated the line of march in what was one of the most spectacular greetings the city has ever given to any visitor.

Having been feted at the round of receptions, balls, and dinners, the prince, weary of official functions, sought diversion in less conventional ways. After one particularly tedious dinner party, the night maids wandering through the halls of the Fifth Avenue Hotel were astounded to see the young prince and several of his attendants in the middle of the corridor playing leapfrog. Another evening, the prince discreetly suggested that he would welcome a night off to see the town. James Gordon Bennett of the *New York Herald* rose to the challenge, directed the prince to retire early, and said he would arrange everything. At eleven thirty, the fire department put a ladder under his window. The prince slipped out, successfully eluded the press and public, and spent the night in a notorious brothel.

When his absence was discovered the following morning, panic seized officialdom and the police were summoned to comb the city for the missing future monarch. At about eight thirty in the morning, the prince walked in looking thoroughly pleased with himself. Many years later, when the present duke of Windsor first visited New York as the prince of Wales, he asked if he could be treated to a night out on the town as his grandfather had been.

The prince's visit was historically significant in that it put an end to the anti-British sentiment prevalent in the country since the revolutionary war.

AFTER THE PRINCE'S VISIT, THE FIFTH AVENUE HOTEL BECAME A POLITICAL AS WELL AS A SOCIAL CENTER

The Fifth Avenue Hotel became headquarters for Union supporters during the Civil War and retained its political character throughout its history. Such men as Jay Gould, Jim Fisk, Commodore Vanderbilt, Larry Jerome, Henry Clews, Horace Greeley, Hamilton Fish, and Henry Ward Beecher gathered to discuss the fate of the nation.

The plan to elect Ulysses S. Grant president of the United States was proposed in the hotel by Hamilton Fish. President Andrew Johnson was once attacked by a furious woman who tried to horsewhip him in the lobby, because her husband had been dismissed from his government position. Grover Cleveland's political name was made in the hotel. The Amen Corner, so-called because Tom Platt, the Republican boss gave his orders here, became the appointed meeting place for political leaders. It was in the Amen Corner that Theodore Roosevelt was chosen to be the vice-presidential nominee, despite his energetic protest. Every president from Buchanan to McKinley stayed at the Fifth Avenue, and almost every political personality of the era dropped in at the Amen Corner during its half century of existence.

When the hotel opened, the charge per room was $2.50 a day, including four meals. Even on the last day of operation, in 1909, the hotel continued to add that extra meal—a late supper. If a resident or visitor of the hotel cared to invite a guest for a meal, no charge was made. To the end, diners sat at long family tables twenty or thirty at a time.

IN 1861, DELMONICO'S MOVED UP-TOWN TO FIFTH AVENUE AND 14TH STREET AND REMAINED AT THAT LOCATION UNTIL 1876 WHEN IT MOVED NORTH AGAIN TO THE MADISON SQUARE AREA AT 26TH STREET

Delmonico's Restaurant, recognized throughout the world as the finest in New York and among the finest in the world, figured prominently in Fifth Avenue history for nearly seventy-five years. In 1861, the first year of the Civil War, Lorenzo Delmonico bought and moved into the Grinnell mansion at 14th Street and Fifth Avenue and turned it into the uptown branch of his famous downtown restaurant. One of its first visitors was President Abraham Lincoln.

An amusing anecdote about the famous restaurant is related by Ward McAllister in *Society As I Have Found It*. Henry Lukemeyer, a rich German who had arrived in New York to open a bank, needed to prove his solvency. He arranged a dinner at Delmonico's, invited seventy-two guests, and paid $10,000 for an endless procession of gourmet delights and wines. The table was decorated with millions of tiny violets set in great fields of greenery surrounding an oval pond thirty feet long on which swam four graceful swans, brought from Brooklyn's Prospect Park. The swans had been drugged, but, as the dinner wore on, the drugs wore off. At first the swans were content to take a few stabs at the sweet violets, but eventually one of the tipsy creatures made a lunge at a middle-aged matron. The lady ducked and the swan lunged at another swan. A fierce battle ensued in the pond and diners fled in panic from the table. Help was secured, and the swans were hustled out of the dining room and back to Brooklyn.

Delmonico's was also the setting for the first coming-out balls held outside Fifth Avenue mansions. By 1872, virtually all the ranking debutantes were introduced in the ballroom.

Another notable dinner given at Delmonico's was in honor of Professor Samuel F. B. Morse, the inventor of the telegraph. In the grand ballroom a connection was made with the first cable to Europe, and Professor Morse telegraphed the first cablegram from his table. In forty minutes an answer came back and, followed by tremendous applause, was read to the 350 persons present.

GRACE EPISCOPAL CHURCH, ALTHOUGH AT BROADWAY AND 10TH STREET, WAS NONETHELESS AN IMPORTANT PART OF FIFTH AVENUE HISTORY

Grace Episcopal Church, designed by young James Renwick, Jr., later to design St. Patrick's Cathedral, was consecrated in 1846. Controversy raged over the architecture. The ever-garrulous

George Templeton Strong, a classmate of Renwick's at Columbia College, wrote of the structure: "I instituted a minute examination this afternoon into Renwick's new church. It will certainly look well when completed and the pipe-cleaners of columns that support the clerestory will . . . impress the congregation with . . . the uncertainty of human life . . . it's positively frightful to behold them . . . a Samson who can grasp two of them at once would have but little to brag of in bringing the whole clerestory down with one jerk."

Just a month after the consecration, Strong described meeting Renwick at a party at the home of his future father-in-law, Mr. Ruggles: "At Ruggles soiree last night . . . walked down with the most windy of all bags of conceit and coxcombry that ever dubbed themselves Architect, Jimmy Renwick [Jr.], and most entertaining was the monologue with which he favored me . . . If the infatuated monkey showed the slightest trace or germ of feeling for his art, one could pardon and pass over blunders and atrocities . . . the vanity and pretension that are endurable and excuseable in an artist are not to be endured in a mechanic, and especially not in one who . . . degrades, vulgarizes and pollutes every glorious idea and form of the successive eras of Christian art that he travesties and tampers with."

Nonetheless a year later, Strong married Ellen Ruggles in Grace Church amidst all the "blunders and atrocities" of "Renwick's pasteboard abominations."

One of the most colorful characters to emerge from Grace Church's history was Isaac Hull Brown, sexton of the church. He preceded Ward McAllister as society's arbiter. His unusual height, together with one of the most prominent and well-fed paunches in the city, made him a most impressive personage as he walked down the aisle of the church. At the same time, his manner was so proud and courteous that Nathaniel Parker Willis, editor of the *Home Journal* once said, "His manner would well become the nobleman who is Gold Stick in Waiting at the Court of Her Majesty, Queen Victoria of England."

Although Brown was not in New York society, he well knew that his church contained so many of its members that he would be able to capitalize on them both socially and financially. He was the city's most prominent undertaker, and because of his knowledge of proper ritual at funerals, he was much in demand. He was said to have remarked soberly a few days before Ash Wednesday, "The Lenten season is a horridly dull season but we manage to make our funerals as entertaining as possible."

Peter Marie, a wit of the day, wrote of him:

O Glorious Brown! Thou medley strange,
     of churchyard, ballroom, saint and sinner
Flying in morn through fashion's range,
And burying mortals after dinner.
Walking one day with invitations,
Passing the next with consecrations.
Tossing the sod at eve on coffins;
With one hand drying the tears of orphans,
And one unclasping ball-room carriage,
Or cutting plum cake up for marriage:
Dusting by day the pew and missal;
Sounding by night the ball-room whistle,
Admitting free through Fashions' wicket,
And skilled at psalms, at punch, and cricket.

Mrs. Burton Harrison, in her diary, wrote of "arrogant" old Isaac Brown: "A fashionable lady, about to have a fashionable gathering at her house, orders her meats from the butcher, her supplies from the grocer, her cakes and pies from the confectioner and her invitations she puts in the hands of Brown. He knows whom to invite and whom to omit. He knows who will come and who will not come, but will send regrets. In case of a pinch he can fill up the list with young men, picked up about town, in black swallow tailed coats, white vests and white cravats, who in consideration of a fine supper and dance will allow themselves to be passed off as the sons of distinguished New Yorkers. The city has any quantity of ragged noblemen, seedy lords from Germany and Hungarian barons out at the elbow, who left their countries for their country's good, who can be served up in proper proportions at a fashionable party when the occasion demands it. No man knows their haunts better than Brown."

The last words Brown was said to have uttered when he died in 1881, as the march of the great houses continued northward, were "I cannot undertake to control society above Fiftieth Street."

In early 1863, President Lincoln had just issued the Emancipation Proclamation and the bloody battle of Gettysburg was only months away. The nation, weary of the tragic Civil War, found welcome diversion in a wedding that took place in Grace Church on February 10. Tom Thumb took two-foot eight-inch Lavinia Warren as his bride. The two-foot ten-inch bridegroom was born Charles Sherwood Stratton to normal-sized parents in Bridgeport, Connecticut, on February 4, 1838. At eighteen months he had stopped growing and by the time he was ten was discovered by P. T. Barnum.

Barnum presented the couple at levee daily up to one week before the wedding. He had offered them a staggering sum to appear right through the final week, but reason and devotion overcame greed and the couple retired to prepare for their wedding. And what a wedding! It was to be a "small family affair," but the couple yielded to pressure and expanded the guest list to two thousand of "the elite, the creme de la creme, the upper ten, the bonton, the select few, the very FF's [first families] of the City nay of the Country," according to the *New York Times*. There was no ballroom fodder at this affair. Astors, Vanderbilts, Belmonts, Roosevelts, along with senators, congressmen, and diplomats were in attendance. In the meantime, some fifteen thousand people made application, offering as much as $50 a ticket to view the service. Others sent extravagant gifts, hoping to receive an invitation. Several days before the event, the uninvited began to leave town "on the advice of the doctor" to avoid the embarrassment of not having been included among the chosen few. Finally, a public notice appeared in the papers: "The wedding is no more a money matter than is that of any of the readers of this notice, and therefore money will not purchase wedding cards."

On the morning of the wedding, before dawn, people jammed the street near Grace Church. Every window, door, and balcony in the vicinity was packed with spectators. Broadway had been blocked from Ninth Street to 12th Street, and the police set up barricades and formed human chains to contain the immense crowd. People on nearby Fifth Avenue who were not invited were in a fury over the inconvenience caused them. At noon, the wedding carriage drew close to the church. Cheers went up, and crowds surged toward the carriage. The police had to give way, but did manage to control the spectators.

The *New York Herald* said: "If we had thought it a delicious jam outside, what shall we say of within? Here indeed was the true vision of fair woman. Here was the carnival of crinoline, the apotheosis of purple and fine linen. Never before was the scarlet lady seen to such advantage. Babylon was a rag fair compared to it." The *Observer* said: "It is the event of the century, if not unparalleled in history."

In the church, thousands of tulips were banked along the altar and aisles, where an honor guard of policemen stood at attention. The organist augmented the traditional wedding music with the tempestuous overtures to *William Tell* and *Oberon*. There were several false alarms but finally, at twelve thirty, half an hour late, the great Barnum himself, delayed en route from his Fifth Avenue mansion by the crowds, made his way up the aisle with several members of the immediate family. Pandemonium ensued as New York's most elegant citizens abandoned all breeding. Shouts of "They come!" rang up to Renwick's rafters. Grande dames and budding socialites leaped upon pews for a better look. Even Mrs. Astor, in a fit of school-girl glee, jumped onto a stool that she had placed on the pew, craning her neck for a better look. Sedate matrons were seen shinnying up on their hushusbands' backs for a view of the lilliputian pair. Many ignored the solemnity of the occasion and giggled vociferously during the ceremony.

The *New York Times* reported: ". . . the service was done decently and in order. After Dr. Taylor gave the benediction, the General honestly kissed his wife, and in the presence of the entire audience feasted upon her the 'killing' glance with which he has in days gone by, captivated so many equally susceptible damsels." These included Queen Victoria and the queens of Belgium, Spain, and France.

The presents that the couple received were magnificent and included many diamond-encrusted pieces of jewelry from Fifth Avenue residents named Astor, Belmont, Vanderbilt, and Gould, and even President and Mrs. Abraham Lincoln sent a gift.

The wedding caused much controversy among the congregation. An exchange of correspondence between William Rhinelander Stewart of Lower Fifth Avenue and the Reverend Dr.

Taylor about admission to the church during the ceremony is worth noting.

> The Revd. Dr. Taylor
> Sir:
>
> The object of my unwilling addressing you this note is to inquire what right you had to exclude myself and other owners of pews in Grace Church from entering it yesterday, enforced too by a cordon of police for that purpose. If my pew is not my property I wish to know it, and if it is I deny your right to prevent me from occupying it whenever the Church is open even at a marriage of mountebanks, which I would not take the trouble to cross the street to witness.
>
> Respectfully
> Your obt. servt.
> William Stewart

Dr. Taylor replied:

> 804 Broadway, New York
> February 16, 1863
>
> Mr. William Stewart
> Dear Sir,
>
> I am sorry my valued friend that you should have written me the peppery letter that is now before me. If the matter of which you complain be so utterly insignificant and contemptible as "a marriage of mountebanks which you would not take the trouble to cross the street to witness" it surprises me that you should have made such strenuous, but ill-directed efforts to secure a ticket of admission: and why, permit me to ask in the name of reason and philosophy, do you still suffer it to disturb you so sadly?
>
> It would perhaps be a sufficient answer to your letter to say that your cause of complaint exists only in your imagination!
>
> *You have never been excluded from your pew!* As *Rector* I am the custodian of the Church, and you will hardly venture to say that you have ever applied to me, for permission to enter, and been refused!
>
> Here I might safely rest, and leave you to the comfort of your own reflections in the case. But, as you in common with many other worthy persons, would seem to have very crude notions, as to your rights of *property* in Pews,—you will pardon me for saying that a Pew in a Church is property only in a peculiar and restricted sense. It is not property as your house or your horse is property. It invests you with no fee in the soil, you cannot use it in any way, and in every way, and at all times, as your pleasure and caprice may dictate. You cannot put it to any common or unhallowed uses: you cannot move it, nor injure it, nor destroy it. In short you hold by purchase, and may *sell* the *right* to the undisturbed possession of that little space within the Church Edifice you call your *pew,* during the hours of Divine Service! But even that right must be exercised decorously, and with a decent regard for time and place, or else you may at any moment be ignominiously ejected from it. I regret to be obliged to add, that by the law of *custom,* you may during those said hours of Divine Service (but at no other time) *sleep in your pew.* You must however do so noiselessly and never to the disturbance of your sleeping neighbors! Your property in your Pew, has this extent and nothing more.
>
> Now if Mr. William Stewart were at any time to come to me and say "Sir, I would that you should grant me the use of Grace Church for a solemn service (a marriage, a baptism or a funeral as the case may be) and it is desirable that the feeling of the parties should be protected as far as possible from the impertinent intrusion and disturbance of a crowd from the streets and lanes of the city, I beg that no one may be admitted within the doors of the Church, during the very few moments that we expect to be there, but our invited friends only!"—It would certainly in such a case, be my pleasure to comply with your request and to meet your wishes in every particular; and I think that even "Mr. William Stewart" would agree that all this would be entirely reasonable and proper.
>
> Then tell me, how would such a case differ from the instance of which you complain? . . .
>
> I tell you sir, that wherever and from whomever such an appeal is made to my Christian courtesy although it should come from the humblest of the earth, I would go calmly and cheerfully forward to meet their wishes although as many William Stewarts as would reach from here to Kamsohatka clothed in fuss and frowns should rise up to oppose me. . . .

> Respectfully submitted by
> Your obd. servt.
> Thomas House Taylor,
> Rector of Grace Church.

Years later, William Rhinelander Stewart in his comprehensive *Grace Church and Old New York,* published in 1924, expresses regret that the parish records of the thirty-three-year rectorate of Thomas House Taylor "are so meager that little of interest has been gleaned from them."

LATER THAT YEAR, THE PASSAGE OF A DRAFT LAW RESULTED IN THE MOST INFAMOUS INCIDENT IN THE CITY'S HISTORY

On the morning of July 13, 1863, Fifth Avenue and New York awakened to a bright, clear, midsummer day. None could suspect that by sunset the city would be in the midst of a bloodbath. Behind the riots was resentment of the Civil War draft law that included a "rich man's" clause allowing those who did not wish to serve the option of paying $300 for a substitute.

The trouble began in the morning at a local draft board on Third Avenue and 46th Street. When some two dozen names had been drawn, a crowd numbering about fifty persons commenced to shout violent disapproval. Within moments the crowd swelled, grew more disorderly, and began to storm the building. Windows and doors were smashed, and a mob made its way into the main office where books, papers, records, and lists of eligible draftees were destroyed. The drafting officers were set upon with clubs and forced to flee from the room through a rear exit. Suddenly smoke started to belch out of the upper windows. The crowd continued to stone the building. Firemen arrived, only to be met with savage beatings.

Constantly increasing in numbers, the mob moved on, setting fires at the Second Avenue Armory. Shots were fired when the police attempted unsuccessfully to restore order and the violence gained momentum as police were viciously attacked, many being beaten to death and even dismembered.

A shout was heard from the crowd, "Now for the Fifth Avenue Hotel—there's where the Union Leaguer's meet." (The Union League had supported the draft law along with the Union cause.) By this time the streets were thronged with women and children, who goaded on the rioters to storm the Fifth Avenue Hotel. Iron doors and blockades were thrown up in front of the hotel in a successful effort to keep the crowds out. Other targets of attack were not so fortunate.

At four o'clock, the mob attacked the Orphan Asylum for Colored Children on the west side of Fifth Avenue between 43rd and 44th streets. Thousands of rioters ransacked and plundered the building from cellar to attic. When it became clear the mob intended to burn the building, the directors of the orphanage appealed to the crowd in the name of humanity, but in vain. Despite brave efforts of the fire department to quell the flames, the building burned to the ground. Fortunately most of the children were evacuated, although one little girl was discovered by the drunken rioters under a bed and beaten to death.

Black people of the city became the targets for violence. Eighteen were hanged from trees and many of their bodies were savagely mutilated and burned, while women and children danced beneath them. Others were drowned in the East and Hudson rivers.

The charming Croton Cottage, across from the reservoir at 42nd Street and Fifth, was burned and the Allerton Hotel at Fifth and 44th Street followed. Mayor Opdyke's house at 15th Street and Fifth became a target and the crowd forced the front door open and hurled rocks through most of the windows before the police were able to contain the rioters.

For the next three days, avenging mobs roamed a lawless city, burning, looting, and murdering. More than twelve hundred people were killed; another eight thousand were seriously injured; and more than one hundred buildings were burned to the ground.

ON APRIL 15, 1865, FIVE DAYS AFTER THE END OF THE CIVIL WAR, ABRAHAM LINCOLN WAS ASSASSINATED IN WASHINGTON; THE FOLLOWING WEEK, EN ROUTE FROM THE CAPITOL TO SPRINGFIELD, ILLINOIS, HIS BODY LAY IN STATE IN NEW YORK'S CITY HALL

On an unseasonably warm April day, more than a million mourners jammed the City Hall area and lined the processional route up Broadway and Fifth Avenue to bid farewell to the martyred president. They stood twelve to fifteen feet deep along the streets and faces peered from every window, rooftop, tree, and post. Throughout the city, flags flew at half staff and many buildings were draped in mourning black.

At noon, after thousands of persons had passed before the bier, members of the veterans reserves removed the coffin from its place of honor in City Hall, carrying it to a dais on the steps of the building. Troops presented arms, drums rolled, colors were dipped, and the thousands of men in the square bared their heads. The coffin was then placed on the funeral car and the somber procession uptown to the 13th Street Railroad Station began. Sixteen magnificent gray horses, each led by a black groom, drew the funeral car. The car, sixteen feet long by six feet wide, was covered with black broadcloth embroidered with silver shields and stars, and surmounted with a "temple of liberty" from whose gilded dome the national colors waved. Heavy mourning plumes draped the vehicle.

Along Broadway from City Hall to 14th Street, regiments stood at attention as a seemingly endless parade of blue-clad troops filed past the onlookers. Finally, the funeral car, preceded by the Seventh Regiment as a guard of honor, passed solemnly by. At its rear marched dozens of ethnic, mercantile, and political groups.

AFTER THE CIVIL WAR, CONSTRUCTION OF ELABORATE BUILDINGS ON FIFTH AVENUE RECOMMENCED

An influential figure in postwar New York society was A. T. Stewart, who had made his millions in the department store business. In 1864, he purchased the northwest corner of 34th Street and Fifth Avenue from Dr. Sarsparilla Townsend. Stewart announced that he would spend more than $1 million to erect a mansion for himself, and when the house was finally completed in 1868, it was reputed to have cost $3 million. Built entirely of the finest white Carrara marble, Italian artists were imported to carve the friezes and decorate the ceilings. The halls were filled with unmistakably parvenu art. Unquestionably the showiest and most costly house in town at the time, the newspapers referred to it as a palace and it soon became a great attraction for tourists.

In 1876, Steward died, leaving his widow to manage the house. The old lady, alone and pathetic, was wont to sit throughout the day in front of her mirror, trying on different wigs and making up her face. She once asked her maid, "Where is the fountain of youth? I will pay a million dollars for a small bottle of its waters." In the evenings, she would put on her grandest gowns and descend the staircase into her empty drawing room. Carrying a lamp in one hand and a wine glass in the other, she would talk to the paintings that hung on the walls. As time wore on, she took to weeping as she paraded through the musty corridors of the mansion. She died, forlorn and afraid, in 1886. The house stood empty for many years until the Manhattan Club leased the property. Rudyard Kipling lived there until the club, because of the cost of maintenance, abandoned the house. It was finally torn down toward the end of the century, with much of its marble then incorporated in the Church of Our Lady of Lourdes at 142nd Street near Amsterdam Avenue.

Just up the Avenue, on the northeast corner of 36th Street, stood the Rose Hill Nurseries. Siebrecht and Wadley, the proprietors, boasted, "Flowers by telegraph to any part of the world." This bit of rural Fifth Avenue survived until the 1890s.

Farther up the Avenue, at 40th Street, William H. Vanderbilt, son of the commodore, purchased the site of Croton Cottage. There he built the first of many Vanderbilt family residences on the Avenue on land that cost $80,000. The house stood on the property until 1920. At one time or another, members of this family lived at 489, 640, 642, 645, 647, 660, 666, 680, 742, 744, 746, and 1025 Fifth Avenue.

North of the Vanderbilt home, the Rutgers Female College, the first seminary for the higher education of young ladies of gentle birth in New York, moved in 1866 into a row of buildings known as the House of Mansions, located where the New York Public Library now stands.

During this period, the area between 46th and 47th streets was the site of a cattle market known as the Bull's Head. Cattle drivers led their stock down from Westchester County and Connecticut to pen them in the fenced lot. Butchers came from First Avenue, selected their beefs, drove them off, and slaughtered them. Tyson's Market at Fifth Avenue and 43rd Street and Brandie's on 42nd Street were both butcher shops that catered to housewives of the period.

On the southwest corner of Fifth Avenue and 44th Street stood a little frame house called Ye Olde Willow Tree Inn. Built in 1850, this cottage and the solitary tree from which it derived its name stood as recently as 1905.

In 1868, the infamous Jay Gould moved into his thirty-five-room brownstone mansion on the northwest corner of Fifth Avenue and 47th Street. After the millionaire had disrupted the financial affairs of the nation by attempting to corner the gold market, the Avenue in front of his house became the scene of a riot on Black Friday, September 24, 1869. Thousands of angry persons gathered and called for Gould, some with sticks and stones, but the crafty tycoon had slipped out of town to a retreat in New Jersey.

The Gould House was leased to Gimbel Brothers in 1942 for the use of the Kende Galleries, an auction house. Eleven years later, in 1953, this house, the last of the mansions below 59th Street, was razed to make way for an office building.

Although the block between 57th and 58th streets was considered inaccessible wilderness in 1869, Mary Mason Jones, the daughter of a banker, decided to build what became known as Marble Row there. Her cream-colored marble houses were significant architecturally because they marked the passing of the era of the brownstone front on Fifth Avenue and the introduction of French design. Modeled after the Palace at

Fountainbleu, the houses were gigantic in scale with many large rooms. The expression *keeping up with the Joneses* has been attributed to the influence of these houses as many residents of the Avenue copied the architecture in later years. Mrs. Paran Stevens later bought the houses from Miss Jones. The last house in the row was torn down in 1929.

In 1869, one of the few remaining areas of parkland on the East Side was built up. Hamilton Square, which lay between Fifth and Third avenues from 66th Street to 68th Street, was closed, and cross streets were pushed through, despite the promise of the City Corporation that the square would be "kept open forever" for public use.

IN 1868, CHARLES DICKENS AGAIN VISITED NEW YORK AND SUCCEEDED IN MENDING FENCES WITH THE CITY HE HAD VILLIFIED SOME TWENTY-FIVE YEARS BEFORE.

The time had come to show Charles Dickens that New York had outgrown the provincialism he had scorned in 1842, and Delmonico's on 14th Street was selected by the New York City Press Club as the place to do it. Lorenzo the Great, as he was referred to by the gourmets of the city, knew only too well how to raise a mere banquet into the realm of art.

The pretensions of the earlier dinner were abandoned. The occasion was planned to be as pleasant, casual, and sociable as possible. The dinner, however, was unsurpassed in artistry, for Delmonico's chefs turned it into a festival of Dickens's characters. Sugar confections were fashioned into replicas of Uriah Heep and Little Nell; Sairy Gamp, Betsy Frig, and Captain Cuttle emerged from the charlotte Russe, and Tiny Tim was presented as a paté de foie gras mold. A hidden orchestra played, and Horace Greeley, president of the Press Club, introduced the honored guest.

The menu, compared with that of the 1842 banquet, did indeed reflect a greater degree of sophistication. Economy, order, and smooth progression of courses replaced the absurdly unwieldy order of service of 1842. The total number of dishes was reduced from sixty to a manageable thirty, and the nineteen main entrées were cut to six. Heavy boiled meats were not served and two vegetables, endive and artichoke, not known in New York in 1842, were featured. An English translation of the French menu was omitted. New York had arrived, and Charles Dickens knew it.

The author responded to the honor in the following words: ". . . what I have resolved upon . . . is, on my return to England, in my own person to bear . . . such testimony to the gigantic changes in this country as I have hinted at tonight. Also, to record that wherever I have been, in the smallest places equally with the largest, I have been received with unsurpassable politeness, delicacy, sweet temper, hospitality, consideration, and with unsurpassable respect for the privacy daily enforced upon me by the nature of my avocation here and the state of my health. This testimony, so long as I live, and so long as my descendants have any legal right in my books, I shall cause to be republished as an appendix to every copy of those two books of mine in which I have referred to America. And this I will do and cause to be done, not in mere love and thankfulness, but because I regard it as an act of plain justice and honor."

LATER IN THE YEAR, ON NOVEMBER 20, GENERAL ULYSSES S. GRANT WAS OFFICIALLY HONORED AT A RECEPTION AT THE FIFTH AVENUE HOTEL

What was intended to be a dignified dinner and reception in honor of Grant turned into an embarrassing fiasco. The general, coming to town to claim his share of the glory of victory, was honored by more than 150 people, who had paid $100 per plate to attend. Unfortunately, those who organized the affair lost control of the guest list, and more than 2,500 people jammed the halls, corridors, and reception rooms of the hotel. Among the crashers were a group of religious fanatics. Directly after one prominent businessman had been introduced to the general, the group of enraptured souls threw themselves at his feet, offering up hosannas for the salvation of his soul. Others insisted on bringing their children, and thrust them forward to greet the general. One precocious moppet sang a chorus of "The Battle Hymn of the Republic" out of tune. To add to the confusion, those who fought their way through the melee to be formally presented were announced by a ridiculous little man who consistently mispronounced their names.

Although slightly put out by the fiasco, Grant managed to salve his vanity by eating his share of the oysters and canvasback duck and drinking far more than his share of wine and liquor.

DURING THIS PERIOD, NEW YORKERS BECAME MORE INTERESTED IN ART AND THE KNOEDLER GALLERY MOVED TO FIFTH AVENUE

The Knoedler Gallery, founded in 1846, was the first of the commercial art galleries to move to Fifth Avenue, locating at 22nd Street in 1869. In those days the gallery showed primarily paintings of the French Barbizon and American schools.

In 1877, the gallery moved to 355 34th Street, the present site of B. Altman and Company. Among their clients were Cornelius and William H. Vanderbilt, William Waldorf, John Jacob Astor, Henry M. Flagler, H. O. Havemeyer, S. V. Harkness, William Rockefeller, and Leland Stanford. Jay Gould bought twenty-two pictures in two days during this period. By 1900, Henry Frick, P. A. B. Widener, Charles Taft, and Andrew Mellon were dealing with the gallery.

In 1911, the gallery again moved, purchasing the old Lotos Club at 556 Fifth, where it remained until 1925. Among the famous pictures that passed through Knoedler's hands were Van Eyck's *Annunciation,* Botticelli's *Adoration of the Magi,* Velázquez's *Head of Pope Pius X,* Vermeer's *Lady Writing,* and his *Young Girl with a Flute.*

Chapter Four

THE SEVENTIES AND EIGHTIES

CHRONOLOGY

1870   New York City population is 1,478,103.

Work begins on Brooklyn Bridge.

Equitable Life Assurance Society Building opens at 120 Broadway, first office building in the city to use passenger elevators.

1871   Steam trains appear on the Greenwich Street elevated.

Grand Central depot opens.

New York Cotton Exchange incorporated.

Tweed Ring of corrupt politicians is overthrown.

1872   East New York annexed to Brooklyn.

Jim Fisk shot.

1873   Panic on Wall Street.

Towns of Kingsbridge, Morrisania, and West Farms are added to New York, extending the city limits to Yonkers.

1874   P. T. Barnum opens Great Roman Hippodrome at 27th Street and Madison Avenue.

Governments of the city and county are again consolidated.

1875   Rapid Transit Commission is created.

1876   First train service from New York to San Francisco.

Central Park is completed.

1877   First high-wheeled bicycle appears in New York.

The American Museum of Natural History opened by President Rutherford B. Hayes.

First tenement building around a central court completed in Brooklyn.

1878   Sixth Avenue elevated opens from Rector Street to Central Park.

New York Symphony Society is organized through the efforts of Leopold Damrosch.

1879 St. Patrick's Cathedral consecrated by Cardinal McCloskey.

Operetta *Pinafore* given its first performance in New York.

First Madison Square Garden is opened.

1880 New York City population is 1,911,698.

Metropolitan Museum of Art opened by President Rutherford B. Hayes.

Broadway is electrically lighted for the first time, with British arc lights.

Elevated railroad system completed to the Harlem River.

1881 Cleopatra's Needle, a gift of the khedive of Egypt, is presented to New York, its transportation and pedestal in Central Park paid for by William H. Vanderbilt.

1882 Joseph Pulitzer founds the *New York Morning Journal.*

The Edison Company begins operation, inaugurating the first commercial lighting by electricity in New York City.

The Metropolitan Opera House, at Broadway and 39th Street, is opened.

1883 Brooklyn Bridge, the longest suspension bridge in the world, is opened.

Dakota Apartments open at 72nd Street and Central Park West.

New York Telephone and Telegraph Company is incorporated.

Centennial of the British evacuation of New York is celebrated, and the statue of Washington on the steps of the Subtreasury Building is unveiled.

Metropolitan Opera House formally opened with a performance of *Faust.*

1884 Report made to legislature recommending acquisition of park and parkway land in the Bronx.

Long-distance telephone service established between New York and Boston.

John Singer Sargent begins painting portraits in New York.

Leopold Damrosch inaugurates the first season of German opera in New York.

1885 First cable cars operated on Amsterdam Avenue.

First law passed regulating the height of buildings in New York.

Fifth Avenue Bus Line is inaugurated.

General Grant dies in New York. Funeral procession escorts his body to the temporary tomb on the site of the present Grant's Tomb on Riverside Drive.

1886   Statue of Liberty, a gift to the United States from the people of France, is unveiled.

Elevated railway links the Bronx with Manhattan.

1887   Joseph Pulitzer founds *New York Evening World* and Charles A. Dana founds the *New York Evening Sun*.

Electric streetcars are used for the first time.

1888   First modern "steel skeleton" structure is erected, the Tower Building at 50 Broadway.

Fulton Street elevated line is completed in Brooklyn.

Electric trains are installed on the New York elevated railway lines.

1889   Centennial of Washington's inauguration is celebrated in New York.

In the decades following the Civil War, New York City's merchant class, which had thrived during the conflict, consolidated its position and defended its ranks against the newly arrived millionaires whose fortunes had been made in the West. By 1870, the city had a population of 1,478,103, and the politically corrupt rule of William Marcy ("Boss") Tweed was about to be ended by the efforts of the chairman of the Democratic state committee, S. J. Tilden.

The first subway, one block long, running from Murray Street on the south to Warren Street on the north, opened to the delight of New Yorkers. The elevated railroads were commissioned with those on Third and Sixth avenues the first to begin operations. Real estate values increased as the northern reaches of the city became more accessible. Commodore Vanderbilt constructed the tracks for the New York Central Railroad on Park Avenue and both the American Museum of Natural History and the Metropolitan Museum of Art were founded. The first telephone had appeared, as had the first electric light. Central Park was completed in 1876 and St. Patrick's Cathedral was consecrated in 1879.

The ladies had turned from hoop skirts to bustles and could be seen strolling up and down the Avenue wearing colored stockings and immense ostrich feathers in their hats. Horse-drawn buses had begun running up and down the city's thoroughfares, and etiquette required that the gentlemen either stand or take the ladies on their knees. The gentlemen of the era wore moustaches; goatees, imperials, Vandykes, walruses, muttonchops, ironsides, Dundrearies, and many other designs were as requisite to the man of fashion as his Prince Albert coat. Bicycling and ice-staking became popular, and one of the sights of the period were the trained bears who roamed the streets with their masters. Usually imported from the mountains of Austria, the bears were led through the streets with rings in their noses and danced on their hind legs for the delight of the children.

IN 1870, JUST OFF FIFTH AVENUE ON 23RD STREET, THE EDEN MUSÉE OPENED

What Fifth Avenue needed to complement its human waxworks was a chamber of horrors. After a semipublic gala for society on a Friday night in 1870, the Eden Musée was opened to the general public. Despite disparaging comments about the wax figures, it eventually became a "must" on any tour of the city. The musée never achieved the status of Mme. Tussaud's in London although one critic commented: ". . . it is Frenchy when it should be American: but it will become Americanized by and by when we get a popular murderer or two in the Tombs, and as it is opened to stay, there will be plenty of time for the improvements and additions." Twenty years later the Eden Musée closed its doors forever.

DURING THE 1870S, A PROCESSION ON FIFTH AVENUE WELCOMED THE GRAND DUKE ALEXIS OF RUSSIA

On November 19, 1871, the Grand Duke Alexis of Russia visited New York and was wined and dined extravagantly on the Avenue. His reception at the Battery was followed by a parade up Broadway and Fifth. When the procession finally reached the Clarendon Hotel just off Fifth Avenue on 25th Street, the grand duke was delighted to find that a private residence connected to the hotel had been converted into a replica of the Imperial Palace for his visit. The entire city was combed for priceless pieces and paintings to furnish the grand duke's quarters.

The visit went smoothly, culminating in a sumptuous dinner at the New York Yacht Club and a grand ball at the Academy of Music.

THE MOST SIGNIFICANT EVENT OF THE DECADE WAS THE OPENING OF CENTRAL PARK IN 1876

Central Park, even before it was officially opened, became the showplace for trotting horses and splendid equipage, providing the residents of Fifth Avenue ample opportunity to parade in their elaborate carriages drawn by expensive horses. Commodore Cornelius Vanderbilt, William H. Vanderbilt, William Rockefeller, General Grant, and Leonard Jerome were all seen regularly driving up the Avenue to the park.

By 1870, Jim Fisk, already established as one of the most notorious of the robber barons, owned the largest stable of carriage horses in New York. He rode up and down Fifth Avenue in an imposing barouche, with a six-foot four-inch coachman and an equally imposing footman in attendance. He always drove six perfectly matched horses, three blacks and three whites. An elegant Dalmatian dog, known in those days as a coach dog, ran beside the horses under the pole. It is recorded in Fifth Avenue annals that on New Year's day, 1871, Fisk paid his calls in a magnificently appointed chariot, drawn by six horses, with four smart footmen dressed in ostentatious livery. When he stopped before a favored house, a lackey descended, unrolled a carpet, laid it from the carriage steps to the door, and then, as the footmen stood at attention on each side, their master walked to the house. During this period Fisk imported a bevy of French divas and opéra-bouffe queens, whom he installed in his Grand Opera House at Eighth Avenue and 23rd Street. He was frequently observed progressing up Fifth Avenue in an open carriage with one or more women of vivid complexion at his side. On one of these trips his companion was Celine de Montaland, a singer whom he had engaged for his opera house. As they made their way through the vastness of Central Park, he informed the star that these were the grounds of his New York estate. The singer was greatly impressed and promptly informed the millionaire that a man of such vast *richesse* could certainly afford to pay her higher wages. She demanded a new contract and Fisk was forced to triple her salary.

Fisk's taste for great beauties ultimately cost him his life. In 1871, he consorted with Josie Mansfield, an actress who had been a favorite of Edward Stokes. Fisk became more and more flamboyant in his attentions and was soon seen riding publicly up the Avenue with Josie at his side. The blatant affront inflamed the jealous Stokes. In January, 1872, as Fisk descended the staircase of the Broadway Central Hotel where Josie lived, Stokes shot him in the back and killed him. Stokes was tried and convicted, but was eventually freed through his political influence. Josie lived in Paris until the early 1930s where she died at the age of eighty.

During the early days of the park, several attractions that have long since disappeared provided popular diversion. A miniature steam railroad ran the length of the park along Fifth Avenue, and at 110th Street and Fifth, an immense toboggan slide drew many a devotee of winter sports. Ice-skating, of course, was a major diversion in those days. As recently as the 1920s, Fifth Avenue and Madison Avenue buses carried the traditional red ball on the front whenever the ice was safe for skating.

At about the time that the park was opened, the Coaching Club of New York was organized. Founded by nine gentlemen who sought to emulate the English revival of coaching as sport, the club had as its leading spirits Colonel William Jay and Colonel Delancey Astor Kane. The group's stated purpose was simply "to encourage four-in-hand driving in America." The club held its annual spring parade, signaling the end of the social season in New York, to and from the Hotel Brunswick on Fifth Avenue.

The parades were, however, far from uppermost in the hearts of the club members. Public coaching was their real interest. Public coaching meant regularly scheduled trips to various points in and around the city over a specified route with passengers who had paid a fare. Anyone could reserve a seat on these coaches and for an extra fee could ride directly beside Delancey Astor Kane or even Alfred Gwynne Vanderbilt. Favorite runs were to the Westchester Country Club, then at Pelham, to the Getty House in Yonkers, and to the Ardsley Club at Ardsley overlooking the Hudson. These drives could be made comfortably in one day, leaving ample time for a leisurely lunch before the return trip. The fare

was $3 for one way, $5 for the round trip. The longest run made in this country was in 1894, between the old Waldorf Hotel and the Stratford in Philadelphia, a distance of more than one hundred miles. The run was sponsored by the coaching clubs of New York and Philadelphia. The halfway point was Princeton, New Jersey, where lunch was taken at the old University Hotel.

The tradition continued into the twentieth century but vanished after World War I. Mrs. Marise Blair Campbell remembers the excitement of the coaching days of her childhood: "Since there were no lights on the corners on Fifth Avenue in those days, there was always a guard on the rear of each coach, blowing a horn to warn the police that we were coming. It was thrilling to hear the sound of those coaching horns coming down Fifth. If the police stopped us, the guards would have to jump off and stop the horses. There was always a class of coaches in the Horse Show and at that time there was a race to Tuxedo Park. That meant driving the coach to the Fort Lee Ferry, getting the horses on the ferry and then crossing the Hudson and progressing on to Tuxedo. There were always two teams, the men's and the ladies' and surprisingly enough, the ladies' usually won the race." Many of these coaches are now on display in the Shelburne Museum in Vermont.

NEW YORK CITY BEGINS TO BUILD
THE METROPOLITAN MUSEUM OF ART

John Taylor Johnston's first public art gallery had created a demand for a larger and more public institution, and, acting on the suggestion of John Jay, a group of civic-minded New Yorkers elected to establish an art museum for the people. A board of trustees was named and a campaign was launched to raise $250,000 to build the museum. William Cullen Bryant was named chairman of the campaign committee.

Eventually the trustees acquired property in

Central Park along the Avenue between 80th and 85th streets. At the time a squatter's camp named Seneca Village occupied the site. The shanties were torn down, and work was begun on the museum. Until the first building was ready for occupancy, two houses sheltered the growing collection temporarily. The first was at 681 Fifth Avenue in a house that was once the home of the Allen Dodsworth's Dancing Academy. As the collection outgrew the house, it was moved to a

The Waldorf-Astoria Hotel, built on the site of Mrs. William Astor's residence.

The Palm Garden of the Waldorf-Astoria Hotel in 1893.

The dining room of the William K. Vanderbilt house, 1880.

The twin Vanderbilt residences on Fifth

Avenue between 51st and 53rd streets in 1894.

The drawing room of the William H. Vanderbilt house

at the northwest corner of Fifth Avenue and 51st Street.

The view south and east from the front of the Plaza Hotel at 59th Street in the late 1890s. The Cornelius Vanderbilt house stands where Bergdorf Goodman is today. Across the street is Marble Row, the houses built by Mary Mason Jones.

The residence of William K. Vanderbilt, just to the north of the twin mansions,

in 1893. It was here that Mrs. W. K. Vanderbilt's famous ball was held.

The funeral procession for General Ulysses S. Grant on August 8, 1885, shown south of Croton Reservoir at 42nd Street.

Mrs. Cornelius Vanderbilt costumed as an electric light at the Vanderbilt ball, March 26, 1883.

Fifth Avenue and 13th Street after the blizzard of

1888. The Church of the Ascension is on the right.

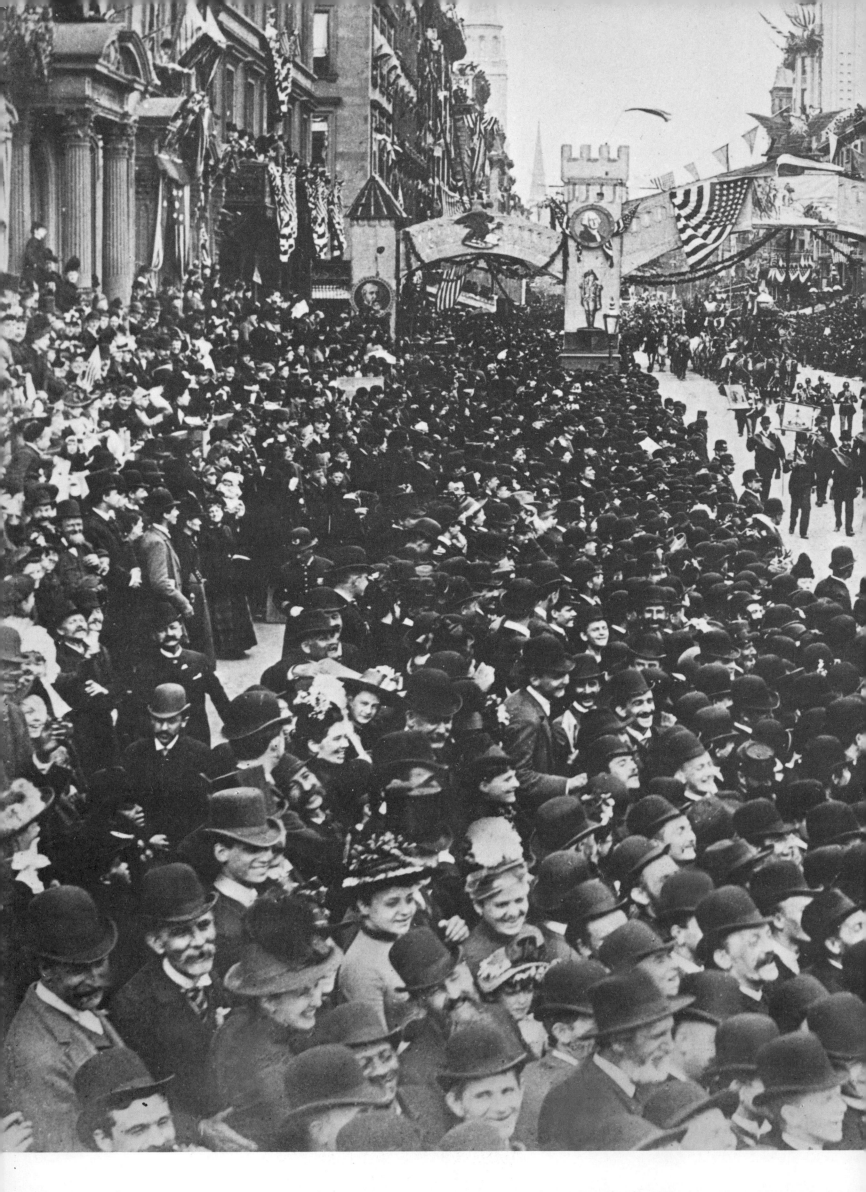

The parade commemorating the centennial of George Washington's inauguration,

April 29-May 1, 1889. Madison Square and the Brunswick Hotel are on the right.

mansion on the south side of 14th Street just west of Sixth Avenue.

Finally, on March 30, 1880, the first wing, a red brick structure designed in the Tuscan Gothic style, was dedicated by President Rutherford B. Hayes. As the years went by, the museum expanded and, in fact, is still the subject of controversy for its proposed encroachment on Central Park land.

The nucleus of the original permanent collection was provided by William T. Blodgett and John Taylor Johnston, the first president of the Metropolitan. Blodgett had been in Europe during 1870 prior to the great upsurge in popularity of Old Masters, and had bought three important private collections. He offered them to the trustees of the Metropolitan for exactly what they had cost him, $116,180.27. One hundred and seventy-four pictures were involved, mostly Dutch and Flemish seventeenth-century works, with a few Italian, French, English, and Spanish paintings from various periods. Johnston thought the purchases "somewhat rash," but his confidence in Blodgett's judgment was such that he assumed half the cost. Some of the pictures have been discredited by art critics, but by and large, the collection has stood up surprisingly well. Frans Hals's *Malle Babbe,* included in the group, has remained continuously on exhibition for over one hundred years.

During subsequent decades, the museum expanded its facilities. In 1888, the southwest wing and facade, designed by Theodore Weston, was added. In 1894, the north wing was added, and in 1902, the Fifth Avenue wing, designed by Richard Morris Hunt and finished by his son Richard Howland Hunt, was completed. In 1906, the side wings by McKim, Mead and White were constructed.

In the meantime, bequests and acquisitions multiplied. In 1877, the Cesnola Curium treasures from Cyprus, consisting of more than 10,000 objects, were acquired. In 1889, Mrs. John Crosby Brown donated her collection of 270 musical instruments, and by 1906, she had added to the collection bringing its total to 3,500 pieces. In 1889, the Moore Collection of Greek and Etruscan vases, the Bishop Collection

of Chinese jades, and Catharine Lorillard Wolfe's Salon and Barbizon pictures joined the collection. In 1889, the first two Manet's ever to be hung in a museum were acquired.

Subsequent additions include the Duc de Dino Collection of armor in 1904; the Hearn bequest of American paintings in 1906; the Cesnola, Pulitzer, and Altman bequests from 1909 to 1913; the Riggs armor bequest in 1913; the Davis Collection of Egyptian objects in 1915; the 1917 Fletcher bequest including Rembrandt's *Head of Christ*; the great Morgan bequest in 1917; the W. K. Vanderbilt gift in 1920, the Huntington, Marquand, and Havemeyer bequests during the 1920s; the Friedram bequest in the 1930s as well as the Blumenthal bequest. The great Bache Collection was given to the museum in 1949 and more recently the Robert Lehman and Nelson Rockefeller collections have been donated. John D. Rockefeller's Cloisters, which was built during the 1930s, was perhaps the most important single gift to the museum.

In 1961, the museum made history when its director, James J. Rorimer, bid $2.3 million for Rembrandt's *Aristotle Contemplating the Bust of Homer* at a Parke-Bernet auction. The price was the highest ever bid at auction for a work of art at the time.

In 1963, as a gesture of friendship toward President John F. Kennedy, André Malraux, the French minister for cultural affairs, loaned the famous *Mona Lisa* by Leonardo da Vinci to the Metropolitan for display. An estimated one million persons filed passed the masterpiece to gaze upon the lady with the enigmatic smile.

During the centennial year in 1970, plans were unveiled for the future expansion of the museum. The Robert Lehman Collection will be housed in a special pavilion built onto the west side of the museum. The Temple of Dendur, presented to the United States by Egypt in return for United States aid to help preserve Abu Simbel and other Numian monuments threatened by the Aswan High Dam, will be housed in a glass enclosed temple to the rear of the building. The Rockefeller Collection of Primitive Art will also have its own pavilion.

IN 1876, DELMONICO'S OPENED A NEW RESTAURANT ON THE WEST SIDE OF FIFTH AVENUE AT 26TH STREET AND THE HOFFMAN HOUSE, THE ALBERMARLE, AND THE BRUNSWICK HOTEL ALL OPENED THEIR DOORS IN THE VICINITY

The opening of Delmonico's at 26th Street in 1876 marked the final decline of Lower Fifth Avenue as the social center of the city. Madison Square had now unquestionably claimed that distinction, and the uptown Delmonico's became the nexus of social events.

That year, Captain Alexander S. ("Clubber") Williams of the New York City Police Department was transferred from the Gas House District on the Lower East Side to the Madison Square area. Receiving news of his transfer, he came in to dine at Delmonico's and announced to Charles Delmonico: "I've been living off chuck steak for a long time. Now I'm going to get a bit of the tenderloin." Hence the Tenderloin District, which comprises the area around Madison Square, got its name.

Another attraction of the Madison Square area was the Hoffman House, opened at 25th Street and Fifth Avenue about 1870. Within a few years, it was known throughout the civilized world. Its bar was a magnificent structure of carved mahogany; the mirrors that lined the walls were said to be the largest in the United States; the ceiling was lofty; and no expense was spared on the furniture and fixtures.

Edward Stokes, the man who assassinated Jim Fisk, was one of its proprietors and spent thousands of dollars on the magnificent paintings that covered the walls. An immense picture, *Nymphs and Satyrs,* the most celebrated work of the French painter Bouguereau, then notorious for his erotic paintings, was bought at auction for $10,000 and hung over the bar. Visitors from the far corners of the earth came to see it. It was probably the biggest single attraction for any hotel in the history of this country. One day a week was declared ladies' day, and any lady calling at the hotel was met by a page with a printed catalog describing the house and its works of art. Ladies were escorted through the bar, unless they declined.

Just after the turn of the century, Carry Nation closed the Hoffman House bar—for one night on September 2, 1901. The tempestuous leader of the temperance movement had swung her hatchet in many of the city's saloons and she and her disciples invaded Madison Square for a temperance demonstration.

Rumors reached the management of the Hoffman House that the teetotalers planned to invade the café at nine in the evening, intent not only on smashing the bar and its bottles but also on destroying the *Nymphs and Satyrs* and other art objects worth $100,000. At six in the evening, the Hoffman House was boarded up and the bar sealed as tight as a drum in anticipation of the attack. Mrs. Nation never arrived, but the event is an example of her power to intimidate saloonkeepers.

The Hoffman House was torn down in 1915, and New York lost another of its colorful treasures.

The Brunswick Hotel, across the street from Delmonico's at the northeast corner of 26th Street and Fifth, did not share the racy reputation of the Hoffman House. The Brunswick was an ultraexclusive hostelry that catered to visitors from Britain and to New York's horsey set. On the

27th Street side of the hotel was a *jardin d'été,* the first sidewalk café to open in the United States. Soon after the opening, outdoor cafés dotted Fifth Avenue.

Members of the New York Coaching Club, just up the street, used the hotel as the starting point for the runs to New Rochelle. The members always created a sensation as they gathered in front of the hotel before the drive up the Avenue, appearing in natty club suits of forest green with brass buttons. During the Horse Show, which took place just across Madison Square at the garden, the hotel was invariably draped in blue and yellow bunting, the official Horse Show colors.

The hotel enjoyed enormous popularity until the late 1880s. Because of a single incident, it fell out of favor overnight, never to recover. One bright wintry morning, a tall, well-dressed man, whose speech distinguished him as a gentleman, entered the Brunswick and arranged with a clerk for the entertainment of a number of friends at dinner that evening. He took a large roll of bills from his pocket and offered payment in advance, but the clerk, impressed by his manner and appearance, refused it. Late that night, an immense four-horse sleigh drew up in front of the hotel and a swarm of men and women, the likes of which had never been seen in the Brunswick, entered the dining room and took their seats at a long table. There was nothing to do but serve the party, although the waiters were in shock. The man was none other than Billy McGlory, the proprietor of a disreputable Lower East Side establishment called Armory Hall, of whom his guests were habitués. The newspapers carried the story and ruined the name of the hotel. Its traditional clientele was incapable of taking the affair in stride. The Brunswick closed its doors in 1890.

IN 1877, A STRANGE SIGHT APPEARED IN MADISON SQUARE, AS THE TORCH-BEARING ARM OF THE STATUE OF LIBERTY WAS UNVEILED TO PROMOTE FUND RAISING FOR THE PEDESTAL TO BEAR BARTHOLDI'S GIANT STATUE

As the centennial celebration of the American Revolution drew near, the people of France, under the guidance of author Edouard René de Laboulaye, sought a suitable way to mark the occasion. At a meeting with the sculptor Frédéric Auguste Bartholdi, the mammoth Statue of Liberty was commissioned.

A quarter of a million dollars was raised in France by public subscription and the sculptor began his work. Although the statue was not completed in time for the Centennial Exposition, Bartholdi shipped the torch-bearing right arm to Philadelphia for the celebration. In 1877, the arm was sent from Philadelphia to New York where it was exhibited in Madison Square Park. It remained on view until 1884, when it was returned to Paris to be fitted to the rest of the figure.

Because the French public had paid for the statue, Americans thought it only fitting that the pedestal should be paid by public subscription here. The American public was not enthusiastic about this plan, and donations lagged shamefully.

Finally, Emma Lazarus, the daughter of wealthy parents of Portuguese-Jewish descent, organized an extensive drive and by October 28, 1886, the day of the dedication, the money had been raised.

IN THE 1870S, A BIZARRE DEATH ON FIFTH AVENUE SOLVED A MYSTERY OF THREE DECADES

On the corner of Fifth Avenue and 52nd Street stood a distinguished house that became an object of attention during the 1870s. On almost any day, a grim-faced, fashionably dressed woman could be seen descending the high front stoop with a brisk gait that belied her advancing age. At the foot of the stairs an imposing coachman led her to her carriage for her afternoon drive through the park. The moment the wheels began to turn, a garrulous group of street urchins invariably charged around the corner screaming derisively, "Ha! Ha! Your house is built on babies' skulls!" Madame Restell was an abortionist, and a legend had grown up surrounding the house. It was said that the skeletons of dozens of babies were interred in the cellar. The woman never flinched, but looked sternly ahead, ignoring the taunts of the children.

When the woman died, her estate was officially valued at more than $1 million. Word soon spread, however, that she had not died of natural causes. She had added one more life to those that she had taken by killing herself in the bathtub of her palatial home.

During the years immediately before her death, Madame Restell, or Madame Killer the Abortionist, as she was also known, had been relentlessly attacked in print by Anthony Comstock. It was said that he had driven her to suicide, but another motive for her action was revealed by the *National Police Gazette*. Some thirty years before, there had been a sensational murder and suicide across the Hudson River in New Jersey. Mary Rogers, a cigar-store girl, had become engaged to Daniel Payne, a young naval officer of a prominent New York family. Evidently, the girl had become pregnant and had sought Madame Restell's assistance in the latter's establishment on Greenwich Avenue. The girl died during the operation, and her body was later found in a meadow in Hoboken. The young officer was cleared of what appeared to be murder. But only two weeks later, he went to the spot where the young girl's body had been found and committed suicide. The *Gazette* said that the abortion had indeed been performed by Madame Restell. The obvious conclusion was that, after many years of living with this unsavory incident, as well as others, on her conscience, Madame Restell could simply no longer endure her life.

The mystery, incidentally, was the subject of Edgar Allan Poe's story "The Mystery of Marie Roget," although he changed the locale and the names of the characters.

After the death of Madame Restell, James Gordon Bennett of the *New York Herald* claimed he had a list of her clients and threatened to publish it on the front page of his newspaper. Fifth Avenue residents were uneasy for months, and more than one prominent man about town offered money to Bennett to dissuade him. The list was never published, but Bennett reprinted a cartoon from *Puck* on the front page of his newspaper entitled "Before and After Madame Restell." The "before" cartoon depicted Fifth Avenue filled with promenaders and horses, and the "after" scene was filled with women and nursemaids pushing baby buggies.

ON MAY 25, 1879, ST. PATRICK'S CATHEDRAL WAS FORMALLY CONSECRATED

The cornerstone of the cathedral, which was designed by James Renwick, Jr., was laid in August, 1858, by Archbishop John Hughes. The building was to occupy the square block from Fifth Avenue to Madison Avenue between 50th and 51st streets. The following year, the contract for construction of the entire fabric of the cathedral was signed, but building operations were suspended during the Civil War.

The cathedral grounds were the site of an elaborate fair in the fall of 1878 during which nearly $200,000 was raised to defray the cost of construction. In May, 1879, St. Patrick's was formally opened, complete except for the spires.

Among the little-known objects of interest in the cathedral today is its collection of red hats. It is traditional that, when a cardinal dies, his hat is suspended from the vault of his cathedral church where it hangs until it falls of its own accord. The hats of McCloskey, Farley, Hayes, and Spellman all hang within St. Patrick's.

Among the altars of the cathedral is one that was donated by the Bouvier family. Within, of course, is a statue of St. Patrick, with a book in one hand and a shamrock in the other. St. Patrick, as everyone knows, is the man who drove the snakes from Ireland. Most people are not aware, however, that he was not Irish at all, but a Scot who was sent from Rome to convert the Irish to Catholicism.

Directly north of the cathedral, at 51st Street and Fifth Avenue, stood the Roman Catholic Asylum. This institution opened at the Fifth Avenue address in 1853 and remained there until the last days of the nineteenth century.

The year of the opening of the cathedral, New York's best-known parade, the annual St. Patrick'sDay Parade, moved to Fifth Avenue. It was originally primarily a civil rights demonstration, but that element in the procession disappeared with the irish accession to political power in New York.

The original parades on St. Patrick's Day were much more rowdy than those of today. In 1961, the late Brendan Behan was refused permission to march in the parade by the vice-chairman, Judge James A. Comerford, who was born in Kilkenny, Ireland. "We don't want a personality who has been advertised so extensively as a common drunk," the judge said. In the 1880s, an edict of this sort would probably have caused a riot.

The longest parade in the city's history was held in 1890 when the Irish marched up Fifth Avenue from Washington Square to the Polo Grounds at 155th Street, a distance of nine miles. It was an impressive spectacle as hundreds of horse-drawn carriages proceeded along the Avenue. Irish maids employed in the great mansions were generally given the day off. As they watched the procession from the upstairs windows, they showered the marchers with fruit and cakes.

SARAH BERNHARDT LED THE PROCESSION OF STARS ENTERTAINED ON FIFTH AVENUE IN THE 1880S

Bernhardt, at the time of her American debut, was already a legend in France. Although well-known in America as a superb actress, she was probably better known for the scandal that had touched her life. Despite the uncertainty of her reception, the Divine Sarah arranged to visit the city in January, 1880.

As she made her descent down the gangplank of the ship docked at the Battery, she was confronted by a horde of hysterical fans and curiosity seekers. Her unruly admirers, brandishing scissors or with grasping fingers, tried to secure a piece of her hat, a snip of her hair, or a ruffle from her bustle. Protected by her manager and bodyguard, she ultimately came safely through the pandemonium to her closed cab where she composed herself while driving uptown to the Albermarle Hotel on the west side of Fifth Avenue north of Madison Square.

Henry Abbey, the star's New York producer, saw to it that she was surrounded with proper splendor. He had booked an elegant second-floor suite, with a balcony overlooking the main entrance on Fifth Avenue. The manager of the hotel informed the actress that General Grant himself had occupied these quarters just before her arrival. Bernhardt was unimpressed. The interior, however, was more to her liking. Abbey had had it redecorated to remind her of her home in Paris. All the clutter, Victorian froufrou, and bad taste of the period were thrown together in eclectic vulgarity. Potted palms, Turkish ottomans, cozy corners, immense flower arrangements, bearskin rugs, and the ubiquitous grand piano covered with a Spanish shawl were elements of the decor. The Divine Sarah was suitably impressed.

As she gazed around the salon, she noted three busts on marble shafts—one of Molière, one of Racine, and one of Hugo. With a shriek of delight she kissed the cold bronze cheek of Hugo. Michael Knoedler of the art gallery had brought them over. After greeting him effusively, she declared that she was totally exhausted and must have an hour's rest. At that moment three reporters appeared in the door and began to ask questions. Bernhardt turned on her heels, uttered one of her death-scene cries, and threw herself onto the floor, legs flailing and fists beating the carpet. The men left only to return with several more reporters. This time Sarah ran into an adjoining room, locked the doors, pulled the bureau in front of the door, and recommenced her tantrum. Her manager politely told her that antagonizing the New York press was most certainly

not a good idea, and that she had better come out and give them audience. The actress screamed through the door that, if she did not have her way, she was quite capable of throwing herself out of the window of the hotel onto the street below. He agreed to let her have a short rest.

After her nap, the reporters confronted her and learned that she did not feed live quails to her pet lion, nor did she sometimes dress in drag and smoke cigars, nor did her dressmaker keep a skeleton in her workshop on which to fit the creations she made for her. They also learned that she ate nothing but mussels three times a day and that it was none of their business how much her jewelry was worth. The following day a number of cruel caricatures of the actress appeared in the newspapers, including one that portrayed her as a seductive boa constrictor.

Bernhardt's first impressions of New York were not at all favorable. But after touring the city to view Fifth Avenue, Central Park, the El, the Brooklyn Bridge, and some of the taller buildings, she commented, "I returned to my hotel, reconciled to these great people."

After her opening at the Booth Theater, crowds followed her carriage up Fifth Avenue to the Albermarle where they cheered her below her balcony. Bernhardt stepped outside and blew kisses to her fans. The band played the "Marseillaise," while Sarah stood at attention.

Within a week, Sarah Bernhardt candy, cigars, eyeglasses, and jewelry all made their appearance in the city. The newspapers printed accounts of her every move. The Divine Sarah was, however, never accepted in the drawing rooms of Fifth Avenue. Her reputation, her several ex-husbands, and the illegitimacy of her son made that quite impossible. James Gordon Bennett, however, did arrange an evening for her; he planned an after-theater supper party in a private room at Delmonico's in her honor. With the exception of Sarah, all the guests were men. Word spread next day that an orgy had taken place in Delmonico's back room. In order to set things straight, Bennett beseeched the Union League Club to entertain the actress. They did, but again the only guests who arrived were men. Sarah, however, never cared. She had many devoted friends in this city and was hardly concerned with society's elite.

After her farewell tour of the country, she returned to Paris. Before her death in 1922, the Divine Sarah had made eight "final" farewell tours of the United States.

IN 1882, OSCAR WILDE CAME TO NEW YORK, LECTURED AT CHICKERING HALL, AND MADE THE ROUNDS OF TEAS AND DINNERS AT THE GREAT HOUSES

From the start, Fifth Avenue's hostesses competed to entertain "Lady Wilde," as he was called, at their dinner tables and in their parlors. The New York press was eager to attack him. Needless to say, the combination was devastating, with both Wilde and Fifth Avenue society the target of a corps of journalists bent on outdoing one another with clever poems and brutal dialogue.

Wilde had come to America to lecture. He already had a reputation as an outrageous fop and had been portrayed walking around gazing wistfully into the lilies and sunflowers that he held in his hand. His appearance was outlandish for the period: long hair, velvet knee breeches, frilled shirts, velvet frock coats, and flamboyant handkerchiefs tucked here and there. Neither the press corps nor the people of Fifth Avenue had ever seen anyone quite like him.

For weeks before his lecture at Chickering Hall, at 18th Street and Fifth, society feted him with teas and receptions. He was introduced at the home of Augustus Hayes, Jr., a rich, effete, young travel writer, who decorated his house in the Wildian manner for the afternoon reception. Heavy curtains were drawn against the pale winter light. Wilde received standing before a Japanese umbrella "like a heathen idol" telling London stories to his admirers. Other prominent citizens too invited him to their homes. John Bigelow, General George B. McClellan, and the Century Club all entertained him.

Despite his overcivilized appearance, Wilde secured the admiration of the masculine half of the city's elite at a stag party. He accomplished this feat through sheer monumental gluttony, having put down mounds of oysters, chops, eggs, cheeses, and endless glasses of whiskey and soda. When dawn finally arrived, others at the party rose from the table, gripping at phantom chairs and stepping over fleeting shadows on the floor. Through the alcoholic haze, they noted that Wilde was standing as straight as a column, leading them firmly down stairs and through doors while they stumbled and fell. When they finally all reached the street safely, one of the men asked Wilde if he would like a ride home. He politely replied, "Really, it's a wonderful night for a stroll." So he strolled, as the others assisted one another into hansom cabs.

On the evening of January 6, Wilde attended the smash hit *Patience* at the Standard Theater in the company of Colonel and Mrs. Samuel F. B. Morse. One of the characters satirized Wilde and everyone in town was eager to know if he would react. He did, by saying to Mrs. Morse, "Caricature is the tribute which mediocrity pays to genius."

As the night of his lecture drew near, he was besieged with invitations, and bouquets of lilies arrived at his door by the dozen. Crowds of people followed him on his daily walk up and down Fifth Avenue. One day, he reportedly dressed himself in a white suit exactly like the one that

Mark Twain customarily wore and sat himself down on Twain's bench in Madison Square, poking fun at the American humorist.

Unfortunately for Wilde, his lecture was an anticlimax and far too long-winded. Occasionally he spoke artful compliments such as, "There is something Hellenic in your air, something that has a quicker breath of the joy and power of Elizabeth's England about it than our ancient civilization can give us." But some members of the audience were departing, and Wilde finally had the sense to cease talking. The newspapers were not complimentary. He departed on an extensive tour of the provinces.

LILY LANGTRY FOLLOWED WILDE TO NEW YORK FOR HER AMERICAN DEBUT

Henry Abbey, who had arranged Bernhardt's American tour, was also responsible for bring actress Lillie Langtry to New York. After his success with Bernhardt's tour, he sought to duplicate his triumph with Langtry. He arranged a grand reception at the Albermarle on Fifth Avenue where Bernhardt had stayed and booked the same suite for the Jersey Lily.

Lillie's crossing on the *Arizona* was highly publicized because Christine Nilsson, the Swedish soprano, was on another boat that left Europe at the same time. Nilsson wished to beat Langtry to New York to secure the more triumphant reception. The *Arizona,* however, won the race and Langtry received the kudos. The band at the dock welcomed her with a rendition of "The Girl I Left Behind Me."

Oscar Wilde returned to New York from the West especially to greet the actress and boarded the *Arizona* wearing a cowboy hat over his long hair. The *New York Times* commented: "He was dressed as probably no man in this world was ever dressed before."

New Yorkers received the actress with enthusiasm. Hundreds of bouquets arrived daily at the Albermarle, and young men by the score courted Lillie. Letters asked her advice on beauty, love, marriage, and husbands. When she entered Delmonico's, waiters were in such a flurry that they dropped bottles of champagne and trays full of dishes. Sarony, the photographer, had her sit for him and printed thousands of souvenir photographs. Langtry is reputed to have said to him, "You have made me pretty. I am beautiful."

During the week preceding her debut, gossip flourished as Wilde was seen constantly at her side. "Lillie is through with her husband. Wilde is mad about her," repeated the newspapers day in and day out. Well connected up and down the Avenue, Wilde maneuvered countless teas, dinners, and receptions at the great houses for his enamorata.

Finally the evening for her debut arrived. At five o'clock, after a final rehearsal, the actors, David Belasco, and Abbey were sitting in her suite at the Albermarle when Pierre Lorillard raced into the room crying out, "I'm afraid the Park Theater is on fire." The Park was just down West 25th Street on Broadway, within view of the Fifth Avenue balcony of the Albemarle. They all rushed to the windows and saw the roof of the theater ablaze, billows of smoke belching through the eaves. Fire bells rang, and David Belasco saw "Miss Lillie clench her hands and wipe the tears from her eyes." She stood and watched a signboard on the roof, the board with her name on it. She said, "If it stands, I'll succeed. If it burns, I'll succeed without it." After the fire was extinguished, Mrs. Langtry turned to Abbey and said, "Well, we'll try again some other day." She did, about a week later at Wallack's Theater. Needless to say, the performance was a triumph.

IN APRIL, 1882, P. T. BARNUM BROUGHT JUMBO THE ELEPHANT OVER FROM LONDON TO THE DELIGHT OF ALL NEW YORKERS

P. T. Barnum had contracted with the Royal Zoological Society in London to buy Jumbo, the largest elephant in captivity for $10,000. The society, pleased to receive the money, could not have imagined the furor that the sale would precipitate in England. Thousands wrote letters begging Barnum not to take their elephant friend from them. Many complained that newly rich America was robbing England of its treasures. Queen Victoria herself asked Barnum to call off the deal, as did the prince of Wales.

The commotion may appear to have been a storm in a teacup, but Jumbo was an extraordinary animal and universally loved. He was enormous, standing close to twenty feet in height, and in contrast to his great strength and bulk, he was exquisitely tender with children. With near human intelligence, if he spotted a child in his path, he would stop and carefully nose the tot to safety.

The English dismally prophesied that the Americans would not know how to feed an elephant properly, and in the meantime, twenty thousand people a day swarmed to the London Zoo for a last look at Jumbo.

On the morning of April 10, the *Assyrian Monarch,* the steamship selected for the elephant's crossing, anchored in New York harbor. Barnum and company embarked and went to view their prize. Then came the task of getting the elephant off the boat and up to Barnum's garden at Madison Square. A huge hoisting crane was set up at the dock as some ten thousand spectators watched the operation from the roofs, doors, and windows of nearby buildings. Eventually, Jumbo's box was raised from the deck of the ship and lowered to the dock. The crowd cheered, and Jumbo trumpeted back in response. After that, the wheeled cage was attached to sixteen horses and pulled uptown toward Madison Square Garden. At one point, the box got stuck and two elephants were brought down from the garden to assist the horses. Up Broadway the strange procession went, followed by thousands of curiosity seekers. Finally at one twenty in the morning, the procession turned into the garden. Just across the street at the Fifth Avenue Hotel, a large party celebrating the arrival of the elephant was in progress, with every window of the hotel jammed with reveling well-wishers. As Jumbo stood in his box before the entrance to the garden, a gentleman from the *Assyrian Monarch* presented Barnum with the constitution of the Jumbo Club, which had been formed on board by the passengers. Each member was required to "look as wise as an owl, as meek as a newly ordained parson and as hypocritical as a temperance reformer." Barnum, a confirmed temperance advocate, groaned, and the crowd cheered.

The following day, Jumbo was released from his cage, and with the gentleness of a lamb, he stepped onto the wooden floor of the circus. The floor gave way with a resounding crash, and the elephant retreated. The hole in the floor was covered with heavy boards, and the creature was led to a side area where he was fastened to an iron spike. With no apparent effort, he gave one gentle tug and yanked the spike from the floor. A larger, more permanent spike was then installed, and the elephant was permanently attached. That day thousands of presents began to arrive: cases of champagne, bales of hay, and impractical gifts such as tobacco, pipes, and a sewing machine. One woman was so enthralled by the elephant that she named her baby after him.

During the following four seasons, Jumbo was exhibited to more than four million children and sixteen million adults. He became as beloved to Americans as he had been to the English. Then one day in 1886, Jumbo met his death, and two continents mourned. His end was particularly sad, as it resulted from his concern for the safety of others. An approaching train was about to crash into a baby elephant in the troupe. In a vain attempt to rescue the threatened youngster from danger, the immense creature received the total impact of the oncoming train himself, and in a few minutes died from his injuries. His skeleton is preserved in the American Museum of Natural History, and his skin is mounted and rests in a museum at Tufts College in Massachusetts.

DURING THE 1880S, THE ASTORS AND THE VANDERBILTS MOVED ONTO FIFTH AVENUE AND SOCIAL FEUDING REACHED EXTRAVAGENT PROPORTIONS AS NEW MONEY STROVE TO CRASH SOCIETY

Caroline Schermerhorn Astor, known along the Avenue as "the" Mrs. Astor, was the wife of William Astor, the second son of William Backhouse Astor. "The" Mrs. Astor unfortunately lacked both beauty and brains and, in fact, wore a black wig because she was nearly bald. She was, however, worth $50 million and had an old New York family background and a determined personality.

In 1880, on the southwest corner of Fifth Avenue and 34th Street, Mrs. Astor built a four-story mansion at a cost of $1,500,000 and a further cost of $750,000 to furnish. In the ballroom of this house the supreme event of the social season was held. On the third Monday of January every year, she gave a ball, limiting her guest list to four hundred people. The term *the Four Hundred* derives from her list. Ward McAllister, her social arbiter, once told a reporter, "There are only about four hundred people in fashionable New York society. If you go outside the number, you strike people who are either not at ease in a ballroom or else make other people not at ease. See the point?"

At her annual gala she received while standing in front of a full-length oil portrait of herself. Her jewels, including an immense diamond stomacher said to have belonged to Marie Antoinette, were worn in excessive and vulgar display. After her death, it was learned that her famous rope of pearls was partly fake; only every other pearl was genuine.

Just to the south of Caroline Astor lived John Jacob Astor II with his wife, Charlotte Gibbs Astor. Mrs. J. J. Astor was, in contrast to her sister-in-law, in every sense a lady. She was cultivated, gracious, well traveled, a benign philanthropist, and possessed the most extraordinary diamonds in the United States. The ladies shared a common ballroom at the rear of the two houses. When John Jacob Astor died in 1887, Charlotte withdrew, so Caroline alone ruled the roost. Her nephew-in-law, John Jacob Astor III, was ambitious for his wife, Mary Paul Astor of Philadelphia, and resented deeply his aunt's domination of society. After losing two political elections in his district, he decided to move to London. Before doing so, however, he tore down his father's house and constructed the Waldorf Hotel on the site, much to his aunt's chagrin. Ultimately, Mrs. William Astor tired of living in the shadow of a hotel and moved into her new house, designed by Richard Morris Hunt, on the southeast corner of 65th Street and Fifth Avenue. On the site of her former home the Astoria Hotel was constructed. On the advice of her lawyers, the Astoria was combined with the Waldorf to form the Waldorf-Astoria Hotel, but Mrs. Astor stipulated that, should she change her mind, the hotels could be separated. On every floor where doorways were constructed to combine the two buildings, provisions also were made for sealing them up again. The Waldorf-Astoria remained at that site until 1929, when it was torn down to make way for the Empire State Building.

During the decade, the Vanderbilts, who were much more prolific than the Astors, began to settle up and down the Avenue. The first to build had been William H. Vanderbilt, the second son of the commodore. William H. had doubled the family fortune, but like his father, he was not in the slightest socially ambitious. His wife too had simple tastes and it was finally their daughter-in-law who entered the social arena to jockey for position for the family.

When the time came for William H. Vanderbilt and his family to move from the reasonably modest house built on the site of the old Croton Cottage, the block on the west side of Fifth Avenue between 51st and 52nd streets was selected. Isaiah Keyser maintained a vegetable garden on the site and lived in a small three-story farmhouse set back from the street. William H. Vanderbilt bought the property and built the twin mansions. The houses cost considerably more than $3 million, which did not include the price of the furnishings or the many paintings bought to cover the walls. He and his wife lived in one of the houses while his daughters, Mrs. Elliott F. Shepard and Mrs. William D. Sloane, lived in the other. More than six hundred artisans worked for one and a half years on Vanderbilt's house, and sixty sculptors were imported from Italy to carve the conglomeration of cornices, pilasters, entablatures, and arched openings. Built in a modified Italian Renaissance style, the house had doors that were copies of those by Ghiberti at the Baptistery in Florence.

After the opening, William H. Vanderbilt commissioned Edward Strahan to prepare a series of elaborate portfolios picturing all the rooms in the house. The lofty tone of his text was amusing: "In these volumes, we are permitted to make a revelation of a private home which better than any other possible selection may stand as a representative of the new impulse now felt in the na-tional life. Like a more perfect Pompeii, the work will better the vision and image of a typical American residence, seized at the moment when the nation begins to have a taste of its own . . . The country, at this moment, is just beginning to be astonishing." Some sixty years later, when David O. Selznick was looking over photographs to find a sufficiently spirit-blighting interior for Rhett Butler's alcoholic binges in *Gone With the Wind,* he decided that the Vanderbilt mansion was exactly the jewel he sought. It was, in terms of the taste of today, ghastly.

Despite, or probably because of, the opulence of the place, Mrs. William H. Vanderbilt was not very pleased with it. The *New York Tribune* wrote in 1885, quoting Mrs. Vanderbilt: "We don't need a better home, and I hate to think of leaving the old house where we have lived so comfortably. I have told William that, if he wants a finer place for his pictures, to build a wing to which he could go whenever he felt inclined; this is too good a house to leave. I will never feel at home in the new place. I remember the first picture we ever bought. We paid ninety dollars for it, and we were afraid to let our friends know how extravagant we had been. I have the picture yet, and there is more pleasure to me in looking at it than all the Meissoniers and other great pictures in the house."

The main house stood until 1947, when it was finally vacated by a later Mrs. Vanderbilt. During the years after World War II, passersby often noticed Mrs. Vanderbilt's curtains flapping through the open windows, torn and shopworn, frayed ghosts of a once glorious past. The house that William H. Vanderbilt built for his daughters was torn down in 1926 to make way for De Pinna's store and a subsequent era in the history of Fifth Avenue.

If Mrs. William H. Vanderbilt was a woman of simple tastes, her daughter-in-law, Mrs. William K. Vanderbilt, née Alva Smith, the daughter of an Alabama cotton planter, was not. The William K. Vanderbilt house was built on the northwest corner of 52nd Street and Fifth Avenue in 1881. It cost more than $3 million, was designed by Richard Morris Hunt, and had limestone exterior imitative of the Chateau at Blois. The entrance and staircase were of Caen stone, and there was a two-story paneled dining hall and a Moorish billiard room on the second floor.

Louis Sullivan, one of the greatest of American architects, came to New York shortly after the house was completed and wrote: "Must I show you this French chateau, this little Chateau de Blois on this street corner here in New York and still you do not laugh? Must you wait until you see a gentleman in a silk hat come out of it before you laugh? Have you no sense of humor? No sense of pathos? Must I tell you that while the man may live in the house physically (for a man may live in any kind of house physically), he cannot possibly live in it morally, mutually or spiritually, that he and his home are a paradox, a contradiction, an absurdity, a characteristically New York absurdity; that he is no part of the house, and his house is no part of him?"

As the house was being constructed, the architect, Richard Morris Hunt, had no knowledge of the instructions to the contractor concerning the figure to be placed on the highest pinnacle of the mansion. Work went forward in the interior, and Hunt paid little attention to a small, cloth-enclosed booth that appeared in the dining room. Finally, aware that it was the center of much talking and laughing, he stated: "That thing must go. Why cannot all work be done out in the open?" Then he was admitted to the secret. The contractor had employed a sculptor to carve a statue of Hunt himself dressed in working clothes with a chisel in hand. The statue actually adorned the place designed for it for a time. Later it was taken down and given to Hunt's heirs.

Alva Vanderbilt was determined to unseat Mrs. Astor as queen of society, and her plan was well thought out. First, she quietly entertained in her house for two years. Mrs. Astor ignored her. Then she planned the most sumptuous costume ball that had ever been given in the United States for the night of March 26, 1883. Miss Caroline Astor, daughter of the "queen" and the future Mrs. Orme Wilson, assuming that she would be invited, began to organize a star quadrille in which she and her friends would appear as pairs of stars in yellow, blue, mauve, and white. Mrs. Vanderbilt, hearing of young Caroline's plans, let word drop that, as Mrs. Astor had never paid her a call, it would be unfortunately quite impossible for her to invite the young lady. "The" Mrs. Astor finally bowed, summoned her carriage, left her card at the Vander-

bilt mansion, and in so doing, symbolically surrendered her social crown to Alva Vanderbilt.

The night of the grand ball arrived, and through the portals of William K. Vanderbilt's house strode Mrs. Astor's Four Hundred, plus another eight hundred persons also invited. The costumes were unbelievably elaborate. Mrs. Pierre Lorillard wore a Worth gown costuming her as a phoenix; as she paraded toward the vestibule, she scattered tinsel ashes and sparks before her. Mr. and Mrs. Bradley-Martin came as Louis XV and Mary, queen of Scots, and Mrs. Ogden Goelet was dressed as a Polish equestrienne. Mrs. Cornelius Vanderbilt II, however, stole the show. Illuminated cosumes were in vogue, and she strode into the ballroom dressed as an electric light.

Armies of decorators placed thousands of blossoms throughout the house. It was the fashion to open all balls with quadrilles. The first was a hobby horse quadrille in which the dancers, dressed in riding habits, appeared to be mounted. It had taken two months to construct the props, for the horses were of life-size and covered with genuine hides. Following this performance came a Mother Goose quadrille, Caroline Astor's star quadrille, and a Dresden quadrille.

When it was all over, the newspapers reported the cost of the party:

Costumes	$155,730
Flowers	11,000
Carriages	4,000
Hairdressing	4,000
Champagne, catering, music	56,270
	$231,000

In 1880, Cornelius Vanderbilt II, another son of William H. Vanderbilt, began to build his house on the west side of Fifth Avenue between 57th and 58th streets where Bergdorf Goodman now stands. When the house was enlarged in 1894, the carriage entrance faced Grand Army Plaza. The two lots were purchased by the family in 1850 for $1,230. The house was demolished in 1927 and all that remains of it today are the north gates, which were reerected in Central Park at

105th Street and Fifth Avenue. The house was every bit as elaborate as that of his brother William K. on 52nd Street, with a ballroom that measured sixty-four by fifty feet. Thirty servants staffed the house, which was furnished with late nineteenth-century copies of French furniture.

Shortly after the statue of *Abundance,* which stands today before the Plaza Hotel, was unveiled, Cornelius II complained to the city, as his bedroom fronted on a rear view of the statue. The city refused to remove it, so Vanderbilt moved his bedroom to the rear of the house.

IN MARCH, 1888, THE FAMOUS BLIZZARD STRUCK THE CITY AND FIFTH AVENUE WAS BURIED IN SNOW

Sunday, March 11, was a cloudy warm day in New York. The city had just experienced one of the mildest winters in decades. Spring was in the air, the forsythia and chinaberry in Central Park were budding, and the bluebirds had come back to town. At about two in the afternoon, it started to drizzle. An hour later, the drizzle became a steady rain, which then exploded into a cloudburst. Slowly the temperature fell. By ten o'clock, the rain had changed to sleet, and by midnight the city was besieged by swirling clouds of dry snow. By seven o'clock Monday morning, all railroad service in and out of the city had ceased. The temperature was 21° F, and the wind had increased to around ninety miles an hour, or hurricane force.

That morning, Roscoe Conkling, a prominent Republican politician, left his suite at the New York Club in the Hoffman House and proceeded downtown to his office on Wall Street. J. P. Morgan made his way down Fifth from his house at 36th Street and Madison Avenue. Everyone else had the sense to stay home. By the time the business day had begun, eighteen inches of snow had piled up, and in some places drifts rose to thirty feet. Fifth Avenue was deserted. Even the English sparrows had sensibly stayed out of the storm; flocks of them flew through the open doors of the Fifth Avenue Hotel, where thousands roosted undisturbed until the storm was over.

By midafternoon, Conkling and Morgan each decided that he had better head for home. Conkling later wrote about his journey: "There wasn't a cab or carriage of any kind to be had. Once during the day I had declined an offer to ride uptown in a carriage because a man wanted fifty dollars, and I started up Broadway on my own pins. It was dark and it was useless to try to pick out a path, so I went magnificently forth, shouldering through drifts and headed for the north. I was pretty well exhausted when I got to Union Square, and wiping snow from my eyes, I tried to make out the triangle there. It was impossible. When I reached the New York Club at Fifth Avenue and 25th Street, I was covered all over with ice and packed snow, and they would scarcely believe that I had walked all the way from Wall Street. It took three hours to make the journey."

After being lost for two hours in Madison Square, Conkling arrived at the Hoffman House, stumbled through the doorway, and collapsed onto the floor. As a result of his ordeal, he developed pneumonia and mastoiditis and died a month later. The very morning of the blizzard the *New York Herald* had published an editorial proposing Conkling for the presidency of the United States.

Morgan also had a harrowing experience, although it did not result in his death. He sensibly retained a cab and was driven as far as 36th Street and Fifth but could go no farther. The great man struggled through the drifts to his home, only a block away, but was so exhausted when he arrived that he barely managed to ring the doorbell before he collapsed. A servant opened the door and dragged him inside.

That night was one of the strangest New York had ever seen. Almost all the streetlamps in the city had been blown down; those that remained standing were of no use for the gas lines had frozen; and not a soul was to be seen on the streets.

At Madison Square Garden, P. T. Barnum had scheduled the opening of his circus. Drifts of snow more than five feet high blocked the entrances, but workers kept the main doors clear. Although fewer than two hundred spectators came to the opening, Barnum decided that the show must go on. As the circus procession began, the old man sent champagne to the reporters who sat ringside. Soon they were leaping into the ring to give their own performance. The clowns and circus folk all took seats and watched the shenanigans.

At the Hoffman House, Maurice Barrymore, father of John, Ethel, and Lionel, climbed onto a table in the bar and recited Mark Antony's funeral oration from *Julius Caesar*. One drunk tried to silence him and a brawl broke out.

The following morning the temperature read minus 1° F and the snow had stopped. The blizzard was over, but hundreds had perished and damage totaled approximately $25 million.

IN APRIL, 1889, THE CENTENNIAL OF THE INAUGURATION OF GEORGE WASHINGTON WAS CELEBRATED IN NEW YORK WITH A PARADE DOWN FIFTH AVENUE TO WASHINGTON ARCH

On April 30, 1789, in New York City, George Washington was inaugurated as the first president of the United States, and one hundred years later, a festive celebration commemorated the event. The climax was the dedication of the Washington Arch in Washington Square Park, the only arch in the world erected by private subscription to mark a historical event. Designed by Stanford White, the temporary arch was built of wood. Two years later, it was removed and the permanent arch, built of marble and also designed by White, was erected. For a number of years, the pedestals on the north front of the arch were vacant, but in 1913 money was raised to provide two marble statues. The eastern pedestal, showing Washington as general of the Continental Army, was dedicated in May, 1916. The western pedestal, showing Washington as president, was placed in February, 1918, and was designed by A. Stirling Calder, the father of sculptor Alexander Calder.

Chapter Five

THE GOLDEN AGE OF FIFTH AVENUE (1890-1917)

CHRONOLOGY

1890   New York City population is 2,507,414.

Second Madison Square Garden, designed by Stanford White, opens.

Coney Island annexed to Brooklyn.

1891   Carnegie Hall and New York Botanical Garden open.

1892   Ellis Island replaces Castle Garden as immigration station.

Grand Boulevard and Concourse in the Bronx proposed.

Cornerstone of the Cathedral of St. John the Divine is laid.

400th Anniversary of Columbus's discovery of America is celebrated. Italian citizens of the city unveil the Columbus Monument at 59th Street.

Mrs. Astor gives her famous ball.

1894   Citizens vote to merge counties into Greater New York and to extend rapid transit to them.

1895   Bronx area east of Bronx River annexed to city.

Drawings of Charles Dana Gibson, especially the Gibson Girl, become popular.

Theodore Roosevelt is made police commissioner.

1896   Columbia College becomes a university.

Aquarium opens in old Castle Garden.

1897   Grant's Tomb dedicated.

First trolley car crosses Brooklyn Bridge.

Waldorf-Astoria Hotel completed at Fifth Avenue and 34th Street.

1898   Greater New York is established.

Harlem speedway is opened.

1899   Bronx Zoo opens.

Reservoir at 42nd Street and Fifth Avenue demolished to make way for public library.

1900   New York City population is 3,437,202.

Subway construction begins in New York.

First automobile show held in Madison Square Garden.

Floradora Sextette appears in New York.

Blacks begin to replace Italians and Jews in Harlem.

82,652 tenements house 70 percent of the city's population.

Twenty-six-story Park Row Building is erected, the tallest in the world.

1901   Institute for Medical Research established by John D. Rockefeller.

Tenement House Law passed, ending "dumbbell plan" and beginning so-called New Law tenement.

1902   Flatiron Building is completed.

Williamsburg Bridge is opened.

1903   Sherman statue unveiled at Grand Army Plaza.

Enrico Caruso makes his debut at the Metropolitan Opera House in *Rigoletto*.

Stock Exchange Building at Broad and Wall streets is completed.

All immigrant records broken, as 857,046 foreigners come to New York.

1904   New York City subway system opens from City Hall to West 145th Street.

Lenox Avenue subway opens.

1905   Staten Island ferry service inaugurated with a five-cent fare.

Mark Twain celebrates his seventieth birthday at a dinner at Delmonico's.

1906   Stanford White murdered by Harry K. Thaw in Madison Square Garden roof theater.

Fraunces Tavern is reconstructed as it appeared at the time of Washington.

1907   Custom House in Bowling Green is completed.

1908   Pennsylvania Railroad Tunnel is opened.

Fifth Avenue Association is formed.

Academy of Music in Brooklyn opens.

East River Tunnel connecting Lower Manhattan with Brooklyn is completed.

McAdoo Tunnel, first of the Hudson Tubes, opens from Manhattan to Hoboken.

Broadway line of IRT extended to Kingsbridge in the Bronx.

1909   Queensboro and Manhattan bridges open.

Hudson-Fulton Celebration is held in New York.

Grand Concourse opened in the Bronx.

1910   New York City population is 4,766,883.

Pennsylvania Station opens.

Gimbel Brothers opens in New York.

1911   Hall of Records in City Hall Park is completed.

New York Public Library, established by joining the Astor, Lenox, and Tilden bequests, is opened on Fifth Avenue and 42nd Street.

Triangle Shirtwaist Company fire at Washington Place and Greene Street kills 145. Reforms in garment industry and fire codes result.

1913   Present Grand Central Station is completed.

Armory Show at Sixty-ninth Regiment Armory proves a sensation as U. S. sees "modern" art for the first time.

1914   Federal Reserve Bank is established in New York.

Panama Canal opened, spurring traffic between New York and Pacific coast.

1915   Blue, white, and orange city flag is adopted, the colors of Maurice, prince of Orange, in the time of Henry Hudson.

Alexander Graham Bell talks over the telephone from New York to San Francisco.

German submarine *Deutschland* makes a first visit to New York. It is seized on second visit in 1916 and interned during World War I.

1916   Permanent lighting installed in the Statue of Liberty.

First zoning resolution in country takes effect in New York.

1917   Catskill water system is opened.

United States declares war on Germany, and New York becomes chief port of embarkation for the American Expeditionary Force.

1918   Regular air service is instituted between New York and Washington.

New York celebrates the return of peace on November 7, in a false Armistice Day, and on November 11 when the verified news is received.

The period from 1890 to the beginning of World War I was the Golden Age of Fifth Avenue. Literally hundreds of new buildings rose on sites formerly occupied by brownstones and on the vast stretches of vacant land fronting Central Park.

One by one the older houses, clubs, and churches were torn down and mercantile buildings were erected. Billboards appeared advertising everything from bunion pads to corsets, and the upper stories of loft buildings were converted to sweatshops. The area from 14th to 27th streets became a center for the garment industry, and only Lower Fifth Avenue, the area south of 14th Street, retained its original character. Madison Square was unrecognizable, as the Fifth Avenue Hotel, the Brunswick Hotel, the Hoffman House, and the Albermarle Hotel were all abandoned, and either torn down or marked for demolition. The Ladies' Mile, the elegant shopping district on Broadway near Madison Square, disappeared as the fashionable stores were moved to the area between 23rd and 38th streets on Fifth Avenue. At 42nd Street, the old Croton Reservoir was torn down in 1902, and the New York Public Library was constructed in its place.

In 1908, Fifth Avenue was widened, and almost all its Old World charm vanished as sidewalk cafés, gardens in front of houses, and the old Dutch stoops were removed. That year the Fifth Avenue Association was formed to save Fifth Avenue. Zoning rules were established, and commercial invasion was halted below 34th Street.

North of 42nd Street, the mansions built in the previous two decades dominated the Avenue and exclusive clubs, hotels, and restaurants were opened. Above 49th Street, Millionaire's Row attracted the attention of America as one millionaire after another erected an extravagant house to prove his wealth.

Ostentation on Fifth Avenue reached its peak as elaborate entertainments occupied the time and ambitions of the residents. Informed by detailed newspaper accounts, the public was alternately fascinated and censorious. Public criticism of "big spending" literally forced some individuals to leave the country.

During the period from 1870 to 1910, the population of the city rose from 1.5 million to nearly 5 million persons as floods of Italian, Russian, Greek, Polish, and Scandinavian immigrants settled in the city. Although Fifth Avenue was the showplace of the nation, thousands of tenement buildings were constructed on its northern reaches to house the new arrivals, destroying the rural pockets that had survived until that time.

The streets were noisily alive with hansoms, victorias, four-in-hands, buggies, sulkies, and phaetons. Later in the period the automobile assumed preeminence. This was the era of the Gibson Girl, made famous by Charles Dana Gibson in his cartoons in the old *Life* magazine. With hair piled high in a pompadour and with a starched shirtwaist, she epitomized the American girl. The Gibson man also wore a starched shirtwaist, was clean-shaven, and had classic features. The interiors of the houses of the rich were filled with tasteless bric-a-brac, including plaster casts of the Venus de Milo and the Winged Victory, bisque statuary, wax flowers, cattails, and peacock feathers; Turkish and Moorish cozy corners too had their place in these domiciles.

ON JUNE 16, 1890, THE NEW MADISON SQUARE GARDEN ACROSS MADISON SQUARE FROM FIFTH AVENUE OPENED

During the Gay Nineties and in fact until it was torn down in 1924, Stanford White's exquisite cream-colored Madison Square Garden was the center for New York extravaganzas, both social and public. The new garden, which replaced Gilmore's Garden, was modeled after the Giralda in Seville, Spain. The *New York World* on June 17, 1890, wrote of the opening: "It was lifted into the importance of a social event. The rabble was there, of course, and swarmed like ants all over the ground floor, but all the boxes and conspicuous places in the vast enclosure were occupied by men and women prominent in society."

Mrs. Paran Stevens, who lived on Marble Row at 57th Street and Fifth, and who never missed any event, postponed the annual fete at her Newport cottage in order to attend the opening. When the new Metropolitan Opera House opened in 1879, she had amused New Yorkers by dividing her time between the Academy of Music on 14th Street and the new hall. She could be seen speeding back and forth on Fifth Avenue during intermissions, trying to cover two openings in one evening. General William T. Sherman took a front box for the garden's opening and Eduard Strauss, the brother of the Waltz King, Johann, came from Vienna to lead the orchestra.

After the opening, the Horse Show was the first important event to take place in the garden, and thereby secured a place of prominence in the social life of the period. The garden was the site of the famous balls of the period (the Arion, the Old Guard, and the French Ball) as well as six-day walking and bicycle races, cakewalks, Buffalo Bill's Wild West Show, boxing matches, political pageants, mass meetings, religious revivals, flower shows, fruit shows, antique shows, cat shows, poultry shows, and the circus. The first bicycle show, automobile show, and motorboat show were all held in the old garden.

In addition to the main arena of the garden, there was also a Garden Theater. This theater was the scene of the murder of Stanford White, who designed the garden as well as many other significant buildings still standing on Fifth Avenue. On the night of June 25, 1906, Mr. and Mrs. Harry K. Thaw and their two male guests arrived at the theater to attend the opening of *Mamzelle Champagne,* a frivolous musical comedy typical of the era. Mrs. Thaw, the former show girl Evelyn Nesbit, had a clandestine alliance with White. During the performance, Thaw rose from his table. When a member of the cast began singing "I Could Love a Million Girls,"

three pistol shots suddenly cracked, and first-nighters turned to see a man slump in his chair and fall to the floor. Police disarmed Thaw, and chorus girls flocked to White's body, which lay in a pool of blood. Six months later the sensational trial began.

The trial revealed that Evelyn, a simple girl from Pennsylvania, had led a disreputable life. At fourteen, she had become an artist's model and subsequently a show girl in the popular musical *Floradora*. White had arranged to have her come to his apartment, gave her drugged champagne, and seduced her. She became his mistress, and nightly he realized his personal fantasies by having her sit naked on a red velvet swing, while he pushed her to and fro. After a few years, she tired of White and became Thaw's mistress, eventually marrying him. Thaw was a sadist and mercilessly whipped his wife several times a week. Evelyn played one man against the other, and eventually Thaw's jealousy provoked him to murder.

The first trial resulted in a hung jury. The second declared that Thaw was insane, and he was committed to Matteawan State Hospital for the Criminally Insane. In 1924, he was released and thereafter lived quietly until his death in 1940.

Evelyn fared badly after the trial. She started the long trail downhill with divorce, suicide attempts, and second-rate nightclub acts. As recently as 1955, she was hired as a consultant for a film, *The Girl in the Red Velvet Swing,* a motion picture patterned on her life. She died a few years later at the age of eighty-two in a convalescent home. In her last years, she said, "Stanny White was killed, but my fate was worse, I lived."

Augustus Saint-Gaudens's copper statue of Diana crowned the garden's tower for a time. The statue, which stood eighteen feet, six inches high and weighed two thousand pounds, was raised to its place atop the tower on November 1, 1891. The night of the unveiling "great lamps in and about the goddess were lighted for the first time," reported the *New York Tribune*. Across the square at both the Fifth Avenue Hotel and the Hoffman House, crowds gathered to toast the new landmark.

However, not everyone was pleased with Saint-

Gaudens's work because the goddess was depicted clad only in a ribbon of copper that was looped and appeared to float behind her. One reporter wrote: "During the past two weeks, there has been a marked change in the character of Madison Square. Formerly this beautiful little park was the gathering place of children. Now all this is changed. Occasionally a stray child may still be seen, but more generally what children come there are rushed through at breakneck speed in the tow of a nurse or some older person. Their place on the Square is now thronged with clubmen, armed with fieldglasses. Where babyhood once disported itself, today elderly gentlemen, Delmonico elegants, casino Johnnies and every variety of local dude linger in restless idleness."

As a result of the criticism, the statue was removed and sent off to a fair in Chicago. However, sentiment changed in New York, and in 1893, a second Diana was mounted atop the garden where she stood until 1924, when the garden was pulled down. The statue was acquired by the Philadelphia Museum of Art in 1932.

IN 1902, THE FIRST SKYSCRAPER TO APPEAR ON THE AVENUE WAS ERECTED AT THE INTERSECTION OF BROADWAY, FIFTH AVENUE, AND 23RD STREET

In 1902, the George Fuller Company hired the architectural firm of D. H. Burnham and Company to design a building for a site described as a "stingy piece of pie" at the junction of Fifth Avenue, Broadway, and 23rd Street. This building has survived and is known today as the Flatiron Building. Through the years, it has been in and out of vogue in architectural circles. When it was built, there were sharply divided opinions regarding its merit, but today it is recognized as one of the great examples of early skyscraper architecture in the city.

Sir Philip Burne-Jones, after his visit to New York in 1902, wrote of the building: "One vast horror, facing Madison Square, is distinctly responsible for a new form of hurricane, which meets unsuspecting pedestrians as they reach the corner, causing them extreme discomfort. When its effects first became noticeable, a little rude crowd of loafers and street arabs used to congregate upon the curb to jeer and gloat over the distress of ladies whose skirts were blown into their eyes as they rounded the treacherous corner. Hanging about this particular spot soon became a recognized and punishable offense." As the years wore on, the girl watchers continued to congregate and the policemen on 23rd Street continued to shoo them away. The expression *twenty-three skidoo* was inspired by this corner.

During the early days of this century, the Flatiron Building served as a giant projection screen on which election returns were flashed as they poured in from all parts of the country.

The temporary arch constructed in 1876 for the centenary celebration of American Independence. The present arch replaced this one in 1892.

A commercial building at Fifth Avenue and 24th Street.

The Flatiron Building at the intersection of 23rd Street, Fifth Avenue, and Broadway.

Detail from the
Flatiron Building.

Detail, inspired by the Porch of the Maidens, on a building at 91 Fifth Avenue.

Bicycling on Fifth Avenue in 1897, near Mount Morris Park at 124th Street.

The new building for **B. Altman and Company**, on the east side of Fifth

Avenue between 34th and 35th streets, shortly before its completion in 1906.

Detail from the New York Public Library.

The New York Public Library, designed by

Carrère and Hastings in 1898, as it looks today.

Charles Scribner's Sons, at
597 Fifth Avenue between
48th and 49th streets, designed by Ernest Flagg in
1913.

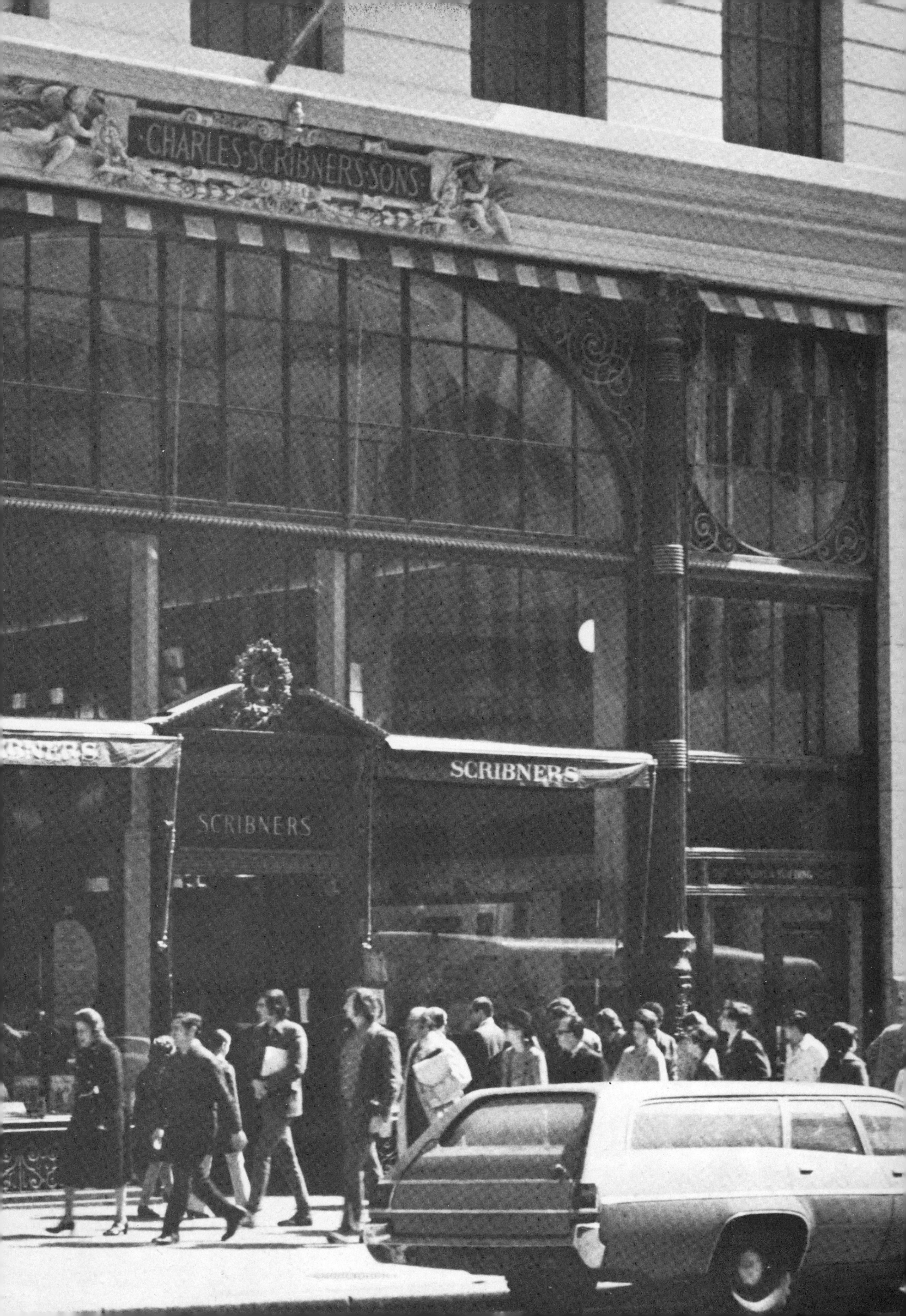
CHARLES·SCRIBNERS·SONS·
SCRIBNERS
SCRIBNERS
SCRIBNERS

Detail from the Plaza Hotel.

On the left, the University Club, at the northwest corner of Fifth
Avenue and 54th Street, designed by McKim, Mead and White;
and on the right, the Gotham Hotel, designed by Hiss and Weeks.

Detail from the Gotham Hotel.

Grand Army Plaza and the Plaza Hotel.

The start of the New York to St. Louis tour in the spring of 1904 is pictured in front

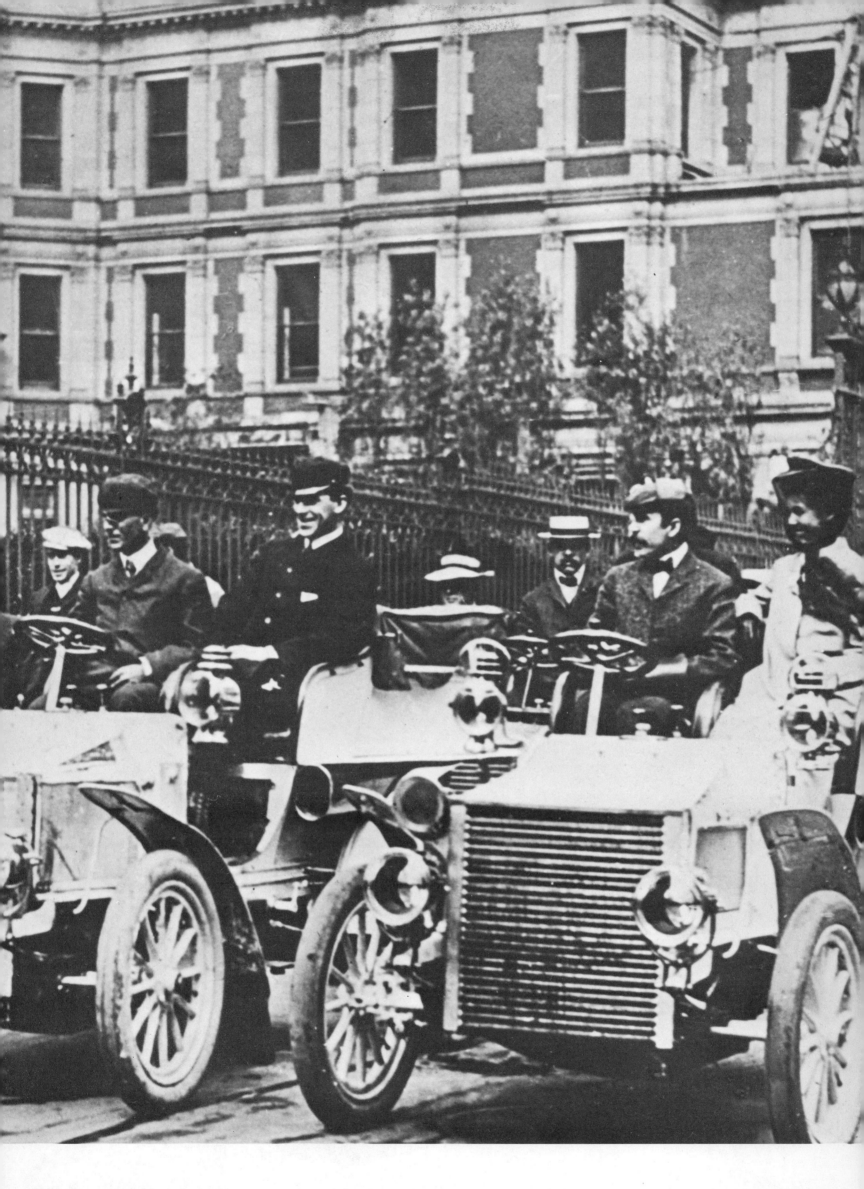

of the Cornelius Vanderbilt mansion at West 58th Street, just off Fifth Avenue.

Fifth Avenue looking north from below 65th Street

in 1901. John Jacob Astor's house and others.

Cartier, Inc. formerly Morton F. Plant residence at the southeast corner of 52nd Street.

On the left, the Augustus Van Horne Stuyvesant mansion, now the Ukranian Folk Museum. In the center, the McCook house, now occupied by the Eastern States Mission Home of the Mormon Church; and on the right, the Harry Payne Whitney house, now the French Cultural Services of the French Consulate. This row of great houses is one of the few remaining on Fifth Avenue today.

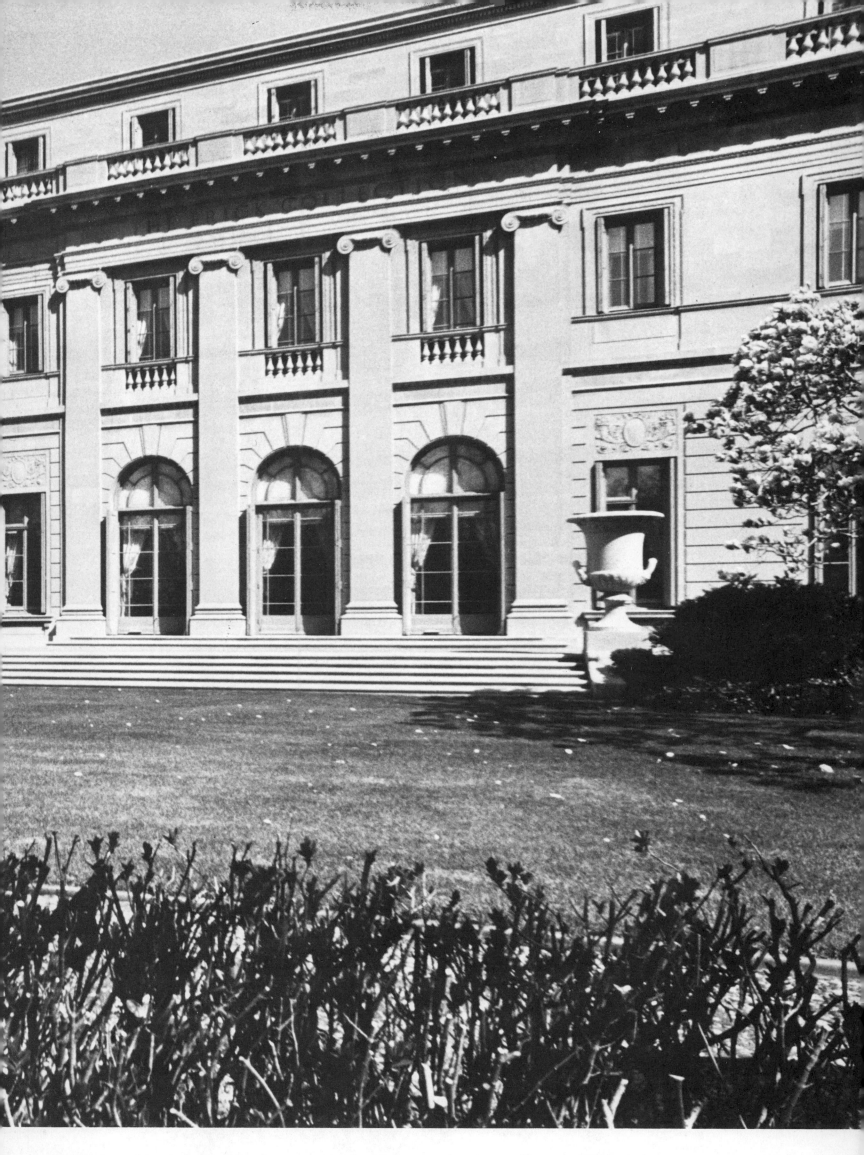

Frick Collection, formerly the Henry Clay Frick mansion on Fifth Avenue between 70th and 71st streets. This house was designed by Carrère and Hastings in 1914 and was opened to the public as a museum in 1935.

The Isaac V. Brokaw residence on the northeast corner of Fifth Avenue and 79th Street.

THE FIRST DEPARTMENT STORE, B. ALTMAN AND COMPANY, OPENS ON FIFTH AVENUE

In 1903, Benjamin Altman's department store stood at 301 Sixth Avenue between 18th and 19th streets. That year Altman purchased the property at the northeast corner of 34th Street and Fifth, hired Trowbridge and Livingston as architects, and built a new department store. Residents of the neighborhood were outraged. In an effort to appease homeowners in this prime residential area, Altman had the building designed to look as much like a Florentine palace as possible. The building was completed in 1906 and precipitated the opening of a flock of fashionable stores on the Avenue above 34th Street. Best and Company built on the southwest corner of 35th Street in 1910. The building stands today as 366 Fifth Avenue.

In 1905, construction began at 390 Fifth Avenue on the southwest corner of 36th Street as Gorham Jewelers erected a building that was designed by McKim, Mead and White. At the southeast corner of 37th Street, Tiffany's put up a large structure modeled after the Palazzo Vendramini in Venice. The building, completed in 1906, was also designed by McKim, Mead and White. The 37th Street side of this structure retains its original three ranks of columns supporting a broad cornice. In 1914, Lord and Taylor moved into their present building, designed by Starrett and Van Vleck, at the northwest corner of 38th Street.

Benjamin Altman's decision to build his store on Fifth Avenue initiated the fourth era in the history of the Avenue—that of retailer's showcase. The millions of Americans who visited the city could now take a Fifth Avenue label home with them.

IN 1902, THE CROTON RESERVOIR WAS DEMOLISHED AND CONSTRUCTION OF THE NEW YORK PUBLIC LIBRARY WAS BEGUN

The architects John Merven Carrère and Thomas Hastings were commissioned by the city in 1902 to design the 42nd Street library. The city provided the land and contracted to maintain the library, while the trustees of the New York Public Library, Astor, Lenox, and Tilden foundations promised to establish a free circulating branch and a public library and reading room. Five million dollars was donated by Andrew Carnegie toward these ends. The library, which cost $9 million, was built of marble from Vermont, Tennessee, Greece, Italy, France, Germany, and Belgium. Alan Burnham, the architectural critic, stated: "[It] probably comes closer than any other [building] in America to the complete realization of Beaux-Arts design at its best." The handsome terraces and the well-known lions, which according to legend, roar only when a virgin passes, provide an impressive facade for the building. The interior, with its vast space and grand staircases, is one of the finest in the city.

The library was opened on May 23, 1911, in a ceremony presided over by President William Howard Taft. He commented: "This day crowns a work of national importance." Today it is the most widely used research library in the world, visited by over three million persons a year. In addition, the reading room is the largest in the world with the collection ranking third in the country, standing behind the Library of Congress and Harvard University.

Among the treasures contained in the library's immense collection are a handwritten copy of George Washington's Farewell Address, the first Gutenberg Bible brought to this country, the Dongan Charter of New York City issued in 1686, and a 1726 copy of the *New York Gazette,* the first paper published in New York City.

DELMONICO'S DESERTED MADISON SQUARE DURING THE LAST DAYS OF THE NINETEENTH CENTURY AND MOVED TO 45TH STREET AND FIFTH AVENUE, WHILE SHERRY'S, UNDER THE DIRECTION OF LOUIS SHERRY, OPENED AT 37TH STREET AND FIFTH

When Delmonico's moved uptown to 45th Street, it signaled the start of society's exodus from Madison Square. A few years later, when Sherry's opened at 37th Street, fashionable people had unquestionably deserted the lovely greensward. Both restaurants became the scene of social functions, including some of the most extravagant of galas. Before the Avenue was widened in 1908, both restaurants had terraces and cafés that fronted on the street level. The histories of these two glamorous establishments were, however, short-lived. With the advent of Prohibition, both were forced to close, and with their demise, the era of fabulous public entertaining ended on the Avenue.

ABOUT 1890, THE BANK OF NEW YORK OPENED A BRANCH AT 44TH STREET AND FIFTH AVENUE

The Bank of New York was probably the first bank in the city to personalize the business of handling money. It sought the business of ladies by installing a special counter for their convenience and by maintaining a lovely little parlor for them on the first floor, where maids in crisp uniforms served tea.

Together with many outstanding artists, writers, actors, and musicians of the last century, most of the great singers of the Metropolitan Opera Company had accounts at this bank. Caruso was a depositor. One day he came into the bank at the noon hour to cash a check, and a new teller decided he was an impostor. Caruso had an inspiration. He placed one hand on his chest and sang an aria from *Tosca,* then bowed, took his money, and departed amid the cheers of customers and clerks.

To the north, at 597 Fifth Avenue between 48th and 49th streets, Charles Scribner's Sons commissioned architect Ernest Flagg to design a store. The architect used a large glass front to reveal the handsome two stories of the interior of the bookstore. Opened in 1913, the building still stands and is still occupied by the Scribner bookstores.

The building presently occupied by Cartier, Inc., the jeweler, was formerly the Morton F. Plant residence. Situated at the southeast corner of 52nd Street, it was designed by Robert W. Gibson and built in 1905. In 1917, it was remodeled, and the house next door, at 4 East 52nd Street, was combined with the Plant house for the jewelry concern. The terms of the purchase were

unusual. In exchange for the building, Cartier's bartered a long two-strand pearl necklace, valued at $1.5 million.

In 1899, McKim, Mead and White built the University Club at 1 West 54th Street, on the northwest corner of Fifth Avenue, formerly the site of St. Luke's Hospital. The University Club had been founded in 1865, but its origins go back to 1861 when a group of Yale men who had been intimate friends in college met regularly. The club was unique in the city's social history because implicit in membership was the possession of a college degree. In 1879, the club moved to a house at the corner of Fifth and 34th Street where it remained for five years. When that lease expired in 1884, the club moved into the Jerome mansion at the corner of 26th Street and Madison Avenue. This building was earlier occupied by the Union League and Turf Clubs. Later, this building housed the Manhattan Club.

In 1896, the club purchased its present site. The building, designed largely by Charles F. McKim, who was a devoted member of the club, is in fifteenth-century Florentine style. The murals in the beautiful library were painted by H. Siddons Mowbray in 1904 and are an adaptation of the work of Pinturicchio in the Borgian apartments of the Vatican. The library is one of the few rooms remaining in the city that is closed to women.

DURING THIS PERIOD, HOTEL CONSTRUCTION ALL ALONG THE AVENUE COMMENCED

In 1902, on the southeast corner of 55th Street, the Astor family built the St. Regis Hotel, which was designed by Trowbridge and Livingston. The hotel opened in 1904 and at the time was the tallest in the city. The furnishings came from France, the bathroom fixtures were of silver, and Waterford crystal chandeliers were placed throughout

the building. Bronze elevators in the Art Nouveau style carried the guests from the lobby to their suites.

Colonel John Jacob Astor decided to include a library on the main floor, an innovation in hotels. This room was designed by Elsie de Wolfe, later Lady Mendl, the first of the interior decorators, and is still in its original form. Astor commissioned Scribner's to collect a library of volumes "suitable for gentlemen and gentlewomen" and more than two thousand books were selected.

The King Cole Bar, which formerly fronted on Fifth Avenue, today features Maxfield Parrish's painting of the "merry old soul." Originally the painting, completed in 1900, hung in the old Knickerbocker Hotel, but was moved to the St. Regis upon its opening.

Today, the Watteau suite, also designed by Elsie de Wolfe, contains six panels by Watteau that were brought from the old Ambassador Hotel, later the Sheraton-East, in 1967. They formerly belonged to Consuelo Vanderbilt Balsan who had purchased them from the Chateau de Chambord, which was built by King Francis I during the Renaissance.

Recently the St. Regis has been used as a setting for films and novels. The fictional James Bond always made the St. Regis his home when in New York. Alfred Hitchcock duplicated his favorite suite, 1905, in his film *Topaz*. The painting of four spirited horses in the Oak Room by Lumen Martin Winter was the inspiration for the official Apollo insignia worn by astronauts on their space flights.

The following year, directly across the street on the southwest corner of 55th Street, the Gotham Hotel was opened. The former Cartier Building, at 712 Fifth between 55th and 56th streets, designed by A. S. Gottlieb in 1907, is now occupied by Rizzoli International Bookstore, and the former Coty Building at 714 Fifth Avenue, designed by W. Leeming in 1908, also still stands.

In 1907, the present Plaza Hotel opened. It was designed by Henry J. Hardenbergh, architect of the old Waldorf-Astoria and the Dakota Apartments.

During the early days of the century, the Plaza became famous for tea dancing in the grillroom. It was here that new dances such as the bunny hug, grizzly bear, turkey trot, fox trot, and camel walk were introduced to a somewhat shocked society. The newspapers did not approve. William Randolph Hearst's *American* reported: "New York and Newport society are just at present manifesting a craze for the disgusting and indecent dance known as the Turkey Trot." The *New York Sun* said: "Are we going to the dogs by the ragtime route? This decadent drivel, rhythmically attracting degenerator which hypnotizes us into vulgar foot-tapping acquiescence." Later in its history, the Plaza Grill became the scene for tango teas at which the undisputed queen was the glamorous Constance Bennet.

IN 1903, SHERMAN'S STATUE WAS UNVEILED ON GRAND ARMY PLAZA, AND IN 1912, THE PULITZER FOUNTAIN AND THE STATUE OF ABUNDANCE WERE UNVEILED

During his last years, General William T. Sherman became one of the most loved characters in New York history, and it was fitting that after his death he should be immortalized in bronze. Augustus Saint-Gaudens was commissioned to create the sculpture in 1892 and went to Paris to work on the project. After crossing the ocean twice, the statue was finally finished, cast in bronze, and gilded; then it lay on its side in the snow near the sculptor's Vermont studio.

Finally, in the spring of the year, it was transported on flatcars to Manhattan where it stood in a shack near the Metropolitan Museum of Art as controversy raged over where to place it.

It was first proposed that it stand near Grant's Tomb on Riverside Drive, but General Grant's family objected and that idea was rejected. Then it was suggested that Sherman's statue should occupy the focal point of the mall in Central Park, but that idea was also abandoned. Finally, the present spot on Grand Army Plaza at the entrance to Central Park was selected.

On May 30, 1903, the statue was unveiled, and the inevitable procession up Fifth Avenue took place. Automobiles participated in the parade; many of them backfired, frightening the horses.

New Yorkers generally were pleased with the statue, but some, primarily of Southern origin, felt otherwise. They did not fail to comment on the fact that the statue was led by a winged victory: "Just like a Northerner to send a woman ahead of him—so nobody could shoot," and "Who but a Northerner would let a woman walk while the man rides."

In 1912, as stipulated in Joseph Pulitzer's will, the fountain in front of the Plaza Hotel, designed by Carrère and Hastings and topped by the nude female statue by Karl Bitter, was completed. To this day, New Yorkers speculate about the identity of the woman who posed for the figure. One story has it that a schoolteacher, whose beauty would have been hidden forever under her skirts, was the model. Another story is that Suzy, a famous artist's model of the period, was the inspiration. In April, 1966, another name entered the picture. Mrs. Doris Doscher Baum, an eighty-four-year-old lady who posed for the Miss Liberty twenty-five-cent piece first minted in 1916, confessed on the *I've Got a Secret* TV show that she was the model.

In January, 1900, electric buses, with seats for twelve, replaced the horse-drawn public conveyances on the Avenue. In October of that year, the first parade of automobiles drove up the Avenue from the old Waldorf to Grand Army Plaza. The *New York Times* headlined the story, "Horses look on Unmoved." In August, 1903, a Packard arrived in New York from San Francisco, having made the run in fifty-two days. This was the first automobile to cross the continent under its own power. Still, the automobile was a toy for the rich. A poem that made the rounds at the time was called "The Charge of the 400."

> Half a block, half a block
> Half a block onward,
> All in their motobiles
> Rode the 400.
> Forward! the owners shout,
> Racing car! Runabout!
> Into Fifth Avenue
> Rode the 400.
>
> Forward! The owners said
> Was there a man dismay'd?
> Not though the chauffeurs knew
> Someone had blundered.
> Theirs not to make reply,
> Theirs not to reason why,
> Theirs but to kill or die.
> Into Fifth Avenue
> Rode the 400.

By 1905, the Fifth Avenue Coach Company introduced twenty-four double-deck buses imported from France. In 1906, Woodrow Wilson, then president of Princeton University, said, "Nothing has spread socialistic feeling more in this country than the use of the auto." The Fifth Avenue line was so pleased with this that they bought more buses, and on July 30, 1907, all horse stages were removed from the Avenue. A few months later, the flotilla of taximeter cabs imported from Paris arrived.

By 1910, traffic had become a problem. Plans were discussed to make the Avenue a one-way street. An underpass at 34th Street was also proposed. A plan was even submitted that featured an elevated pedestrian walk above the level of street traffic. In 1915, a law barring trucks from the Avenue was introduced, but failed to pass the City Council. By the time World War I passed into history, the traffic problem on Fifth Avenue was much as it is today.

THE AVENUE FROM 59TH STREET NORTH TO 96TH STREET WAS DEVELOPED, AS LOT AFTER LOT BECAME THE SITE OF A MANSION

It is quite probable that the world had never seen nor will ever see again such a concentration of wealth as that represented by the mansions that were built on Upper Fifth Avenue from 1890 until World War I. Millionaires' residences stretched for a solid mile and a half from 59th Street to 90th Street. Although the predominant architectural style was French, these eclectic creations included every conceivable design from Egyptian to Victorian. Nearly seventy mansions faced Central Park, every one of which housed treasures assembled from the four corners of the earth. The round of breakfasts, luncheons, receptions, teas, dinners, balls, and suppers was uninterrupted, the jockeying for position was ludicrous, and the stories were endless. It was the Golden Age of Fifth Avenue and American capitalism.

Each millionaire tried to outdo the next. The Whiteneys imported a seventeenth-century ballroom from Bordeaux for their house; the Zieglers, an Adam drawing room from London. Some bought whole castles and had them shipped to the United States in pieces. Mrs. John Jacob Astor had a two-ton bathtub cut out of a solid block of marble. Elbridge T. Gerry possessed a superb law library. Henry Havemeyer's house contained a priceless collection of old violins. Up and down the Avenue, old masters hung beside Impressionist canvases, and enormous tapestries graced baronial dining rooms.

Edith Wharton in *The House of Mirth* described the extravagance and frivolity:

> Van Alstyne prided himself on his summing up of social aspects, and with Selden for audience was eager to show the sureness of his touch. Mrs. Fisher lived in an East side street near the Park and as the two men walked down Fifth Avenue the new architectural developments of that versatile thoroughfare invited Van Alstyne's comment.

> "That Greiner house, now—a typical rung in the social ladder! The man who built it came from a milieu where all the dishes are put on the table at once. His facade is a complete architectural meal, if he had omitted a style his friends might have thought the money had given out. Not a bad purchase for Rosedale, though: attracts attention, and awes the Western sightseers. By and by he'll get out of that phase, and want something that the crowd will pass and the few pause before . . . That's the next stage: the desire to imply that one has been to Europe, and has a standard. I'm sure Mrs. Bry thinks her house a copy of the Trianon, in America every marble house with gilt furniture is thought to be a copy of the Trianon."

Millionaire's Row started at East 60th Street. On the northeast corner of Fifth Avenue, McKim, Mead and White built the Metropolitan Club. Designed to resemble an Italian palazzo, the building has an English carriage entrance and courtyard. In the days when young dandies still drove a coach and four, it was thought to be great sport to whip through this courtyard at breakneck speed. The building still houses this club, which J. P. Morgan founded for friends who had been blackballed elsewhere.

Thomas Wolfe also described the Golden Age in *Of Time and the River*. He wrote: "It is the time of the opera and theatre parties, and the Horse Show, and of late jolly suppers in the walnut dining-rooms, it is the time of elegant ladies with long gloves on naked arms, and Welsh rarebit in the chafing-dish, it is the time of the Four Hundred, and the great names of the millionaires —the Vanderbilts, the Astors and the Goulds—it is the time of the powdered flunkies and the twenty-dollar favors; it is the time of Newport, and the canopied red-carpeted sidewalks, and the great mansions on Fifth Avenue, and the splendid gilt and plush marble halls, and the time of the fortune hunting foreign nobleman (London papers please copy)."

At the northeast corner of 61st Street stands the house of Mrs. M. Hartley Dodge, still in the possession of the original owner. It is a rather undistinguished red brick and limestone row house with windows designed to suit the interior whims of Mrs. Dodge. There is reported to be a fine collection of paintings within, many by Rosa Bonheur. The house has been closed, and the windows sealed for many years, and a degree of mystery surrounds it. Periodically, it is rumored that the house will come down. Mrs. Dodge, who is now elderly, resides at her estate in Madison, New Jersey, and has not been inside the Fifth Avenue house for years. A Rockefeller kin, she lost a son tragically during the 1930s, and apparently the house contains memories too sad for her to endure.

On the southeast corner of Fifth and 62nd Street stands the home of the Knickerbocker Club, designed by Delano and Aldrich. Originally the club was housed in the old William Butler Duncan mansion on the southeast corner of Fifth Avenue and 28th Street. The Knickerbocker, organized in 1871 by the descendants of the first settlers of New York, has long served as a bastion of old guard New York society. An early evaluation of New York clubs stated: "[It] is undoubtedly our most exclusive fashionable club. Mere membership is a passport to society."

At 810 Fifth, just north of 62nd Street, stood the Hamilton Fish house. Number 814 Fifth was the residence of Jules S. Bache. It contained an extremely valuable collection of paintings, including works by Rembrandt, Titian, Botticelli, Watteau, Goya, Velázquez, Raphael, Gainsborough, Romney, Reynolds, and Holbein. The house was opened as a museum in 1937. When it was subsequently razed, the pictures were given to the Metropolitan Museum of Art.

When Mrs. Caroline Astor moved from her house at 34th Street and Fifth, she occupied a chateau on the northeast corner of 65th Street, designed by Richard Morris Hunt. Within there was a picture gallery in cream and gold, a baronial dining hall paneled in old oak and hung with French tapestries, and overhead in painted flowers and clusters of fruit the Astor monogram in gold. And of course there was a ballroom that "comfortably" held Mrs. Astor's Four Hundred.

Between 67th and 68th streets stood the house of robber baron Thomas Fortune Ryan. A self-made man, dashing in appearance, Ryan married his employer's daughter and bought a seat on the New York Stock Exchange. From that time on, he had a hand in virtually everything, including the Belgian Congo. When the Ryans moved into the house, Mrs. Ryan was mildly dismayed at the absence of a small garden. Ryan promptly bought the house next door, which belonged to transit king Charles Yerkes, tore it down, and built a garden. He did save the thirty-two white marble columns that had supported the Yerkes grand staircase, and built the garden around it.

Ryan's wife died in 1917, having donated during her lifetime approximately $20 million to charity. In appreciation, the pope made her a countess of the Holy Roman Empire. Nonetheless, two weeks after her funeral Ryan remarried, causing one of his five sons to say publicly, "It is the most disrespectful, indecent thing I ever heard of." The following year, the son, Allan, went bankrupt after losing $32 million in the stock market. Allan's father never lifted a finger to assist him. When the senior Ryan died, he left an estate of $142 million, and of this a set of pearl shirt studs to his son Allan.

On the southeast corner of 67th Street stood the George Gould house. After his father Jay died, George assumed the patriarchal position in the family. When he married, he sent to Versailles for a royal marriage bed that had eight cupids carved into the bootboard. When his bride saw the bed, she said, "I just know I'll have eight children if I sleep in that bed." So she did.

At Fifth Avenue between 70th and 71st streets, the Frick Collection is housed in what was the former residence of Henry Clay Frick, the Pittsburgh coke and steel industrialist. The building was erected in 1913-14 on the former site of the Lenox Library, which had been incorporated in the newly constructed New York Public Library at 42nd Street. The American architect Thomas Hastings designed the building in a style reminiscent of eighteenth-century European domestic architecture. (Hastings of Carrère and Hastings also designed the New York Public Library.) The decorations and sculpture were executed by the

Piccirilli brothers, and the ground floor interiors were designed by Charles Allom in the style of English and French interiors of the eighteenth century. Implicit in the design were the plans to provide a setting for Frick's extraordinary collection of paintings.

Henry Clay Frick, the son of a farmer of Swiss descent, showed an interest in art during his early twenties. In a report submitted by Judge Mellon, of the Pittsburgh banking Mellons, regarding a loan requested by young Frick, he said, "Lands good, ovens well built; manager on job all day, keeps books evenings, may be a little too enthusiastic about pictures but not enough to hurt, knows his business down to the ground; advise making loan."

In 1881, Frick was in Europe with young Andrew Mellon and purchased his first picture, *In the Louvre* by Luis Jiminez, a modest beginning to what became one of the finest of private art collections. During the 1890s his chief interests were French and contemporary paintings. Bouguereau, Breton, Jacque, Bonheur, Alma-Tadema, and the Barbizon School landscapes occupied his attention. Of these, Daubigny's *Washerwoman,* purchased in 1896, is the only picture still in the collection. However, he also bought one portrait by Nattier, one by Rembrandt, and several eighteenth-century English portraits.

In 1901, the industrialist bought several Turners, a Monet landscape, and a Vermeer. During the next few years, he added a Hobbema, a Cuyp, and a Terborch, and portraits by Lawrence, Reynolds, Romney, and Gainsborough. In 1905, El Greco's *St. Jerome,* Vandyke's *Ottavio Canevari,* and Titian's *Pietro Aretino* were added.

In the autumn of 1905, the Frick family moved into the Vanderbilt house at 640 Fifth Avenue and remained there for nine years. During this period Henry Clay Frick acquired Rembrandt's *Self-Portrait* (1906), an anonymous French fifteenth-century *Pieta* (1907), Constable's *Salisbury Cathedral* (1908), El Greco's *Purification of the Temple* (1909), the Vandyke portraits of Frans and Margareta Snyders (1909), Rembrandt's *Polish Rider* (1910), Velázquez's *Philip IV of Spain* (1911), a second Vermeer, *Officer and Laughing Girl* (1911), Holbein's *Sir Thomas More* (1912), pictures by two Veronese, *The*

Choice of Hercules and *Wisdom and Strength* (1912), Vandyke's *The Earl of Derby; His Wife and Child* (1913), and El Greco's *Vincenzo Anastagi* (1913).

In 1914, the family moved into the Fifth Avenue residence, and Frick purchased Hals's *Portrait of a Man,* Gainsborough's *The Mall in St. James's Park,* and some Fragonards and Bouchers from Joseph Duveen. From Knoedler, he purchased the Veronese allegories and two large Turners. Duveen also provided some of the furnishings and objets d'art for the residence, including the Renaissance bronzes, the Limoges enamels, and the Chinese porcelains. After the start of World War I, Frick bought three Goyas, three Whistlers, two large Turners, Degas's *Rehearsal,* Manet's *Bullfight,* and Renoir's *Mother and Children.*

From 1915 to the end of the war, acquisitions consisted primarily of a large collection of drawings and prints. Frick also bought the Fragonard series, *The Progress of Love,* and the Boucher panels, *The Arts and Sciences.* Other purchases, included Giovanni Bellini's *St. Francis in Ecstasy,* Titian's *Man in a Red Cap,* Bronzino's *Lodovico Capponi,* and Vandyke's *Sir John Suckling.* Frick's last purchase, the only one recorded for 1919, the year of his death, was Vermeer's *Mistress and Maid.*

At his death, Frick bequeathed his residence and his works of art to establish a public gallery "for the use and benefit of all persons whomsoever." In addition, he left an endowment, the income of which was to be used to maintain the collection and for any necessary alterations to the building. He also specified that a portion of the income from the endowment be used to continue acquisitions. This income has enabled the museum to acquire paintings by such artists as Duccio, van Eyck, Piero della Francesca, and Ingres.

The official opening of the Frick Collection came on December 16, 1935. Since then, more than five million people have visited the museum.

On the northeast corner of 75th Street and Fifth stands the former residence of Edward Harkness, now occupied by the Commonwealth Fund. The architect, James Gamble Rogers, chose Tennessee marble with which to build this neo-Italian Renaissance mansion in 1906. Much of the original paneling and decoration remains in the house. The interior is graced with a large gallery on the second floor, the walls and stairway are made entirely of marble, and a vestibule dome was constructed in leaded glass. The library of the mansion is exquisite, with a ceiling coffered in wood and painted in Italian arabesques of gold leaf with a millefleurs motif.

Probably the most vulgar of all the houses ever built on the Avenue was that of William A. Clark, a Montana copper king. The house took six years to construct, was made mostly of white granite, and was said to contain 130 rooms. It stood on the northeast corner of 77th Street and was opened in 1904. A poem celebrated its appearance:

> Senator Copper of Tonapah Ditch
> Made a clean billion in minin' and sich,
> Hiked for Noo York, where his money he blew
> Buildin' a palace on Fift' Avenoo.

Remarkably enough, the block between 78th Street and 79th Street still contains most of the buildings erected during the Golden Age. At the northeast corner of 78th Street is the Institute of Fine Arts, a division of New York University, formerly the James Biddle Duke house. Duke's daughter, Doris Duke, who still largely finances the institute, was born in the house. The building, erected between 1909 and 1912, was designed by the architect Horace Trumbauer. It was adapted from the Hotel Labbatiere, a late eighteenth-century chateau in Bordeaux. As first designed, the house consisted of fifty-four rooms, not counting the subbasement and attic. After Duke's death in 1925, the house was vacant, and in 1959, the family gave the building to the institute.

Within the building, vestiges of the original furnishings and decor remain. The Oak Room, originally the library, has been little changed since the house was occupied by the Duke family. The portraits in the main hall (*Lord Gwyn* by Gainsborough over the fireplace; *Gentleman in Red* by Raeburn; *Mrs. Charlotte Dennison* by Hoppner), the marble-topped chests and tables in the main hall and Oak Room, and the gilt chairs and chandeliers in the main hall are all part of the original furnishings.

The mansion at 972 Fifth Avenue presently houses the French Cultural Services of the French Embassy. This building, by McKim, Mead and White, was constructed in 1902 for Harry Payne Whitney. Originally the house included a seventeenth-century ballroom from Bordeaux and eleven marble bathtubs—ten white and one rose pink. The staircase was once said to be the most beautiful in America and inspired those that were photographed for *Gone With the Wind* and *Rebecca.* The entrance hall features a colonnade of eight pairs of columns with a small fountain in the center, the base of which is part of an antique tomb.

Just north of the Harry Payne Whitney house, at 973, is the house originally built by General McCook for his daughter and son-in-law, the count and countess de Heredia of France. Stanford White was the architect. The building is now occupied by the Eastern States Mission Home of the Mormon Church. In 1914, Joseph Fuller Feder, an international banker, and his wife purchased the house and lived in it with their twenty-one servants for thirty years. The house stood empty for many years, until the church purchased it in 1948.

The entrance hall contains an imposing marble mantlepiece from Italy, and the winding oval staircase with its bronze balustrade is one of the most beautiful in the city. When the church purchased the house, there was a large sitting room at the back of the first floor with eighteenth-century wood paneling. Genuine Louis XIV, it came from a chateau in the Loire Valley in France. The carved wood paneling was sold to Princess Marta and Archduke Otto of Austria in 1953, and the room was remodeled into two offices.

On the second floor, the front room is of the Louis XVI period; the mantelpiece is from the salon of Viollet-le-Duc, the great French architect who restored the Cathedral of Notre Dame. All the other mantels in the house are authentic eighteenth century except one of dark green Caen stone that was especially built for the dining room. The rich stained-glass doors leading into the old dining room are church windows of the late sixteenth and seventeenth centuries, from a small church in Evreux, Normandy. They were exchanged by the parishioners for modern windows during the 1920s.

The library, with its beamed hand-painted ceiling, was copied from an old English library, and the original carpet in the room was a gift from the viceroy of India to President Ulysses S.

Grant. The fourth floor front room has Louis XV doors imported from France, and in the back, the door frames are decorated in pure gold leaf. There is a secret staircase connecting the back third- and fourth-floor rooms. Several scenes from *Gone With the Wind* were filmed in this house.

To the north of the McCook house at the southeast corner of 79th Street is the Augustus van Horn Stuyvesant mansion, built in French Gothic style, designed by Stanford White. Today it houses the Ukranian Folk Art Museum, which features historical objects, folk costumes, weaving exhibitions, tapestries, ceramics, and a permanent collection of Ukranian paintings.

Until recently the Brokaw house, built during this period, stood across the street from the Stuyvesant house at the northeast corner of 79th Street. It was torn down in 1969 to make way for an ultramodern apartment building.

At 991 Fifth, between 80th and 81st streets, stands the William Ellis Corey house, built about 1915, now the home of the American-Irish Historical Society. Corey was a steel magnate who late in life divorced his wife and married the actress Mable Gilman. After his remarriage, he and his wife moved into the house, but his relatives and friends refused to receive the new Mrs. Corey, so the couple moved to Paris. In 1940, Corey's son left the house to the present owners.

The house at 998 Fifth Avenue, on the corner of 81st Street, was deisgned by Stanford White in 1910. At the southeast corner of 82nd Street is the home of the offices of the New York Hall of Fame. The upper floors are private apartments.

At 1028 Fifth, on the southeast corner of 84th Street, is the Marymount School, a Roman Catholic elementary and high school. The three houses that comprise the complex include Mrs. Harriet V. S. Thorne's at 1028, designed by P. H. Gilbert, and the houses of the Milbank family.

At 1014 Fifth, between 82nd and 83rd streets, stands the James F. A. Clark house, built in 1909, which is now Goethe House. In 1926, Mrs. Mary Gerard purchased the property, and in 1960, it passed to its present owners. The staircase is impressive, and a large paneled living room occupies the second floor. In the rear of the first floor, a winter garden looks out over a large outdoor garden. Earlier in the century, a twin house stood next door.

At the southeast corner of 86th Street is the former home of Mrs. Cornelius Vanderbilt, originally the William Starr Miller house. Designed by Carrère and Hastings in 1914, the house contains a beautiful paneled living room, now a lecture hall, several smaller library rooms that still retain their original paneling and fireplaces, and a grand staircase. The Yivo Institute occupies the building today.

The National Academy of Design, at 1083 Fifth Avenue at 89th Street, was formerly the home of Archer M. Huntington. Built in 1900 and redesigned by Ogden Codman, Jr., the building was given to the academy in 1940. The academy was founded in 1825, a group "governed solely by artists for the development in this country of the highest standards in the arts." Samuel F. B. Morse, artist and inventor, was its first president. Of its thirty founding members, eleven are represented in the permanent collection of the Metropolitan Museum of Art.

When Andrew Carnegie built his mansion at the northeast corner of 92nd Street in 1901, squatters, who dwelt in dilapidated shanties, had to be dispossessed by his agents before construction could begin. The building, in the French chateau style, was designed by Babb, Cook and Willard.

Carnegie was almost seventy when he took up residence in the chateau, and by that time he had made his millions and was in the process of giving away his money. Every afternoon, he would leave his house, walk twice around the nearby reservoir in Central Park, and return for formal conferences in the impressive library that stretched along the Fifth Avenue side of the house. Over the great fireplace was Carnegie's favorite motto: The Hearth Our Altar: Its Flame our Sacred Fire. When the builder told the millionaire that the motto was too long for the fireplace, Carnegie retorted, "You mean the fireplace is too short for the motto. Make it longer;

and if the room is too small for the fireplace, make the room bigger; and if the house is too small for the room, pull it down and build a bigger one. But at your peril, don't cut a letter out of that motto."

On April 22, 1919, the wedding of Andrew Carnegie's daughter, Margaret, to Roswell Miller took place in the house. Although guests were limited to one hundred, the wedding was festive as pipers played "The Campbells are Coming" and "Annie Laurie." The old tunes of the Scottish Highlands inspired the ailing Carnegie, now only four months from his death, and he danced a few steps with his only child.

Later the house became the property of the Columbia University School of Social Work, and in 1970 again changed hands. It is at present being refurbished as the permanent home of the Cooper Hewitt Museum, a division of the Institute of Decorative Arts of the Smithsonian Institution.

The Jewish Museum, formerly the Felix M. Warburg house, is situated at the northeast corner of 92nd Street and was designed by architect C. P. H. Gilbert in 1908. The house was presented to the Jewish Theological Seminary of America by Frieda Schiff Warburg in 1940. The adjoining modern wing, designed by Samuel Glazer in 1963, is the Albert List Building. The museum is the world's largest and most comprehensive repository of Jewish ceremonial art and other historical Judaica in the fine arts.

Included within is the Harry G. Friedman Collection, including Torah crowns, headpieces, breastplates, candelabra, Passover plates, amulets, Sabbath lamps, and Kiddush cups. The Benguiat Collection includes the Torah ark given to the synagogue of Urbino, Italy, in 1551. The Samuel Friedenberg Collection of great Jewish portraits in metal is also housed in the museum. Until recently, the Jewish Museum was also a center for exhibitions of contemporary art, with such artists as Larry Rivers, Robert Rauschen-

berg, and Franz Kline all having been honored with one-man shows.

The Otto Kahn house is situated at the northeast corner of 91st Street. It was once considered not only the largest private residence in America, but also the finest. Kahn commissioned it in 1914, demanding that no expense be spared. Architect J. Armstrong Stenhouse designed the building in Italian Renaissance style with an interior courtyard. The exterior, made of French limestone imported from Saint-Quentin, bears pilasters on the second floor. The interior halls are made of Caen stone.

The library is paneled in walnut and is today virtually as it was in Kahn's lifetime. The adjacent room, known as the art room, has drawings on the ceiling; in addition, there is a barred opening to a narrow circular stairway overlooking the room. Legend has it that Kahn would peek through the opening and decide whether or not to greet his visitors. The building is now occupied by the Convent of the Sacred Heart. The former ballroom still contains the beautiful chandelier that illuminated Kahn's elegant parties. During World War I, Kahn was subject to much criticism because construction of his house was continued.

At the northeast corner of 94th Street is the house built for Willard Straight by Delano and Aldrich in 1915. Straight was a diplomat, financier, and publicist, who, with his wife Dorothy, founded *The New Republic*. He died three years after the building was completed. Judge Elbert H. Gary, the steel magnate, and Mrs. Harrison Williams, a great beauty frequently mentioned as one of America's best-dressed women during the years before World War II, were subsequent owners. In 1952, Mrs. Williams sold the building to the National Audubon Society. It is perhaps one of the city's best examples of neo-Georgian architecture. Presently the building is for sale, as the Audubon Society has outgrown the space.

DURING THE GOLDEN AGE OF FIFTH AVENUE, BIG WEDDINGS WERE THE VOGUE AS DAUGHTERS OF WEALTHY FATHERS MARRIED EUROPEANS OF TITLE—AT GREAT EXPENSE

The first of the "holy" alliances took place in March, 1895, as Anna Gould, the second daughter of Jay Gould, became the countess de Castellane, wife of Count Paul Ernest Boniface de Castellane of Touraine, France. The ceremony took place at the Gould home, 47th Street and Fifth Avenue, and in deference to the bridegroom's religion was performed by Archbishop Corrigan.

In exchange for the bride's title, the family surrendered millions to bail out the extravagant young count. Years later, when asked about the alliance, the count replied, "Oh it was very simple. Our eyes met, our hands met, our lips met, and our lawyers met."

The day of the wedding the house was elaborately decorated with thousands of flowers. After a lively and lengthy reception, the couple went off to Georgian Court, the Gould estate in New Jersey, which is today a Roman Catholic college for women. Subsequently, they left for Paris. After the first year of the marriage, the count was several million dollars in debt. At one point, George Gould, Anna's brother, found it necessary to advance her several million dollars to pay the bills. Anna never did treat her French husband with much civility, and as the years wore on, he flamboyantly paraded various mistresses about Paris. When Anna found bills coming in for clothes that she had never ordered, she decided to take action. One day, when Boniface was off on "business," she hired an army of packers and movers who, in four hours, emptied the house of all the furnishings, including the telephone and electric fixtures. Anna even turned off the water and the electricity. Shortly afterward, she filed for divorce, with Boniface receiving $2 million plus a monthly allowance.

Subsequently, she married the duke of Talleyrand, a cousin of her first husband, and became a duchess. After the duke's death, she moved to the Plaza Hotel on Fifth Avenue. As she grew older, she became more and more paranoid. Bodyguards flanked the entrance to her suite and never left her side when she was in public, as she desperately feared being robbed or attacked. She died in 1961, a pathetic, frightened old woman.

In November of the same year, Mrs. William K. Vanderbilt married her daughter Consuelo to the duke of Marlborough. This marriage, in contrast to the Gould-Castellane union, was not to the bride's liking, but the bride's mother was determined to make her daughter a duchess. Recently divorced from William K. Vanderbilt, Alva Vanderbilt controlled her daughter's every move. Consuelo had been in love with Winthrop Rutherfurd, a dashing thirty-year-old New York bachelor of good family. But Rutherfurd was not good enough for Consuelo's mother, and she broke up the romance. In the summer of 1895, she had built her fabulous Marble House in Newport, and her reputation provoked society to comment, "A marble palace is the right place for a woman with a marble heart."

Alva invited the duke to the United States for Consuelo's debut at Marble House. The house had been transformed to resemble the Palace of Versailles, and no one, including the press, appreciated the significance of the presence of the ninth duke of Marlborough. Blenheim, his family estate near Oxford, was one of the few palaces in England that could compete with the opulence of Alva's Newport "cottage." To Alva, it seemed to be a good match.

Two weeks later, she announced the engagement of her daughter. On the morning of November 6, at Alva's new house on East 72nd Street, the bridal party assembled. For twenty-four hours before the wedding, young Consuelo had been locked in her room with armed guards to prevent her escape. The wedding party moved down Fifth to St. Thomas Church at 53rd Street and Fifth Avenue. Three hundred policemen had been placed on special duty to maintain order along the route, as thousands of spectators lined Fifth to catch a glimpse of the future duchess. After the party reached the church, there was an embarrassing delay until finally, at twelve fifteen, Consuelo swept up the aisle in cream-white satin and swept down the aisle the duchess of Marlborough.

After the wedding, a legal document was signed by the interested parties. It read: "Whereas a marriage is intended between the said Duke of Marlborough and the said Consuelo Vanderbilt, and whereas pursuant to an agreement made upon the treaty for the said intended marriage, the sum of two million five hundred thousand dollars in fifty thousand shares of the Beech Creek Railway Company, on which an annual payment of four per cent is guaranteed by the New York Central Railroad Company, is transferred this day to the trustees. And shall, during the joint lives of the said Duke of Marlborough, Consuelo Vanderbilt, pay the income of the said sum of two million five hundred thousand dollars, unto the Duke of Marlborough for his life, and after the death of the said Duke of Marlborough, shall pay the income of the said trust fund unto the said Consuelo Vanderbilt for life." Another agreement provided, agreeably, that William K. Vanderbilt should pay $100,000 a year to the couple.

The following year, former President Benjamin Harrison married Mrs. Mary Scott Lord Dimick in St. Thomas Church. Despite efforts to maintain secrecy, word leaked out and a crowd of thousands gathered in front of the church.

The public's thirst for society news was insatiable. In 1903, a near riot occurred at the Goelet-Roxburghe nuptials. St. Thomas Church was the scene of the wedding. (To this day, one can observe a dollar sign carved into the decoration over the bridal entrance and a replica of bags of money carved into the choir loft, both whimsical touches of the sculptor.)

The event was reported in one paper with the following headlines: "Roxburghe Wedding Made Scenes of Mad Confusion among Women in Street. Police Clubbed Them from St. Thomas. Whole Place Looted After the Ceremony. Well-Dressed but Indecently Curious Mb Made Nuptials of May Goelet Memorable." The story said: "The ceremony was simplicity itself, but the scene without and within the church where the wedding took place was oe of the most amazing ever witnessed on Fifth Avenue. Thousands of women, impelled by curiosity and forgetful of gentleness or or ordinary delicacy, pushed, hauled, surged and fought to get into the church; to get close to the carriage of the frightened bride; to carry off souvenirs; to touch the bridal robes and to do a hundred and one other things, creating suh an uproar and confusion that a platoon of police, armed with nightsticks, was actually compelled to charge upon them, and in many instances to use force . . . They fought, scratched, and screeched like a parcel of wildcats disputing a quarry."

The rear of St. Thomas burned on August 8, 1905, and during the fire a strange sound was heard. A tenor bell in the belfry began a mournful dirge high above the raging flames as a powerful stream of water beat upon it.

Soon after the new church was built, the Easter Parade was originated. On Easter Sunday, the choir boys paraded down the Avenue after the service. Parishioners fell into line and followed the procession. The following year, the parade was repeated and in time became one of the great traditions of the Avenue.

IN 1896, LI HUNG CHANG, VICEROY OF CHINA, PRIME MINISTER, MINISTER OF FOREIGN AFFAIRS, SENIOR GUARDIAN OF THE EMPEROR, EARL OF SUH CHI, AND COMMANDER OF THE NORTHERN ARMY, ARRIVED

On August 28, 1896, at about two in the afternoon, the steamship *St. Louis* entered New York Harbor, bearing a distinguished visitor, Li Hung Chang. An armada of pleasure craft and warships was there to greet te viceroy, and the steamship *Mohawk,* which had been chartered by the visitor's countrymen for the occasion, was crowded with jubilant Chinese people. Chinese flags covered the *Mohawk,* and as soon as the *St. Louis* was in sight, a barrage of small firecrackers was launched, followed by the explosion of several large bombs. An army of Chinese beat drums while others screamed at full volume, and a band played Chinese music. On board the *St. Louis,* the viceroy evidently took not the slightest notice of the reception.

After the steamer docked, the viceroy was carried ashore in a red plush chair. He was over six feet tall and wore a bright yellow jacket, a viceroy's cap with a four-eyed peacock feather attached to it, and a scarlet shirt beautifully embroidered with a floral motif. His fingernails were polished till they shone, a huge diamond flashed on his right hand, and he gazed out over the top of a pair of gold glasses. From the steamer, he was carried to an open carriage, which started the journey uptown to the Waldorf at Fifth Avenue and 34th Street.

At Fourth Street and Broadway, the parade turned to Washington Square, and the procession passed under the Washington Arch, which seemed to interest the viceroy. At 19th Street, a small boy threw an old lemon at the visitor, but he dodged it with alacrity. He reached the Waldorf some thirty minutes later and retired to his suite. Among his entourage was a staff of Chinese chefs who were immediately dispatched to the kitchen to prepare his meals. The viceroy also brought his own stoves and several dozen one-hundred-year-old eggs.

That evening a banquet was held in his honor in the dining room of the Waldorf. The viceroy ate sparingly, refusing most of the courses. Only once or twice during a toast did he place the glass to his lips and sip some wine. His staff then brought him a simple dinner of chicken, rice, and vegetable soup. At the end of dinner, he was handed a wooden toothpick six inches long. Later in the parlor, when the viceroy's pipe was lit for him by a lackey, whispers buzzed around the place that he was actually smoking opium. It was, however, merely tobacco in a water pipe.

The following day, President Cleveland received him at the home of Secretary Whitney at Fifth Avenue and 57th Street. The procession from the Waldorf up Fifth to 57th was viewed by thousands.

THE BRADLEY-MARTINS BALL MARKED THE END OF THE EXTRAVAGANT GALAS ON FIFTH AVENUE

The Bradley-Martins came from Troy, New York, but rarely, if ever, mentioned it. Martin, before the hyphen was added to the name, was the son of an attorney whose fortune had been made in the stock market. His wife Cornelia believed in Society. They had gone abroad, bought a house in London and a country place in Inverness, and married their daughter to Lord Craven. Fifth Avenue was the final challenge, and with the encouragement of such social arbiters as Ward McAllister and Mrs. Paran Stevens, the couple set out to establish themselves. One morning, after reading of the conditions in the slums of the city, Mrs. Martin decided to "give trade an impetus" by staging a costume ball. She ended by spending $369,200.

The new Waldorf-Astoria, which had opened at the corner of 34th Street and Fifth Avenue in 1893, was selected for the party. The hotel was turned into a replica of the Hall of Mirrors at Versailles, with furniture in the Louis XIV style. Every flower in the city, as well as most of the blossoms available from Baltimore to Boston, was purchased to decorate the ballroom, and hundreds of blooms of clematis, shipped from Alabama, embellished the sylvan dells and flirtation nooks.

Mrs. Martin appeared costumed as Mary, queen of Scots, and her husband as Louis XV. Belmont donned a full suit of steel armor inlaid with gold, which cost $10,000. Family jewels were borrowed from impoverished Southern aristocrats; the Oglethorpe gems arrived from Georgia and the Fairfax diamonds from Virginia. Mrs. Martin displayed a massive ruby necklace once worn by Marie Antoinette.

Reports of the party both here and abroad were critical. The *London Chronicle* wrote: "We congratulate New York Society on its triumph. It has cut out Belshazzar's feast and Wardour Street and Mme. Tussaud's and the Bank of England. There is no doubt about that." Oscar Hammerstein produced a burlesque of the fete called *The Bradley-Radley Ball*. Soon the pulpit joined the press in attacking the Martins' extravagance. The city authorities then doubled the tax assessments of the Martins' property. The notoriety caused the Martins to move permanently to England.

From the Bradley-Martin experience, newspapers learned that coverage of excessive displays of wealth aroused public interest and measurably increased circulation. Consequently, they accorded extensive and detailed coverage to all elaborate entertaining.

James Hazen Hyde was not exercising discretion when he gave a $200,000 ball at Sherry's, which had moved north from 37th Street and Fifth to 44th Street and Fifth. Adverse reaction from the press forced him into exile in Paris and served to expose the graft and corruption of the insurance companies of the city, one of which had belonged to his father. A classic example of the excesses of the period was Harry Lehr's dog dinner at which his friends' dogs were invited to eat paté and chicken.

Ironically, these parties ultimately served a purpose not intended by their hosts. Inequities were exposed, scandals were bared, and reform ended the Golden Age of Fifth Avenue.

IN 1899, THE ST. PATRICK'S DAY PARADE WAS SUDDENLY INTERRUPTED AS THE WINDSOR HOTEL BURST INTO FLAMES

Built in 1873, the Windsor Hotel, at Fifth Avenue between 46th Street and 47th Street, was the pride of the city. Its interior was embellished with exotic woods and its register inscribed with the names of well-known people from this country and abroad. Because Jay Gould's house was next door, it soon replaced the Fifth Avenue Hotel at 23rd Street as the center of financial dealings in the city. President William McKinley made it his New York headquarters and installed special telephone connections to Washington. Andrew Carnegie lived there for years as a bachelor. William H. Vanderbilt engaged in stock market and horse talk in the lobby. Adelina Patti, the Italian opera singer, had a pool table placed in her suite when she was in town, and Nellie Melba also stayed at the Windsor on her visits to New York.

On St. Patrick's Day in 1899, an unknown guest in the hotel was watching the parade through an open window in his room. The curtains were blowing, and as he lit a cigarette and tossed the still flaming match out the window, the curtains caught fire. They were ablaze in a minute, and the man fled. At that moment, a waiter passing through the halls saw the fire and tried to extinguish it.

Meanwhile, the streets below were jammed with marching Irish, the sidewalks were packed with well-wishers, and hundreds of spectators watched the parade from the windows of the Windsor. The waiter ran down the stairs screaming, "Fire! Fire!" but his voice could not be heard over the din of the marching bands. He dashed outside and ran to a policeman to tell him of the fire, but the policeman evidently could not hear him and ordered him back from the street. Then he ran into the middle of the street shouting, "The Windsor's on fire!" By that time, smoke was pouring out of the windows of the hotel as flames raced through the lobby and engulfed most of the upper floors of the hotel. Thousands on the street stared in horror at the spectacle, as police tried to force them away from the burning building. Terrified screams for help pierced the din as trapped residents shouted from the flaming windows.

Within minutes, the entire building was a blazing inferno. Safety ropes were lowered from many of the windows, but guests lost their grip and plunged to the ground. Others panicked and simply jumped from the windows to almost certain death below. One man who jumped from a sixth-story window fell onto a man on the street; both were killed instantly. A woman appeared at a window with a baby in her arms. She threw the child to the street and then leaped out the window herself to her death. One hour after the fire was discovered, twenty persons were dead, scores were injured and maimed, and the hotel was a gutted shell.

The fire department did its best, but, because of the parade crowds, firemen were unable to reach the building in time. Many tales of heroism were told in the wake of the fire. Guests had climbed to the roof and jumped to the roof of an adjoining building on 47th Street. Human chains were formed by quick-thinking people in the corridors, and many lives were spared.

Just south of the Windsor Hotel was the house of the late Jay Gould, then the residence of Helen Gould, who must be remembered as one of the truly great ladies of Fifth Avenue. Unlike her sister Anna and her robber-baron father, Helen was a woman of great charity. As soon as she realized that the Windsor was on fire, she opened her house as a temporary hospital. All the linen was put at the doctors' disposal, torn up, and made into bandages. Her humanity saved many lives.

ON SEPTEMBER 30, 1899, TWO MILLION NEW YORKERS PAID TRIBUTE TO THE HERO OF MANILA BAY, ADMIRAL GEORGE DEWEY, AS HE PARADED DOWN FIFTH AVENUE

It was a fine autumn day in September when Admiral Dewey was officially received in New York City. Two million people turned out with flags in hand to cheer the returning hero after his victory over the Spanish at Manila Bay. The line of march from Riverside Drive down Broadway to 59th Street, then to Grand Army Plaza, and down Fifth Avenue to Washington Square was covered with welcome signs and red, white, and blue bunting. Kites with red, white, and blue streamers flew in the skies, and when the procession reached St. Patrick's Cathedral, the bells rang out "America" and other patriotic songs. As the parade passed the Fifth Avenue mansions, some occupants showered the marchers with fruit and bonbons.

The triumphal arch erected at Madison Square was flanked with six white columns and was designed by some of New York's finest sculptors. When Dewey reached the square, the crowd became hysterical and had to be forcibly restrained by mounted police.

Dewey later wrote of the celebration in his autobiography: "I knew what to do in command of the Asiatic squadron, but being of flesh and blood and not a superman, it seemed impossible to live up to all that was expected of me as a returning hero. Dewey arches, Dewey flags, and 'Welcome, Dewey' in electric lights on the span of the Brooklyn Bridge! The great city of New York made holiday . . . and they packed the streets for the land parade in token of public emotion, while the gold loving cup which came to me with the freedom of the city expressed the municipality's official tribute."

A month later, Congress appropriated funds to buy the returning hero a house. Dewey specified within a few blocks the district that would be satisfactory to him, and he further indicated that he wanted a modest house with a small dining room that could seat eighteen people. Eyebrows were raised. Then the sixty-two-year-old admiral married a woman much younger than himself, and a Roman Catholic to boot, and deeded the house to his bride. People were outraged. Earlier, there had been talk of proposing him for the presidency, but by this time the papers and the public were laughing at him.

In the meantime, the triumphal arch, which had been built of temporary material by popular subscription at Madison Square, began to deteriorate. It was intended that the arch be made permanent, but when Dewey fell from public favor, donations fell off. As the months wore on, the paint began to peel, the plaster began to fall, and the arch took on the gray color of city dirt. With the passage of time, the arch became a public nuisance, on the verge of collapse and a danger to the safety of pedestrians. One night the sanitation department carried it off to the city dump, and Dewey was forgotten.

IN APRIL, 1906, MAXIM GORKY, THE RUSSIAN NOVELIST, ARRIVED IN NEW YORK WITH HIS BEAUTIFUL ACTRESS WIFE, MME. ANDREEVA, TO RAISE MONEY FOR THE RUSSIAN REVOLUTION OF 1906

Is he or is he not an anarchist? That was the question that intrigued the press and the public for the duration of Maxim Gorky's visit to New York.

The Club A, at 3 Fifth Avenue, was the scene of the first dinner given in honor of the Russian novelist. He and Mark Twain, an ardent admirer, were the principal speakers. At the dinner the American humorist commented: "If we can build a Russian republic to give to the persecuted people of the Czar's domain the same measure of freedom that we enjoy, let us go ahead and do it. We need not discus the methods by which that purpose is to be attained. Let us hope that fighting will be postponed or averted for awhile, but if it must come . . ." Mr. Clemens's pause was significant. He added: "I am most emphatically in sympathy with the movement now on foot in Russia to make that country free. I am certain that it will be successful, as it deserves to be. Anybody whose ancestors were in this country when we were trying to free ourselves from oppression must sympathize with those who are now trying to do the same thing in Russia."

After his speech, a manifesto was read that formally inaugurated the American movement to make Russia free. It was decided that money would be raised for the purchase of arms for the Russian revolutionaries.

Gorky rose, accepted the offer, and spoke of the revolution: "I come to America expecting to find true and warm sympathizers among the American people for my suffering countrymen, who are fighting so hard and bearing so bravely their martyrdom for freedom. Now is the time for revolution. Now is the time for the overthrow of Czardom. Now! Now! Now! But we need the sinews of war, the blood we will give ourselves. We need money, money, money. I come to you as a beggar that Russia may be free."

Seven months later Gorky departed from the United States in an atmosphere quite different from the one he found on arrival. His outspokenness had made many enemies for him and his cause. One newspaper commented: "Maxim Gorky has left us, unwept, unhonored, and, fortunately for him, unhung." Later, Gorky predicted in *In America:* "A revolution of the unemployed will spring one day upon that city [New York] with hands unfettered and unrestrained, and like rapacious marauders reduce all to dust and ashes . . . bricks and pearls, gold and serf-flesh, the unwashed and the idiots, the churches, the dirt-poisoned hotels, and the twenty floor skyscrapers . . . yes, reduce the whole city to a muckheap, a pool of stench and human blood, into the original chaos whereout it came."

IN 1909, THE CITY CELEBRATED THE CENTENARY OF FULTON'S STEAMBOAT AND THE 300TH ANNIVERSARY OF HENRY HUDSON'S DISCOVERY OF THE HUDSON RIVER

One of the most elaborate parades on the Avenue took place in October, 1909. From 50th Street to Washington Square, the Avenue was decorated for the occasion. the entire history of the city was depicted on scores of floats and more than two million people viewed the spectacle. The floats were the most elaborate the city had ever seen, costing close to $500,000. One measured forty feet long and sixteen feet wide. People who had admired pageants in Rome, New Orleans, and elsewhere claimed that they had never seen anything comparable to the Hudson-Fulton celebration.

That evening, New York was turned into a city of light. Hundreds of thousands of electric lights illuminated virtually every building along Fifth Avenue, while the Hudson River was the scene of a pageant in light, fireworks, and illuminated vessels.

ON MAY 18, 1910, FIFTH AVENUE WITNESSED THE SPECTACLE OF A VISITOR FROM OUTER SPACE

It was a clear spring night, and thousands of people turned their eyes to the skies to catch a glimpse of Halley's Comet. St. Patrick's and other churches along the Avenue were filled with people who silently kept vigil through the night. Workingmen stayed at home, believing their last day on earth should be spent with their families. They feared that the famous comet would collide with the earth or the gases in its tail would kill all life on this planet.

But other New Yorkers reveled in the excitement and anticipation of its arrival. In Central Park, crowds assembled to view the spectacle, and at the 59th Street entrance, Telescope Tom cleaned up by charging a quarter a peek to hundreds eager to get a closer look at the phenomenon.

The roofs of most of the hotels on the Avenue were turned into promenades for the event. At the old Waldorf, several hundred men and women gazed at the sky. When a photographer's flashbulb exploded in a brilliant flash of light, spectators were momentarily convinced that the crack of doom had sounded. The Plaza, Savoy, and Netherlands at Grand Army Plaza too opened their roofs for celebrations, as did the St. Regis and the Gotham. On the Gotham roof, a night camp was set up with wigwams and tepees.

The comet did not collide with the earth, nor was this planet smothered by noxious gases, bombarded by meteorites, or even sprinkled with harmless stardust for the reveling romanticists.

LATER THAT YEAR, GIACOMO PUCCINI CAME TO NEW YORK TO ATTEND THE PREMIER OF HIS OPERA *THE GIRL OF THE GOLDEN WEST* AT THE METROPOLITAN

Opening night of *La Fanciulla del West* was one of the most brilliant performances the Metropolitan Opera and its Fifth Avenue subscribers had ever seen. With the composer in the audience, Toscanini conducting, and Enrico Caruso on the stage, the audience thrilled to the Americanized opera, which bore traces of ragtime, Zuni Indian melodies, a George M. Cohan tune. The composer, enervated at the end of the performance, counted more than fifty curtain calls and stood shaking as he was crowned by the management with a silver wreath.

Puccini's New York visit was marked by another satisfaction. He had seen a motorboat in a display window on Fifth Avenue and imagined himself knifing through the waters at Toree del Lago. The boat cost $3,000—to the Italian an unimaginable sum.

Following the opening night, Puccini was guest of honor at a dinner at the Cornelius Vanderbilt mansion on Fifth Avenue where a world-renowned banker approached him. His great desire was to own a manuscript page of "Musetta's Waltz" from *La Bohème,* autographed by the composer. He said that he would pay any price to have the composer write it out for him.

"Any price?" Puccini said incredulously.

"Anything," was the answer.

"Three thousand dollars?" Puccini asked cautiously.

The following day the banker owned the manuscript, and Puccini went out and happily purchased his motorboat.

IN JUNE, 1910, THEODORE ROOSEVELT RETURNED FROM HIS WORLDWIDE WANDERINGS TO A GRAND RECEPTION ON FIFTH AVENUE

In 1909, after his term of office as president of the United States, Theodore Roosevelt embarked on an extensive world tour during which he spent a great deal of time shooting elephants, tigers, and other animals. The following year, he returned to the city, which welcomed him with a five-mile-long parade and a reception. From Washington Square to 59th Street and Grand Army Plaza, the Avenue was draped in red, white, and blue bunting, and an honor guard lined the route.

Spectators welcomed him with signs that read

"Oh, you Teddy," "Welcome Home," and his own characteristic expression, "Deeeeeeee-lighted!" Scribner's decorated their store with a two-story-high poster of the adventurer.

Because he had spared the life of a cub bear on a hunting expedition, the city and the country were swept with a fad for Teddy bears. As one New York newspaper put it: "Isn't the President the hero of every boy who longs to grow big enough to hold a gun to shoot bears and some day do just the very same things that Teddy Roosevelt does? And so Teddy the bears are named, and as Teddy they are known the length and breadth of our country, as well as on the other side of the Atlantic. Stuffed plush Teddies are fairly rampant." The president was not averse to the appellation. Asked for permission to use his name, he replied, "I don't think my name is likely to be worth much in the bear business, but you are welcome to use it."

On the day of he parade, thousands of children appeared up and down the Avenue wearing Teddy-bear masks and carrying little Teddy bears. At one point in the procession, a gaint Teddy bear was strung up with ropes tied to his hands and feet that made him appear to dance a jig high above the Avenue. Seeing the tribute,

Roosevelt took his hat off, saluted, and said, "Deeeee-lightful! Deeeee-lightful!"

As Roosevelt drew close to Grand Army Plaza where a reunion of Rough Riders was to take place, the comments ranged from "Bully for you, Teddy!" to "Eat 'em Alive!" When the former president was confronted with his band of compatriots, he said, "I certainly love my boys!"

During the week of the celebration, a poem by Wallace Irwin ran in the *Saturday Evening Post*.

> Muses lend me an earthquake
> To rattle the big blue dome,
> Or a dynamite bomb
> Or a fierce tom-tom
> Or a bugle call
> Or Niagara's fall—
> Full justice to do
> To the hullabaloo
> Which roared New York and the Country through
> When Teddy came sailing home.
>
> Thunder and smoke
> How the patriots woke
> From Kalamazoo to Nome!
> Your Uncle Sam
> Fell off of the porch
> And the Statue of Liberty
> Swallowed her torch
> When Teddy came sailing home.

DURING THIS PERIOD, THE BATTLE FOR WOMEN'S RIGHTS BEGAN

Women's rights were already in the wind at the turn of the century. The ladies were getting sick and tired of traipsing around in skirts that dragged in the filth and litter of the streets. Bad weather presented particular problems, so a number of ladies formed the Rainy Day Club, organized for the serious purpose of giving mutual moral support to women who had begun to wear the "rainy-day skirt," which in its shortest form reached the shoe tops. Charles R. Lamb, vice-president of the National Sculptor's Society, urged the wearing of such skirts not only on rainy days but on any and every occasion. "The short

skirt," he said, "is the symbol of the emancipation of women."

In 1904, a typical item appeared in the newspapers. A policeman had halted an automobile in which a woman was smoking a cigarette. He said, "You can't do that on Fifth Avenue," and arrested her. In 1908, Mrs. Patrick Campbell, famed for her correspondence with George Bernard Shaw, was visiting New York, and after lunch at the Plaza Hotel, she lit a cigarette. The headwaiter in the tearoom ran to the assitant manager screaming, "It is a scandal. A lady, she smokes in the tearoom." He was told to tell her to desist.

"I do," he replied, "and she only laugh." The manager approached Mrs. Campbell who replied, "I have been given to understand this is a free country. I propose to do nothing to alter its status." Mrs. Campbell smoked until the cigarette went out. The papers took note of the incident, and the *New York Journal* stated that "smoking by women is indecent." A ordinance banning smoking by women in public was introduced at a meeting of the New York Board of Aldermen. Unfortunately, an addendum was added to the bill making it illegal for men to smoke in the presence of women. The measure was defeated on both counts. The Café Martin, however, with its somewhat racy reputation, announced that women would be permitted to smoke in the dining rooms.

A year later, the *New York Herald* printed a headline reading, "Women Smoke on Way to Opera," claiming in a subhead they "Are Discovered Puffing Cigarettes when Electric Light Beams into Their Carriage." On January 21, 1908, the Sullivan Ordinance was finally passed making it an offense on the part of a manager of a public place to allow women to smoke therein. After World War I, cigarette smoking by both men and women became common practice.

On May 4, 1912, despite the fact that most men thought a woman's place was most definitely in the home, the women's suffrage movement staged a great parade up Fifth Avenue. With banners flying and bands playing, the ranks of women stretched from curb to curb, and the solemn march did not cease from dawn to dusk.

All the women marchers were supposed to wear a standard paper hat. Most did not, however, and there were some extravagant gestures on the part of some participants. One woman dressed as Joan of Arc in a suit of shining armor and rode a white horse down the street. Still others wore flowing white gowns and blew long golden trumpets as they paraded. The former Alva Vanderbilt, now Mrs. Oliver Hazard Perry Belmont, who later confessed that the march was the most difficult thing she had ever undertaken, joined the parade at 41st Street with a contingent of shopgirls. The Reverend Antoinette Brown Blackwell, eighty-seven years old and the last of the 1848 suffrage pioneers, rode in an open carriage covered with lilacs and dogwood blossoms.

In addition to social leaders, thousands of shopgirls, typists, factory workers from the East Side sweatshops, and international delegations from all corners of the globe participated. Many men marched too in support of their wives, mothers, daughters, and sweethearts.

Nearly sixty years later, in the summer of 1970, Fifth Avenue was again the scene of a women's march, as supporters of the Women's Liberation movement took to the streets to publicize their demands.

ON APRIL 6, 1917, THE UNITED STATES DECLARED WAR ON GERMANY, AND NEW YORK BECAME THE CHIEF PORT OF EMBARKATION FOR THE AMERICAN EXPEDITIONARY FORCE

World War I was the occasion for the most patriotic demonstrations ever staged in the city. Any excuse to display the national colors served and flags, banners, and streamers were hung everywhere. The Avenue also was bedecked with thousands of flags of the allied nations, a mass of color that has been described as "one of the most beautiful sights New York had ever seen." In 1918 the Avenue was renamed the Avenue of the Allies.

Division after division of American troops paraded on Fifth Avenue before their departure for France. Liberty Loan parades, led by President Woodrow Wilson, marched along the flag-bedecked thoroughfare. Liberty Bond drives generally were opened at Grand Army Plaza, with such luminaries as Mary Pickford, Marie Dressler, and the former Alva Vanderbilt (now Mrs. Belmont) perched on platforms imploring the public to invest in bonds. In 1918, Fifth Ave-nue made war history at a luncheon given by the Fifth Avenue Association, when Liberty Bonds totaling $52 million were sold within forty-five minutes. Mrs. Cornelius Vanderbilt and Helen Gould, among others, donated the use of their Fifth Avenue homes for musical entertainments in aid of the American Red Cross. Receptions were held in many of the great houses to honor the departing doughboys.

ON NOVEMBER 7, 1918, NEW YORK RE-CEIVED ERRONEOUS NEWS THAT THE ARMISTICE HAD BEEN DECLARED AND THE CITY WENT WILD WITH JOY

The managers of the United Press in France sent the following telegram to the New York office on the morning of November 7, 1918.

UNIPRESS, NEW YORK, PARIS

URGENT ARMISTICE ALLIES SIGNED ELEVEN SMORN-ING. HOSTILITIES CEASED TWO SAFTERNOON. SE-DAN TAKEN SMORNING BY AMERICANS.

The message was passed by the naval censor in New York, and by midday all hell broke loose in the city. Whistles started to blow downtown at one, and New Yorkers paused over their lunches to listen. Other sirens began to take up the call. The noise grew from single sirens to a swelling roar that rapidly swept northward over the city in an ever-growing din. Suddenly thousands of newsboys appeared on the street shouting: "Germany surrenders! The war is over!"

By three o'clock in the afternoon, work was abandoned, and thousands of people poured into the streets. Fifth Avenue from Washington Square to Grand Army Plaza was a mass of humanity from curb to curb. The police department had cleared the Avenue of motorcars, but on the side streets could be heard the constant trumpeting of horns, while many drivers purposely back-fired their cars in celebration. Firecrackers were thrown by the thousands, and confetti and ticker tape were showered from windows along the Avenue.

Stores on the Avenue shut their doors and hung out signs reading "Closed for the Kaiser's Funeral." An immense gallows was hurriedly thrown up at 42nd Street and Fifth where an improvised dummy hung with a bucket over his head and a label on his body: "Bad Bill—Gone to Hell!" In front of the Waldorf, more than a thousand men and women stood for over an hour singing the "Marseillaise," "God Save the King," and "The Star Spangled Banner." French and British men in uniform were lifted on the shoulders of crowds and tossed about jubilantly. Churches were filled with silently praying people, and many just stood quietly in the streets with tears streaming down their faces.

As the afternoon wore on, celebrations were spontaneously planned for that evening, but by five o'clock a rumor spread that the jubilation was premature. The war was not yet over.

FOUR DAYS LATER, ON NOVEMBER 11, THE WAR WAS OVER AND AGAIN THE CITY CELEBRATED

The second time, the news came through at four o'clock in the morning. All over town people were awakened by the sound of sirens. Rousing themselves from sleep, they took to the streets in the dead of night to start celebrating all over again. By sunup, Fifth Avenue was a solid mass of cheering people, who wandered about in hysterical joy. Again automobiles backfired and confetti, ticker tape, and effigies of the kaiser were tossed from windows. By eight o'clock, hundreds of bands marched up and down the Avenue playing patriotic music, and in hotels, bars, and restaurants, celebrations were in full swing. At 42nd Street and Fifth, a team of soldiers played touch football with a team of sailors, while someone played ragtime on a battered old piano on the sidewalk.

At sundown the revelry was still picking up speed. As darkness fell, millions thronged the streets and every light in the city was turned on. The real armistice celebration was even more joyous than the first one and continued until dawn the following day.

Chapter Six

BETWEEN THE TWO WORLD WARS

CHRONOLOGY

1920 New York City population is 5,620,048.

1921 Port Authority is established.

Brooklyn's memorial dedicated to the city's soldier dead of World War I is unveiled in Prospect Park.

1922 First wireless communication between New York and Paris.

First aircraft exhibition is held on Staten Island.

1923 The setback law, limiting height and configuration of new construction in the city, is adopted.

The Greater City holds a silver jubilee at the Grand Central Palace.

Delmonico's famous restaurant closes.

1924 Sunnyside Gardens in Queens admits first residents.

New York City opens its municipal broadcasting station.

The Museum of the City of New York is installed in Gracie Mansion on the East River.

1925 Bronx River Parkway is opened.

Madison Square Garden is closed and demolished.

1926 First telephone conversation held between New York and London.

Queensborough subway opens.

1927 Holland Tunnel opens.

Colonel Charles A. Lindbergh welcomed home after sensational solo flight across the Atlantic.

1928 The Arthur Kill bridges connecting Staten Island to New Jersey are completed.

Graf Zeppelin arrives in New York, completing the first commercial transatlantic flight.

New York Medical Center is dedicated.

1929   Prices on the stock market fall sharply, leading nation and world into the Great Depression.

1930   New York City population is 6,930,446.

1931   Empire State Building and George Washington Bridge open.

Bayonne Bridge between Staten Island and New Jersey opens.

1933   Fiorello La Guardia elected mayor.

Independent subway to Queens opens.

1934   New York City Housing Authority established.

1935   Work begun on East River Drive.

1936   Triborough Bridge opens.

1939   New York World's Fair opens in Flushing Meadow Park, Queens.

Hitler invades Poland and World War II begins.

1940   New York City population is 7,454,995.

Queens-Midtown Tunnel opens, and construction starts on Brooklyn-Battery Tunnel, but is interrupted by war.

1941   U. S. enters World War II.

1945   U. S. Army bomber crashes into Empire State Building between seventy-eighth and seventy-ninth floors.

War ends and Atomic Age begins.

The end of World War I signaled the beginning of a devil-may-care era during which the youth of the period liberated themselves from Victorian morality. Women bobbed their hair, and wore short skirts, rolled stockings, cloche hats, and long strings of pearls. They also smoked and drank. The flappers' counterpart, the sheik, wore four-in-hand ties, plaid wool hose, plus fours, and bell-bottomed dinner clothes. The energetic Charleston took over in the ballrooms, and thousands of speakeasies, where illegal liquor was consumed, opened almost overnight. The high spirits found expression in part in jubilant welcoming parades that took place with ever-increasing frequency. After Mayor James J. ("Gentleman Jimmy") Walker took office, the slightest excuse for a celebration brought out thousands of spectators.

During this period, the great black immigration took place as the German and Italian tenement areas in East and West Harlem changed into black ghettos. The Lower East Side was still inhabited predominantly by European Jewish and Catholic immigrants. The financial community had settled on Wall Street, Greenwich Village was attracting its share of "bohemians," and the West Side was built up as an elegant residential area.

At the same time, the Golden Age of Fifth Avenue came to a close. Famous mansions came down by the score, to be replaced by high-rise apartment buildings and a shopper's paradise of exquisite shops and department stores, entirely changing the face of the Avenue in midtown.

After the devastating market crash in 1929, little activity took place on the Avenue, as it, as well as the nation and the world, went into the eclipse of the Great Depression.

THE GREAT BUILDING BOOM OF THE MID-TWENTIES ENDS THE GOLDEN AGE OF FIFTH AVENUE, AS APARTMENT HOUSES AND DEPARTMENT STORES REPLACE THE ELABORATE MANSIONS, CLUBS, CHURCHES, AND RESTAURANTS

Early in 1925, boulevardiers looked on in horror at the corner of 44th Street and Fifth Avenue as the walls of the famous Red Room of Delmonico's came barreling down the chutes into a waiting dump cart, and gas torches began to slice through the steel structure around them. Two years before, the famed Sherry's had met a similar fate. Prohibition, coupled with soaring real estate values in the area, had doomed these venerable Fifth Avenue institutions.

One block north, at 45th Street, the Church of the Heavenly Rest, was also being loaded on carts as debris. It too had fallen under the wreck-er's ball for the sake of progress. The new church was built at Fifth Avenue and 90th Street. The following year, the minarets and filigreed stonework of the Temple Emmanu-El at 43rd Street toppled under the same pressure.

Twenty blocks to the north, the palace of "the" Mrs. Astor was about to be carried away stone by stone amid falling plaster and flying dust. Mrs. Astor's death in 1908 ended an era, but the final knell for the Golden Age came when her house crumbled under the wrecker's ball.

By 1924, the patrician citadel of hostelry, the Buckingham, just south of St. Patrick's Cathedral, had come down and in its place was erected the eleven-story Saks Fifth Avenue building which still stands.

In 1925, Stanford White's Madison Square Garden on Madison Square was razed.

By 1926, one of the twin mansions of the Vanderbilt family was toppled, bringing down with it the cupids and the gargoyles that adorned it. The William K. Vanderbilt chateau at the corner of 52nd Street and Fifth, scene of Alva Vanderbilt's costume ball, disappeared among clouds of dust rising from falling plaster. The Cornelius Vanderbilt house, then belonging to Alice G. Vanderbilt, the famed "Alice of the Breakers," was also scheduled for demolition. Bergdorf Goodman was soon to open on the site.

Across from the Plaza Hotel, the old Savoy was coming down floor by floor to make way for the Savoy Plaza, later to be replaced in 1965 by the General Motors Building. And the old Netherland was making way for the present Sherry-Netherland. Everywhere one looked, houses, mansions, churches, and landmarks were falling.

Along Millionaire's Row, the scene was devastating. Dozens of mansions were boarded up, and dozens of others were in process of demolition. In addition to the homes of Collis Huntington, William Rockefeller, Frank W. Woolworth, and Senator Clark, the list in 1926 included the following Fifth Avenue houses:

Ellen Bostwick	800 and 802
W. Emlen Roosevelt	804
Mrs. Hamilton Fish	810
Angelic L. Gerry	816
J. C. Hoagland	817
John W. Sterling	912
Samuel Thorn	914
Laura A. Palmer	922
Mrs. Rosina Hoppin	934
John W. Kaiser	953
Nicholas F. Brady	989
George Ehret	994
R. Fulton Cutting	1010
G. L. Hamersley	1030
Countess Leary	1032
James Cullman	1038
Edward F. Hutton	1107
Jacob Ruppert	1116 and 1120
Mrs. Dorothy Straigh	1128
James Gerard	1134
Al Hyman	1138
Lloyd Price	1140

The reasons for the change were numerous. In 1913 the Sixteenth Amendment, empowering Congress to collect taxes on incomes, was passed, cramping the millionaires' style Further, as space on Manhattan Island was now at a premium, building or maintaining a home on Fifth Avenue was like building a bonfire out of banknotes, spectacular but expensive.

And the social tenor of the Avenue had changed in the decade prior to the war. Society had to contend with Pittsburgh steel barons Frick and Carnegie, copper baron Senator Clark, tin-plate magnate Reid, and Charles T. Yerkes, the rapid-transit king—men who had earned their own wealth rather than inheriting it. As a result, many of the older families felt that Fifth Avenue had become nouveau riche and consequently moved to side streets in less conspicuous areas.

Society had also become nomadic. No longer was the Fifth Avenue "manse" a home. Summers were spent abroad or in Newport, and society wintered in Palm Beach, California, or the West Indies. The great houses were closed for a greater part of the year, except during the fall season when the rich returned to their mansions for a two- or three-month stay. The "servant problem" had become acute, as maintaining fifty-room houses required a staff of some twenty or thirty servants, far too many and too expensive to justify the short occupancy period. More and more people moved into hotels or into smaller, more efficient apartments on Park Avenue. With this new life style, the rich could breeze into town at a minute's notice, put up in a hotel, and expect everything to go smoothly, whereas, in the old days, two or three weeks' notice was needed for hiring a staff and putting a house in order. It no longer paid to keep a house on Fifth Avenue; it was easier, cheaper, and allowed one more freedom to dispense with it.

With the depression, Millionaire's Row came to an end. The few great houses that remained were boarded up, fell into disrepair, were sold at great sacrifice, or were actually given away. Fifth Avenue and the rich man's world had changed forever.

FOLLOWING WORLD WAR I, FIFTH AVENUE RECEIVED RETURNING TROOPS AND HEROES, GRATEFUL EUROPEAN MONARCHS, AND FOREIGN MILITARY PERSONAGES IN GRAND PROCESSIONS, USHERING IN THE ERA OF THE GREAT PARADES OF THE 1920S

As division after division of victorious doughboys returned to New York, week in and week out they paraded up the Avenue to the welcoming cheers of hundreds of thousands of proud and grateful people. Finally on September 10, 1919, ten months after the armistice was signed, General John J. ("Blackjack") Pershing returned to New York for the hero's "welcome of welcomes."

Having already been honored in London and Paris, Pershing and his selected division of twenty-five thousand men paraded down the Avenue from 107th Street to Washington Square. This was the first time in history that a full combat division with full combat equipment appeared on the Avenue. With the marching soldiers were heavy artillery drawn by motor tractors and lighter field pieces drawn by horses. A display of combat wagons, ammunition trains, field kitchens, and other paraphernalia of warfare thrilled the onlookers.

Another first for this parade was registered as airplanes flew up and down the Avenue above the line of march. All along the route, hundreds of thousands of flowers and bouquets were tossed from the windows of apartments, stores, and residences, while the block between 58th and 59th streets was carpeted with laurel blossoms. A blizzard of ticker tape rained down on the returning heroes.

The following day, the general made his way to Central Park amid popular cheers and planted a tree, a custom that had existed before the war but that became compulsory in the subsequent decade.

From 1919 until the stock market crash of 1929, the parades and demonstrations along Fifth Avenue were spectacular. The processions included those demanding Prohibition and others demanding its repeal, as well as the traditional New York welcomes for returning heroes and visiting dignitaries. Paper blizzards, cloudbursts of flowers, and jubilant curbside spectators welcomed the prince of Wales, Lloyd George, Prince Aage of Denmark, Premier Brand of France, Herbert Hoover, Marshal Joffre and Marshal Foch of France, Premier Clemenceau of France, the crown prince and princess of Sweden, the king and queen of Siam, and King Albert, Queen Elizabeth, and Prince Leopold of Belgium. New Yorkers also welcomed Captain Fried, commander of the steamship *President Roosevelt,* who had heroically rescued passengers of a sinking vessel at sea; Commander Richard E. Byrd, after his aerial conquest of the North Pole; Gertrude Ederle, the first woman to swim the English Channel; and Mrs. Clemington Corson, the second woman to swim the channel.

In 1926, James J. Walker was elected mayor of New York City and during his term of office parading assumed absurd proportions. The first to arrive during his first term as mayor was the glamorous Queen Marie of Romania.

After disembarking, the queen was interviewed by the press and named one American author whom she had read. His name, she said, was Henry Ford.

The day of her arrival was a dreary one, and

A row of mansions on Fifth Avenue at 82nd Street,

across the street from the Metropolitan Museum of Art.

Fifth Avenue between 116th and 117th streets in 1893. The area

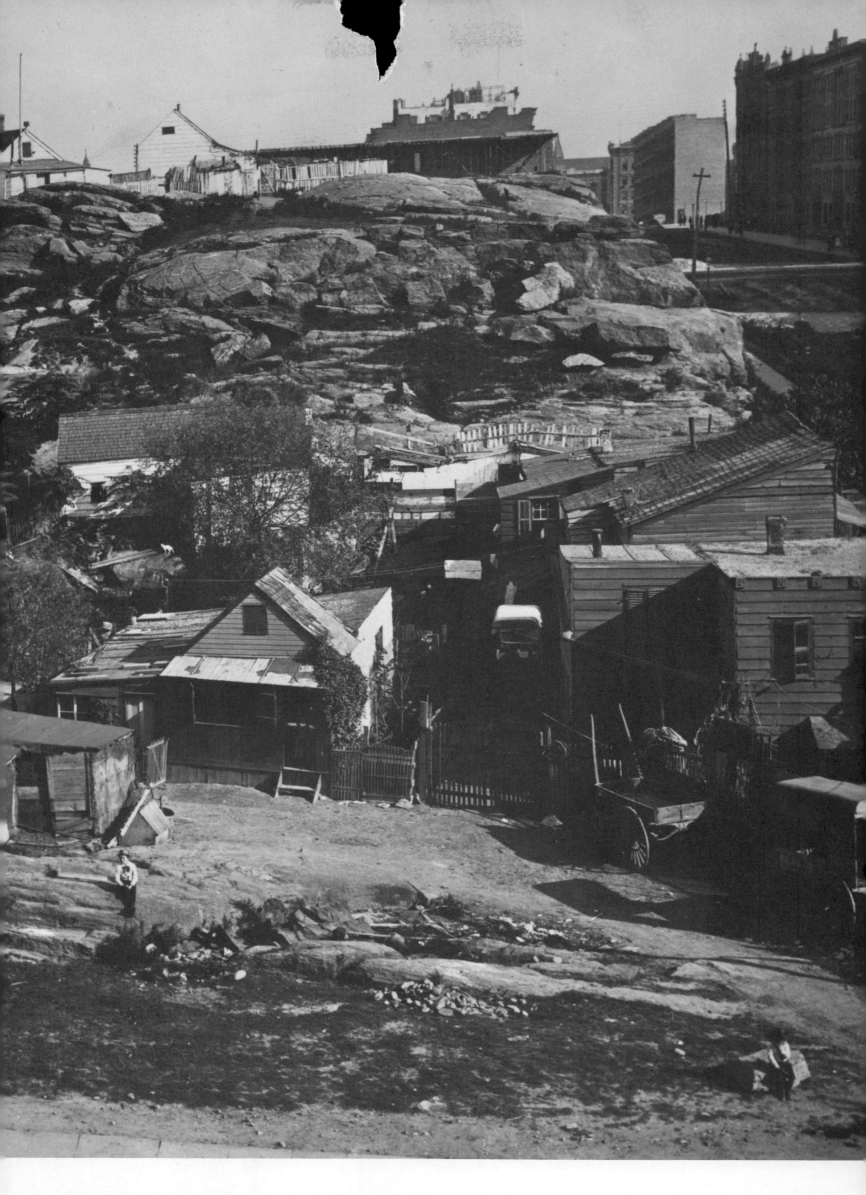

as far south as 88th Street looked like this as recently as 1906.

The Andrew Carnegie mansion at 92nd Street and Fifth Avenue, designed by Babb, Cook and

Willard in 1901. Today the Cooper-Hewitt Institute of Decorative Arts occupies the building.

The Willard Straight house, on the northeast corner of Fifth Avenue and 94th Street, designed by Delano and Aldrich in 1915, now occupied by the Audubon Society.

The fence that surrounds the Andrew Carnegie mansion.

The Sherry-Netherland Hotel on the left
and a corporation building on the right.

The Otto Kahn house at 92nd Street and Fifth Avenue, designed by C. P. H. Gilbert and J. Armstrong Stenhouse in 1918, now occupied by the Convent of the Sacred Heart.

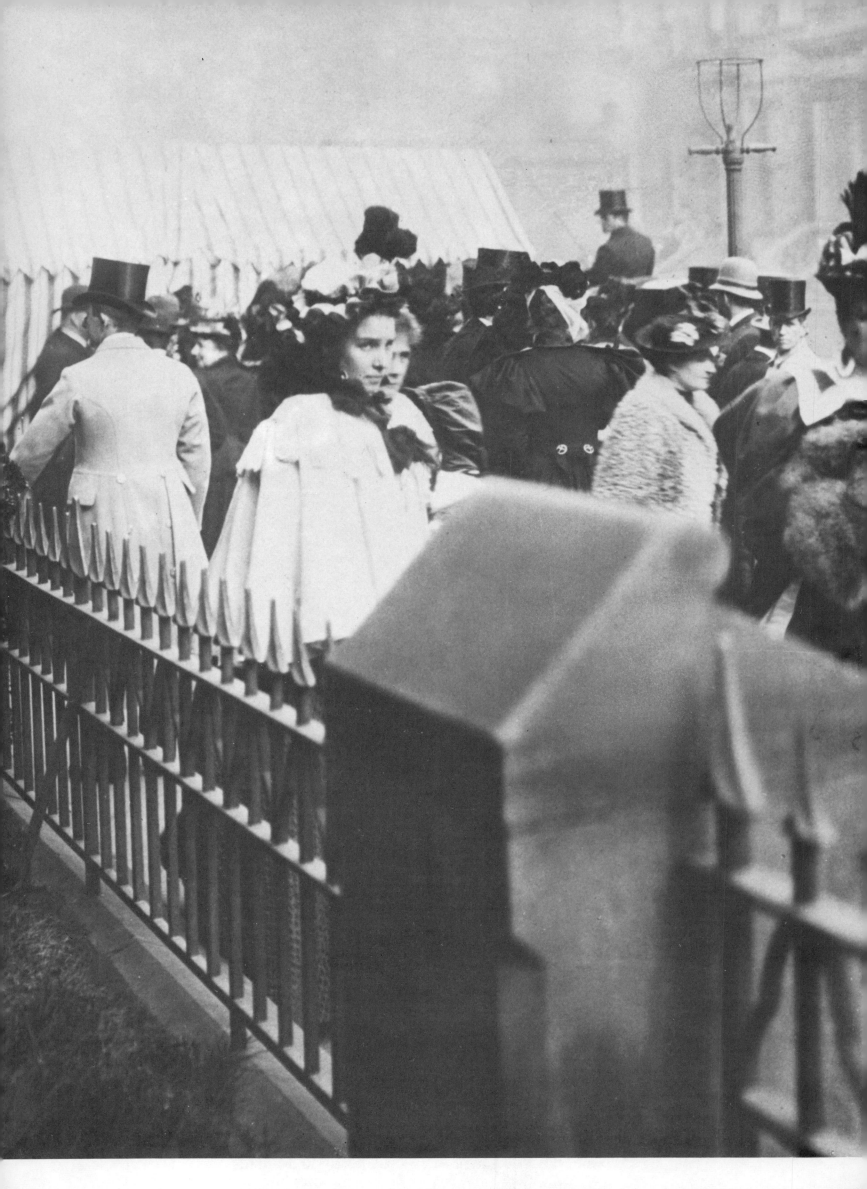

A scene outside St. Thomas Church, Fifth Avenue and 53rd Street, just

before the Vanderbilt-Marlborough wedding on November 6, 1895.

A dollar sign carved into the stone over the bridal entrance
at St. Thomas Church, Fifth Avenue and 53rd Street.

St. Thomas Church at Fifth Avenue and 53rd Street as it looks today.

The Windsor Hotel fire, March 17, 1899. The building was on
the east side of Fifth Avenue between 46th and 47th streets.

The Windsor Arcade, which was built
on the site of the Windsor Hotel in 1902.

the turnout was not so large as expected, but the queen received the traditional ticker-tape welcome. At City Hall, Mayor Walker said: "We have thousands of Romanian stock in this world city, in this the most cosmopolitan city of the world and today . . . may I not beg to assure you that the Romanians have made as fine citizens as this country has within its borders? They have done much for the building of the city of New York." The mayor was generally quite free with his accolades for immigrants, as it is on record that he said virtually the same thing about Turks, Bulgars, Syrians, West Indians, Armenians, Greeks, Poles, Belgians, Serbs, Croats, Basques, Czechs, Hungarians, Norwegians, Swedes, and others.

After the drive up Fifth Avenue, Queen Marie went immediately to Pennsylvania Station to board a train for Washington.

While in the United States, the queen provided the press with a great deal of amusing copy as she literally whistle-stopped across the country. She managed to pick up close to a boxcar full of souvenirs and memorabilia from almost every one-horse town between New York and California. She also received a little cash as she generously endorsed products such as cosmetics, cigarettes, and articles of clothing. A plaque in Cartier's entrance attests to her visit to New York.

A SPECTACULAR CELEBRATION WELCOMED COLONEL CHARLES A. LINDBERGH AFTER HIS SUCCESSFUL FLIGHT ACROSS THE ATLANTIC OCEAN TO PARIS

New York, still somewhat naive when it came to hero worship, turned out four million strong to receive handsome Charles A. Lindbergh on June 26, 1927. His face, figure, and airplane, *The Spirit of St. Louis,* were reproduced everywhere—from half-inch lapel buttons to half-acre portraits draped on skyscraper walls. In Fifth Avenue windows, his picture appeared painted in miniature, life-size, and on a Mount Rushmore scale. His image was engraved on medals, etched on copper, scissored in cardboard, silhouetted in black and white, dyed on dresses, jerseys, and neckties, wrought in mosaic, carved in soap, molded in clay, struck in gold, silver, and bronze, and sewed in needlepoint. One could purchase a model of the airplane, molded in lead "while you wait." In one pastyr shop a giant six-foot cake was crowned with a replica airplane and aviator in frosting. In another window a series of painted watermelons bore his face. Above, in the wild blue yonder, skywriters wrote his name in mile-long clouds of smoke. Automated models of the crossing were set up in dozens of department stores and restaurants.

The entire line of march was a jubilant sea of humanity, vertically as well as horizontally. Every window in every building along the route was jammed with celebrants. People stood precariously on ledges of buildings five hundred feet above street level to catch a glimpse of the hero. Confetti rained down in whirlwinds for miles. Fifteen thousand soldiers and sailors marched before him, and three women dressed in white, blowing golden trumpets, went immediately in front of his open car. Windows along Fifth Avenue had been boarded up to prevent crowds from backing into and breaking them. Trolleys, trucks, buses, and car roofs were covered with people.

At 23rd Street the parade stopped to allow Lucky Lindy to place a wreath at the Eternal Light in Madison Square, erected there following

World War I in memory of those killed during the conflict. Police formed human chains to hold back the immense crowds. Dozens of women fainted, and one young woman who was watching the parade from the roof of a nearby building dropped dead on the spot of a heart attack. The roar of the crowds sounded like swells of thunder as the hero progressed up the Avenue. At one point during the procession, a fragment of a telephone directory landed on the young hero's ear. Lindbergh picked up the piece, examined it, and said to Mayor Walker who stood at his side, "I guess when I leave here, they'll have to print another edition of the telephone book." The Fifth Avenue Presbyterian Church opened its doors so that crowds could fill the entrance, and some people stood on the pews within to get a better look. The young people of the city were even too busy to think of weddings as only thirty-nine marriage licenses were issued at the license bureau in the Municipal Building—the lowest daily figure since the establishment of the institution. Only fifteen couples were married in the chapel of the bureau that day.

The next day, Colonel Lindbergh's reaction appeared in the *New York Times*. He said: "I never expected anything like it. People told me that the New York reception would be the biggest one but I had no idea it was going to be so much more overwhelming than the others. I simply cannot find words to describe my feelings. All I can say is that the welcome was wonderful, wonderful. Perhaps in a few days, maybe a week, I will be able to give a clear picture of how I felt, but just now, at the close of one of the outstanding days of my life, my mind is ablaze with noise, terrific noise, oceans of friendly faces and an electric sort of something that I can't believe happened."

SCOTT AND ZELDA FITZGERALD'S ANTICS WERE CHARACTERISTIC OF THE ERA, AS "FLAMING YOUTH" THREW PROPRIETY TO THE WINDS, SCANDALIZING THE OLDER GENERATION, AND CHALLENGING ALL CONVENTION

The Fitzgeralds, appropriately enough, began their ill-fated marriage on Fifth Avenue, in the chapel at St. Patrick's Cathedral. Zelda first distinguished herself on the Avenue by having her picture taken perched on top of one of the traffic towers that had been installed at major intersections. In her hand, she held a glass of champagne. This antic became the mark for the debs of the era, who would pour out of the Plaza, Waldorf-Astoria, Delmonico's, and Sherry's in the wee hours of the morning to be photographed on top of the traffic towers.

In those days the Fitzgeralds could be seen splashing around in the Pulitzer Fountain in front of the Plaza Hotel or riding up and down the Avenue at breakneck speed atop the fender or roof of sporty motorcars.

After long nights of merrymaking, the Fitzgeralds usually stopped at Child's Restaurant at 57th and Fifth, the "in" breakfast spot for the "flaming youth" of the era.

Fitzgerald, in his short story "May Day," documents one of the parties that he attended at Delmonico's on 44th Street.

So she came out of the dressing-room at Delmonico's and stood for a second in the doorway looking over the shoulders of a black dress in front of her at the groups of Yale men who flitted like dignified black moths around the head of the stairs. From the room she had left drifted out the heavy fragrance left by the passage to and fro of many scented young beauties—rich perfumes and the fragile memory-laden dust of fragrant powders. This odor drifting out acquired the tan of cigarette smoke in the hall, and then settled sensously down the stairs and permeated the ballroom where the Gamma Psi dance was to be held. It was an odor she knew well, exciting, stimulating, restlessly sweet—the odor of a fashionable dance.

At one o'clock a special orchestra, special even in a day of special orchestras, arrived at Delmonico's, and its members, seating themselves arrogantly around the piano, took up the burden of providing music for the Gamma Psi fraternity. They were headed by a famous flute-player, distinguished throughout New York for his feat of standing on his head and shimmying his shoulders while he played the latest jazz on his flute. During his performance the lights were extinguished except for the spotlight on the flute-player and another roving beam that threw flickering shadows and changing kaleidoscopic colors over the massed dancers.

THE THIRTIES BROUGHT A MARKED CHANGE IN ACTIVITY ALONG THE AVENUE AS EVERYTHING GROUND TO A HALT

In October, 1929, the stock market crashed, and Fifth Avenue, New York, the country, and the world entered the Great Depression. The era of exuberant madness on Fifth Avenue came to a close. Public parades during the 1930s were infrequent and were marked by a serious tone.

With the repeal of Prohibition on December 5, 1933, sale of alcohol was legal once again, but the anticipated celebration was a disappointment. There were a few parties in hotels and restaurants along the Avenue, but in general the city took the news in stride.

THREE IMPORTANT BUILDING PROJECTS WERE COMPLETED ON THE AVENUE DURING THE DECADE

The old Waldorf-Astoria was labeled for destruction during the mid-twenties. In 1929, the building was razed and was replaced by the Empire State Building. Designed by Shreve, Lamb and Harmon, it opened in 1931. Until recently, it was the tallest building in the world, originally 1,250 feet high. The tower of the structure was intended to be used as a mooring mast for dirigibles, but, after a few futile attempts at mooring the vehicles, the plan was abandoned because of air-current difficulties. After World War II, a 220-foot TV antenna was added to the top of the tower and is used presently for transmission of

television by all New York City stations. Since its opening, the building has been one of the major attractions in the city.

In 1932, shortly after the opening of the building, the managers found it only half rented. The king of Siam had returned to New York for a second visit and was escorted to the observation tower by Grover Whelan, the city's official one-man welcoming committee. The king commented to Whelan, "We in Siam have a similar possession." Whelan asked the king just what that was. The king replied, "A white elephant."

In 1933, the Empire State Building received

the grand treatment in one of Hollywood's classic creations. King Kong, America's answer to France's Hunchback of Notre Dame, met his end on top of the building as he tried in vain to protect his lady love, Fay Wray, from a squadron of airplanes.

DURING THE HEIGHT OF THE DE-PRESSION, ROCKEFELLER CENTER WAS CONSTRUCTED, PROVIDING WORK FOR THOUSANDS OF UNEM-PLOYED

Until the first decade of the nineteenth century, the site of Rockefeller Center was rough pasture, part of Manhattan's common lands. In 1801, twenty acres in the area were transformed into an oasis of beauty by Dr. David Hosack, who maintained his famed Elgin Botanic Gardens there until 1811, when rising costs made the venture impractical. In 1814, the land was bought by Columbia College, whose trustees still retain title to nearly twelve of the acres occupied by Rockefeller Center today. The university realizes a $4 million rental from the center every year.

Rockefeller Center was built because an opera house was not. In October, 1928, John D. Rockefeller, Jr., spearheading a civic drive to give New York a new opera house, agreed to lease from Columbia University the land on which part of Rockefeller Center now stands. The plan for the new venture called for the central portion of the plot to be made available to the Metropolitan Opera Company, while the remainder of the land was to be leased to private builders for appropriate commercial development. In January, 1929, Rockefeller signed a twenty-four-year lease, with renewal options to 2015, which was extended in 1953 to 2069.

Before the plan could be put into effect, however, the opera company, plagued by legal difficulties and the deepening depression, withdrew from the enterprise and abandoned its plans for a new home. Rockefeller, in 1929, was left with a long-term annual lease commitment of $3.3 million and a difficult decision: whether to abandon the development or to build alone. He chose to build; hence the name Rockefeller Center.

What Rockefeller and his associates built in place of the opera house was a business and entertainment complex, an urban concept far in advance of its period. It had long been the ambition of farsighted architects and real estate men to develop a large plot for business purposes in the heart of Manhattan under conditions that could fully utilize light, air, and transportation. The proposed midtown development offered this rare opportunity, and the center's original architects (Reinhard and Hofmeister; Corbett, Harrison and MacMurray; and Hood and Fouilhoux) rose to the challenge. The result was a pioneering three-dimensional approach to urban design. Skyscrapers were planned in relation to one another and to the open space. The original structures were placed in the three-block plot where they could best contribute to the general architectural plan and provide the fullest exposure to sunlight and the free circulation of air.

Rockefeller Center was the first large real estate project in which extensive landscaping, at both street and rooftop levels, was a planned part of the whole. Fifteen percent of the land was reserved for spacious promenades and plazas. The provision for the Channel Gardens, the six formal beds running from Fifth Avenue to the Lower Plaza, restored Dr. Hosack's dream of maintaining the site as an oasis of beauty in an ever-growing city. Each year more than twenty thousand plants bloom in the gardens, including such favorites as lilies in the spring, tropical plants in the summer, and hardy chrysanthemums in the fall.

The colorful Lower Plaza is the setting for ice-skating in the winter and alfresco dining in the summer. Here distinguished visitors are greeted, important milestones are commemorated, and public service events are held. Band concerts and choral programs entertain the people, and the annual arrival of the "most beautiful tree in the world" signals the start of the Christmas season in Manhattan.

During eight months of the year, beginning with the first springtime floral display in the Channel Gardens and ending with Thanksgiving Day, the flags of the member countries of the United Nations are flown every day, weather permitting, along Rockefeller Plaza and the esplanade around the Lower Plaza. As new countries are admitted to the world organization, their national flags are added to the center's flag display.

On November 1, 1939, John D. Rockefeller, Jr., drove a silver rivet to mark the completion of the "last" building in Rockefeller Center. By the end of World War II, the original fourteen buildings proved inadequate to meet the needs of existing tenants, and the center was expanded across Sixth Avenue and onto neighboring side streets.

IN 1932, THE MUSEUM OF THE CITY OF NEW YORK MOVED INTO ITS PRESENT BUILDING ON UPPER FIFTH AVENUE

When it was founded in 1923, the Museum of the City of New York was housed in Gracie Mansion, the late eighteenth-century town house that is now the mayor's official residence. When it became inadequate for museum purposes, the present Georgian structure was built on Fifth Avenue between 103rd and 104th streets by popular subscription and was opened to the public in 1932. Today, with plans for expansion in the near future, the museum fulfills the unique purpose of documenting three hundred years of the city's history—the growth of New York City from a small settlement on the tip of Manhattan Island to the giant metropolis of today. The permanent collections and exhibitions include theatrical and marine material, costumes, furniture, silver, portraits, prints, toys, and many other treasures rarely seen outside the houses of New York's oldest families.

In addition to its permanent and special exhibitions, the museum has excellent research facilities available by appointment to anyone interested in the city's history. The main library contains more than fourteen hundred works on different aspects of the city. The new Dazian Library, a definitive collection of materials on the visual arts of the stage, is also available for students, historians, and designers.

The range of artifacts in the museum's collections is extensive. The costume, furniture, and silver collections include a large number of distinguished examples of the decorative arts in each of these fields. The print collection numbers half a million items—photographs, paintings, prints, and postcards. The theater collection contains the most complete history of the New York stage ever assembled. The marine museum spans three hundred years of the city's marine history, and the toy collection includes fine examples from the entire area of playthings with the doll and dollhouse collections so richly endowed that they constitute independent collections.

On the fifth floor are two rooms from the John D. Rockefeller house that stood at 4 West 54th Street, currently the site of the garden of the Museum of Modern Art. Rockefeller bought the house in 1884, twenty-five years after it was built. The rooms—a dressing room and a bedroom—were inspired by 1880 designs of an English architect, Charles Eastlake. Satinwood with rosewood woodwork inlaid with mother-of-pearl and intricate carvings are the dominant characteristics, reflecting the grandeur of Victorian taste.

Future plans for the museum include the completion of the pictorial history of the city, a plan that was begun with the Dutch gallery. A British gallery, a nineteenth-century gallery, a twentieth-century gallery, and a twenty-first-century gallery are on the drawing boards.

AFTER THE JAPANESE ATTACK ON PEARL HARBOR, THE UNITED STATES ENTERED THE WAR IN DECEMBER, 1941, AND FIFTH AVENUE ONCE AGAIN REFLECTED THE EVENTS OF THE NATION

Within a month after the United States entered World War II, Fifth Avenue was renamed Street of Mercy as the members of the American Red Cross marched up the Avenue in a plea for contributions to their $50 million National War Fund. Several months later, in May, 1942, the Avenue was to become USO Avenue of Heroes, and portraits of 103 American war heroes were placed on display in shop windows. Throughout the war, parades of troops and bond drive parades could be seen on the Avenue, and in June, 1944, just after D-Day, the Avenue became the Avenue of the Allies. Lampposts bore the names of the allied countries, and flags of all the allied nations flapped before the public library.

During the war the library at 42nd Street and Fifth was the scene of a great intelligence breakthrough. In 1943, American intelligence learned that a secret Japanese naval code was based on a Mexico City telephone directory of the 1920s. A copy of this directory no longer existed in Mexico. The New York Public Library, however, whose collection of city directories and telephone books is unequaled, had a copy, and the naval code was broken.

JUST BEFORE V-J DAY IN 1945, A TWIN-ENGINED B-25 BOMBER EN ROUTE FROM MASSACHUSETTS TO NEWARK LOST ITS BEARINGS OVER MANHATTAN AND CRASHED INTO THE EMPIRE STATE BUILDING

It was close to 10 A.M. on a hazy Saturday, and the tower of the Empire State Building was barely visible through the fog. Suddenly, people on the street below turned their eyes skyward as they heard the sputtering of an aircraft engine. For a second the plane seemed to veer away from the building, but then, lost in the mist, it crashed into the seventy-ninth floor, 913 feet above the street.

A huge ball of fire shot one hundred feet into the air, and the entire top of the building appeared to be on fire. Pieces of the flaming aircraft fell to the street below, as pedestrians quickly dashed into nearby shops and entranceways. Inside the building, the seventy-eighth and seventy-ninth floors were ablaze, and terrified occupants tried to rush to safety. The force of the collision had driven a hole eighteen feet wide in the facade of the building, and the aircraft cut across the entire building to the 33rd Street side. Elevators in the structure plummeted to the ground floor. The three officers in the plane and eleven people in the building were killed. Because it was Saturday and few workers were in the building, many lives were spared.

ON AUGUST 14, 1945, WORLD WAR II ENDED AND FIFTH AVENUE WAS JAMMED WITH CELEBRANTS

The waiting went on for five days. On August 9, all signs indicated that the Japanese were ready to surrender. For five days following the first indication, days of rising hopes and sinking disappointments, New York waited for the end of the war. Then word came. "Official—Truman announces Japanese surrender!" The words appeared on the Times Tower at 7:03 P.M., and within minutes millions jammed the streets of the city.

Chapter Seven

AND TO THE PRESENT

CHRONOLOGY

1946   The United Nations selects New York as its permanent headquarters.

1947   Rockefeller family donates tract at First Avenue north of 42nd Street to the United Nations.

1948   Work begins on permanent UN headquarters.

International Airport at Idlewild, Queens, opens.

1950   New York City population is 7,891,957.

Brooklyn-Battery Tunnel opens.

1952   Lever House opens on Park Avenue, setting trend for transformation of Park Avenue.

1955   Lincoln Center project proposed and approved by city.

1956   Ebbets Field sold as site for housing. Brooklyn Dodgers baseball team leaves New York.

1957   City passes the nation's first fair-housing-practices law, outlawing discrimination.

1958   Seagram Building completed on Park Avenue.

1959   Ground broken for Lincoln Center.

1960   New York City population is 7,781,984.

World Trade Center proposed.

1963   Pennsylvania Station razed.

1964   New York World's Fair of 1964-65 opens.

1965   CBS Building opens.

Great Blackout.

1966   Fifth Avenue made a one-way street.

1968   Robert Kennedy Funeral held in New York.

1969   Vietnam Peace Moratorium held on steps of St. Patrick's Cathedral.

1970   Earth Day celebrated on Fifth Avenue.

After World War II, the second great era of construction in the city's history got under way. New buildings arose like mushrooms in Lower Manhattan. The Third Avenue elevated line was torn down to make way for new housing. Sixth Avenue became a cavern of high-rise buildings, and virtually a ghost town after dark. Park Avenue below 57th Street also saw vast changes as corporation after corporation constructed office facilities on the sites of former apartment houses.

The great middle class exodus occurred, as thousands of New Yorkers fled from the city to the suburbs. During the late 1940s and the 1950s, a new immigrant group settled in the city. Nearly one million Puerto Ricans took up residence in East Harlem and the West Side. To a large extent the city became a place where only the very rich and the very poor lived.

Fifth Avenue changed too as the remaining nineteenth-century landmarks were razed. Lower Fifth lost the Brevoort, the Mark Twain, and the Rhinelander houses and the Brevoort Hotel to apartment houses. Fifth Avenue in midtown lost the last of the mansions that had survived the depression and the war, as the Gould house at 46th Street and the last of the Vanderbilt houses were razed. Farther north, many of the remaining mansions gave way to large apartment buildings.

During the 1960s, sober processions and political demonstrations on Fifth Avenue replaced the extravaganzas, elaborate weddings, and balls of earlier eras. Now, in the 1970s, Fifth Avenue faces a crisis that could end its history as America's Avenue of Avenues.

IN MARCH, 1947, FIFTH AVENUE WITNESSED ONE OF THE MOST BIZARRE EVENTS IN ITS HISTORY

About one o'clock in the afternoon on March 22, the police department received an anonymous telephone tip that a man lay dead in a decaying brownstone at 2078 Fifth Avenue, just north of Mount Morris Park. Arriving at the address, police found a gathering crowd, for this was the home of Homer and Langley Collyer, brothers who were well-known in the neighborhood for their eccentricity. As the police tried to force open the front door, they were confronted with a solid wall of newspapers and magazines. First-floor windows were also blocked with baricades of junk, as were basement doors and second-story windows. Entry to the house was finally gained through a rear window in the basement.

Once inside, the police were appalled by what they saw. The entire house from cellar to attic was filled with junk. The area near the basement door contained an old stove, several umbrellas, numerous packages of newspapers, a gas-mask canister, an old pipe, and a broken scooter. A tiny corridor led through the mess into the cellar, but it was difficult to imagine how anything larger than rats, many of which infested the building, could pass to and fro.

After wandering through the passageways for several hours, police discovered the body of Homer Collyer in a sitting position, wearing only a tattered gray bathrobe. The medical examiner reported that the man had been dead for only ten hours.

The police made a further inspection and reported the building was honeycombed with tunnellike passageways. Neighbors said that Langley, who could not be found, had crawled through these tunnels, placing packages behind him to block the way of intruders. Throughout the house, tin cans rigged to wires and piles of debris formed booby traps for unwelcome visitors.

There were no signs of the seven pianos and the old automobile that, according to rumor, also lay in the building. As the police dug through the debris, however, they discovered, among other trash, broken sleds, an automobile seat, a box of Christmas cards, metal folding chairs, part of a piano frame, and two black hats. Around five o'clock, the junk was put back in the house, and the building was boarded up.

In the meantime, a neighbor protested, saying that Langley was still in the building. Shortly thereafter, the brothers' lawyer arrived and stated that, if Langley were still alive, he would be in touch with him. The lawyer filled in the story. The brothers were good scholars, possessed a great deal of money, and were entirely rational at all times. They had moved into the neighborhood just after the turn of the century when the Mount Morris Park area along Fifth Avenue was quite fashionable.

For nearly half a century, the Collyer brothers had been Harlem's most fascinating mystery. There were no gas, water, electricity, or sewer connections in the house. They admitted no one to their home, and as McMullen, the lawyer, explained, "Langley said they were entitled to live their own lives." Every evening after dark, Langley left the house for a walk, sometimes strolling as far as the Williamsburg section of Brooklyn, to buy food for his brother. Langley had said at one time that his brother Homer was ill, but that they did not believe in doctors.

The following day the search for Langley began. Neighbors stood around gaping and commenting, "He's right up there laughing at you!" The decision was made that, if Langley did not appear by 1:30 P.M., a thorough investigation would be made. Two days later, on March 24, Langley had not turned up, but from one of the rooms of the house the police had removed five pianos, an electric generator, a dressmaking dummy, twenty-five hundred books, gas chandeliers, a carriage top, bed springs, a kerosine stove, a checkerboard, advertisements featuring bathing beauties of the 1900s, a program from a February, 1914, performance of *The Magic Flute,* a box of green toy tops, and a box of half-price tickets for *Angela,* a musical comedy of 1929.

By March 27, rumors were flying that Langley had been seen in Macy's. That day the house re-vealed a potato peeler, a nursery refrigerator, a beaded lampshade, the chassis of an old car, a few more pianos, 6,424 pounds of newspapers, several tree limbs seven feet long, and tickets to an excursion of the Sunday School of Trinity Episcopal Church to Glen Island for July 8, 1905.

Still the search continued. By April 8, 103 tons of junk from the house had accumulated. Then on April 11, Langley's body was finally discovered wedged in a booby trap set to keep out intruders. He was lying in the same room where the body of blind Homer had been found nearly three weeks before. The cause of death was unknown, but apparently he starved or was suffocated through inability to get out of his own trap. Piles of newspapers, books, tin cans, and old furniture filled the room. The two-foot-wide passageway in which the body was discovered also contained a chest of drawers on one side and an old bedspring on the other.

A suitcase, bundles of newspapers, and three metal bread boxes rested on the partly decomposed body, which had been gnawed by rats. The trap was probably tripped by Langley during an illness. By that time 120 tons of junk had been removed from the house, including a total of fourteen grand pianos and a Model T Ford.

Soon afterward, neighbors came forward and gave the police further details about the eccentric brothers. Langley had once told them that a diet of oranges would cure Homer's blindness and bad health. It was said that, together with scraps that he picked up from butchers, grocers, and garbage cans, he and his brother consumed as many as one hundred oranges a week. Langley, formerly a concert pianist, had kept the pianos in the house so that he could play for his brother, and the newspapers were saved for Homer, who would want to catch up on the news when he regained his eyesight.

The brothers, descendants of a family who emigrated to American in 1640, had as many as forty relatives who survived them. Their total assets came to at least $100,000 deposited in banks and twice that amount in stock certificates, which were found in the house. Several years later, Marcia Davenport used some of the Collyers' story in her novel *My Brother's Keeper.*

IN 1957, TIFFANY'S, WHICH MOVED INTO ITS PRESENT BUILDING IN 1940, SUSTAINED A SPECTACULAR ROBBERY

At 5:45 A.M. on August 11, a patrolman, who generally covered the neighborhood at Fifth Avenue and 57th Street, was relieved of his usual duty to reinforce a detail assigned to guard Soviet Foreign Minister Andrei Gromyko. Another patrolman was sent to relieve him, but did not arrive on the beat until 6:05 A.M. Ten minutes later, he discovered the robbery.

Thieves had used sledgehammers to break through two windows on the Fifth Avenue side of the building, where the internationally famous jeweler customarily displayed silver and costly jewels. The glass, five-eighths of an inch thick, with a binder of a cementlike substance, was shatterproof, and the pounding of the instruments on the glass made only a dull noise, not heard at any distance. Two holes, five inches by seven inches, were cut in the glass, and the thieves took two diamond necklaces, a diamond ring, and a diamond clip, worth $163,300. Undaunted, Tiffany's replaced the window glass, and late in the afternoon of the same day placed another display of diamonds worth $130,000 in the two windows. The thieves were never apprehended and the case remains a mystery to this day.

IN 1959, THE GUGGENHEIM MUSEUM, DESIGNED BY FRANK LLOYD WRIGHT, OPENED

Toward the end of 1958, Fifth Avenue waited patiently for the completion of its newest and most controversial structure, the Solomon R. Guggenheim Museum between 88th and 89th streets. The great architect Frank Lloyd Wright had originally wished the museum to be placed in Central Park, but ultimately, after long and bitter arguments with the City Planning Commission over zoning ordinances and after changing his original designs, he agreed to the Fifth Avenue location. To complicate matters further, during the excavation of the site, a meandering brook was discovered, which prevented the construction of a subcellar. Although Wright lived to see the completion of the exterior, he died in May, 1950, and never saw the unique spiral-ramped interior. The museum was opened to the public in October of that year.

To date, the most successful of the Guggenheim's many exhibitions has been the retrospective of the work of Alexander Calder, mounted in 1964. The show featured mobiles and stabiles and a number of mechanical contraptions. Push buttons were installed to set the works in motion. The show was particularly appealing to children, who became "involved" in the works of art. This was probably the first of the participatory exhibitions in the city, and set the trend for many shows of this sort.

The permanent collection includes 130 paintings by Kandinski, as well as many works by Chagall, Klee, Marc, Léger, Calder, Archipenko, and Brancusi.

The Empire State Building on December 16, 1930, with a U.S. Navy blimp flying above it. Originally, the tower was designed as a mooring mast for airships.

A view of Central Park from Fifth Avenue.

Theodore Roosevelt on June 18, 1910, at the parade held in his honor upon his return from a year in Africa and Europe.

The anti-Prohibition parade on Fifth Avenue, July 4, 1921.

Theodore Roosevelt on June 18, 1910, at the parade held in his honor upon his return from a year in Africa and Europe.

Fifth Avenue and 34th Street during the early 1920s, showing the traffic tower and the double-decker buses. It was atop one of the traffic towers that Zelda Fitzgerald had her picture taken drinking champagne.

Tiffany at the southeast corner of Fifth Avenue and 57th Street.

A Tiffany window designed by Robert Rauschenberg and Jasper Johns in the mid-fifties.

The Empire State Building as it looks today.

The tower of the Empire State Building.

The mall at Rockefeller Center.

Detail from the building which stands on the
northeast corner of Fifth Avenue and 57th Street.

Detail, Rockefeller Center.

A view of one of the towers of Rockefeller Center.

The Museum of the City of New York on Fifth Avenue between 103rd

and 104th streets. It was designed by Joseph H. Freedlander in 1932.

Temple Emanu-El at 1 East 65th Street, built in 1929 on the site of "the" Mrs. Astor's house. The huge hall within seats more worshipers than St. Patrick's Cathedral.

Fifth Avenue at Christmas. Lord and
Taylor's light display is on the right.

A horse and carriage at Grand Army Plaza.

The end of Fifth Avenue at 142nd Street in Harlem.

Participants in the Women's Liberation march in August, 1970.

Frank Lloyd Wright's Solomon R. Guggenheim Museum on Fifth Avenue
between 88th and 89th streets. The building was erected in 1959.

The dome of the Solomon R. Guggenheim
Museum, designed by Frank Lloyd Wright.

Bonwit Teller on the northeast corner of Fifth Avenue and 56th Street.

A view from St. Patrick's Cathedral. The now
defunct Best and Company is on the left.

Samuel Paley Plaza, just off Fifth Avenue on East 53rd Street. It was designed by
Zion and Breen, landscape architects, and Preston Moore, consulting architect.

Fifth Avenue at Christmas.

IN 1968, A NEW MUSEUM OPENED IN THE REGION OF UPPER FIFTH AVENUE KNOWN AS SPANISH HARLEM

The Harlem Studio Museum, situated just north of Mount Morris Park on 125th Street at 2033 Fifth Avenue, opened in September, 1968, after three years of planning. It is primarily concerned with exhibitions of African-American and African art. Just to the south in Mount Morris Park stands the lone survivor of many fire towers that once existed in New York. Designed by James Bogardus in 1857, it features "the same post-and-lintel construction [which the architect] used in his cast-iron warehouses."

DURING THE 1960S, FIFTH AVENUE'S DEMONSTRATIONS WERE DECIDEDLY DIFFERENT IN CHARACTER FROM ANY IN ITS HISTORY

Early in the decade, Fifth Avenue's public demonstrations assumed a serious tone. In November, 1963, Fifth Avenue, with the rest of the nation, was draped in black, as pictures of the assassinated John Fitzgerald Kennedy appeared in windows all along the Avenue.

The following year, during the riots in Harlem, a number of Fifth Avenue windows were shattered by marching militants.

In October, 1965, Pope Paul visited New York to address the United Nations on world peace. The first pope ever to visit the United States, His Holiness said mass at St. Patrick's Cathedral.

One month later, Fifth Avenue and the entire northeast were darkened in the Great Blackout. The Palm Court of the Plaza Hotel reverted to nineteenth-century elegance, as hundreds of candles were placed in the sconces and on the tables. Candles burned everywhere that night, which marked the beginning of the breakdown in essential services.

In January, 1966, Fifth Avenue and the rest of the city became the scene of a monumental traffic jam, as the city's transit workers went on strike, closing down all public transportation.

Half a million people from all over the country poured into the city in the spring of 1968 and paraded across Grand Army Plaza in protest against the Vietnam War. In June, the body of assassinated Robert F. Kennedy lay in state in St. Patrick's Cathedral. Tens of thousands of mourners stood in a mile-long line to pay their final respects.

In October, 1969, thousands of people took part in a candlelight vigil on the steps of St. Patrick's Cathedral on the night of the Vietnam Moratorium.

Earth Day was declared in the spring of 1970, and thousands of people turned out onto Fifth Avenue to promenade and to express their concern for the polluted environment.

During that summer, fifty thousand women marched down the Avenue in support of the Women's Liberation movement.

BY 1970, FIFTH AVENUE HAD ENTERED A NEW, AND PERHAPS FINAL, STAGE OF ITS HISTORY

It had become quite clear by autumn of 1970 that, unless something was done immediately, Fifth Avenue was in danger of becoming another cavern of immense corporate offices. Year by year, the retailers had been vacating space that had become too expensive for them, and in their places banks, travel agencies, and airline offices moved in. In 1969, De Pinna closed its doors forever, as the building that it occupied at 52nd Street and Fifth was scheduled for demolition. Georg Jensen moved from Fifth Avenue to Madison Avenue because of too high rent. At 51st Street, late in 1970, Best and Company, a fine retail store and a landmark since the Civil War, went out of business and sold its building to Aristotle Onassis and Arlen Properties, Inc., who plan to build a forty-five-story building on the site.

In March, 1970, a special retail zoning district was proposed for Fifth Avenue by the city's planners through the Office of Midtown Planning and Development. The *New York Times* in an editorial entitled "Can Fifth Avenue Be Saved?" wrote: "[The plan] is a breakthrough being pioneered by New York and watched by the rest of the country. It would save Fifth Avenue as a great shopping street." The plan was passed and features pedestrian circulation, transportation connections, and public amenities that go far beyond the traditional limitations of building size. "These coupled with the objective of a street lined solidly with quality shops topped by new offices andapartments is a brilliant planning triple play," to quote the *Times*.

Implicit in the plan is a retailing area with two or three stories fronting on the street. Ninety percent of the area must be rented to retailers. Banks, airlines, and travel offices may occupy only the remaining 10 percent of the ground floor space. In addition, the office tower, set behind the shops, may also provide for residential floors at the top. Entrances to the buildings must be on the side streets or in a north-south arcade between Fifth and Madison to run the length of the Avenue. The arcade would be lined with boutiques, restaurants, and service stores. In exchange for these amenities, the zoning ordinance would allow the builders bonuses of office space in the towers. It remains to be seen whether or not the plan will work. If successful, it could redeem many of the luxury shops and department stores presently in financial trouble.

Fifth Avenue, as we have known it for the past fifty years, has been given a last chance for survival. With foresight and luck, perhaps America's Avenue of Avenues will blossom into a new and vital stage of its existence.

BIBLIOGRAPHY

Abels, Jules.   *The Rockefeller Billions.* New York: Macmillan, 1965.

Amory, Cleveland.   *The Last Resorts.* New York: Harper, 1952.
                     Who Killed Society? New York: Harper, 1960.

Andrews, Wayne.   *The Vanderbilt Legend: The Story of the Vanderbilt Family—1794-1940.* New York: Harcourt, Brace, 1941.

Benet, Laura.   *Thackeray, of the Great Heart and Humorous Pen.* New York: Dodd, Mead, 1947.

Berger, Meyer.   *New York.* New York: Random House, 1960.

Birmingham, Stephen.   *Our Crowd.* New York: Harper and Row, 1967.
                        The Right People. Boston: Little, Brown, 1968.

Bonner, W. T.   *New York: The World's Metropolis.* New York: Polk. 1924.

Botkin, Benjamin Albert.   *New York City Folklore.* New York: Random House, 1956.

Brock, Henry Irving.   *New York Is Like This.* New York: Dodd, Mead, 1929.

Brown, Henry Collins.   *Fifth Avenue: Old and New—1824-1924.* New York: The Fifth Avenue Association, 1924.
In The Golden Nineties. Hastings-on-Hudson: Valentine's Manual, 1928.
Valentine's Manual of the City of New York for 1916-7. New York: The Valentine Co., 1916.
Valentine's Manual of the City of New York—1917-18. New York: Old Colony Press, 1917.
Valentine's Manual of Old New York—1919. New York: Valentine's Manual, 1918.
Valentine's Manual of Old New York—1920. New York: Valentine's Manual, 1919.
Valentine's Manual of Old New York—1921. New York: Valentine's Manual, 1920.
Valentine's Manual of Old New York—1922. New York: Valentine's Manual, 1921.
Valentine's Manual of Old New York—1923. New York: Valentine's Manual, 1922.
Valentine's Manual of Old New York—1924. New York: Valentine's Manual, 1923.
Valentine's Manual of Old New York—1925. Museum of the City of New York, 1924.

Valentine's Manual of Old New York—1926. New York: Valentine's Manual, 1925.

Valentine's Manual of Old New York—1927. New York: Valentine's Manual, 1926.

Brownstone Fronts and Saratoga Trunks. New York: Dutton, 1935.

The Story of Old New York. New York: Dutton, 1934.

From Alley Pond to Rockefeller Center. New York: Dutton, 1936.

Burnham, Alan.   *New York Landmarks: A Study and Index of Architecturally Notable Structures in Greater New York.* Middletown, Conn.: Wesleyan University Press, 1963.

Churchill, Allen.   *The Upper Crust.* Englewood Cliffs, N.J.: Prentice Hall, 1969.

Crouse, Russel.   *It Seems Like Yesterday.* New York: Doubleday, 1931.

Davis, Kenneth Sydney.   *The Hero: Charles A. Lindbergh and the American Dream.* Garden City, N.Y.: Doubleday, 1959.

Dickens, Charles.   *American Notes and Pictures from Italy.* London: Macmillan, 1893.

Dreiser, Theodore.   *Sister Carrie.* New York: The Heritage Press, 1939.

Dunlop, Agnes.   *The Swedish Nightingale, Jenny Lind.* New York: Holt, 1965.

Ellis, Edward Robb.   *The Epic of New York City.* New York: Coward-McCann, 1966.

Fitzgerald, F. Scott.   *Six Tales of the Jazz Age.* New York: Scribner's, 1950.

Foley, Doris.   *The Divine Eccentric: Lola Montez and the Newspapers.* Los Angeles: Westernlore Press, 1969.

Geller, G. S.   *Sarah Bernhardt.* London: Duckworth, 1933.

Gordon, John and Hills, L. Rust, eds.   *New York, New York—The City as Seen by Masters of Art and Literature.* New York: Shorecrest, 1965.

Hewitt, Edward Ringwood.   *Those Were the Days: Tales of a Long Life.* New York: Duell, 1943.

Holland, Henry Scott.   *Memoir of Miss Jenny Lind – Goldschmidt.* New York: Scribner's, 1891.

Hoyt, Edwin Palmer.   *The Vanderbilts and Their Fortunes.* Garden City, N.Y.: Doubleday, 1962.

James, Henry.   *The American Novels and Stories of Henry James.* New York: Knopf, 1947.

The American Scene. New York and London: Harper, 1907.

Kavaler, Lucy.   *The Astors: A Family Chronicle of Pomp and Power.* New York: Dodd Mead, 1966.

Kouwenhoven, John Atlee.   *The Columbia Historical Portrait of New York.* Garden City, N.Y.: Doubleday, 1953.

Lamb, Martha J. *History of the City of New York.* New York: Barnes, 1877, 1888.

Larkin, Oliver W. *Art and Life in America.* New York: Rinehart, 1959.

Lerman, Leo. *The Museum: 100 Years and The Metropolitan Museum of Art.* New York: Viking, 1969.

Lewis, Lloyd and Smith, Henry Justin. *Oscar Wilde Discovers America.* New York: Harcourt, Brace, 1936.

Lord, Walter. *The Good Years: From 1900 to the First World War.* New York: Harper, 1960.
A Night to Remember. New York: Holt, 1955.

McCague, James. *The Second Rebellion: The Story of the New York City Draft Riots of 1863.* New York: Dial Press, 1968.

McDarrah, Fred W. *Museums in New York.* New York: Dutton, 1967.

Manchester, William R. *A Rockefeller Family Portrait from John D. to Nelson.* Boston: Little, Brown, 1959.

Mayer, Grace M. *Once Upon a City: New York from 1890-1910 as Photographed by Byron.* New York: Macmillan, 1958.

Munsey's Magazine. Many editions.

New York Magazine. Many editions.

Pearson, Hesketh. *Oscar Wilde: His Life and Wit.* New York and London: Harper, 1946.

Ray, Randolph. *My Little Church Around the Corner.* New York: Simon and Schuster, 1957.

Reed, Henry Hope and Duckworth, Sophia. *Central Park: A History and a Guide.* New York: C. N. Potter, 1967.

Ross, Walter Sanford. *The Last Hero: Charles A. Lindbergh.* New York: Harper and Row, 1967.

Shaw, Charles Green. *New York Oddly Enough.* New York and Toronto: Farrar and Rinehart, 1938.

Silver, Nathan. *Lost New York.* Boston: Houghton Mifflin, 1967.

Skinner, Cornelia Otis. *Madame Sarah.* Boston: Houghton Mifflin, 1967.

Smith, Arthur and Howden, Douglas. *John Jacob Astor, Landlord of New York.* New York: Blue Ribbon Books, 1931.

Starrett, William Aiken. *Empire State, A Pictorial Record of its Construction.* New York: William Edwin Rudge, 1931.

Stevenson, Lionel. *The Showman of Vanity Fair, The Life of William Makepeace Thackeray.* New York: Scribner's, 1947.

Still, Bayrd. *Mirror for Gotham: New York as Seen by Contemporaries from Dutch Days to the Present.* New York: University Press, 1956.

Strong, George Templeton.   *The Diary of George Templeton Strong.* Edited by Allan Nevins and Milton Halsey Thomas. New York: Macmillan, 1952.

Sullivan, Mark.   *Our Times: The United States.* Volumes 1-6. New York: Scribner's, 1926-1935.

Talese, Gay.   *New York, A Serendipiter's Journey.* New York: Harper and Row, 1961.

Tillotson, Geoffrey.   *Thackeray the Novelist.* Cambridge: University Press, 1954.

The New York Times.   Many editions.

Tompkins, Calvin.   *Merchants and Masterpieces: The Story of the Metropolitan Museum of Art.* New York: Dutton, 1970.

Torrey, Raymond H.   *New York Walkbook.* New York: American Geographical Society, 1951.

Toth, David Goldsmith.   *The City Within a City; The Romance of Rockefeller Center.* New York: Morrow, 1966.

Towner, Wesley. Completed by Stephen Varble.   *The Elegant Auctioneers.* New York: Hill and Wang, 1970.

The New York Herald Tribune   Many editions.

Ulmann, Albert.   *A Landmark History of New York.* New York: Appleton, 1901.

Valentine, David T.   *Obsequies of Abraham Lincoln in the City of New York.* New York: Edmund Jones and Company, 1866.

Vanderbilt, Cornelius.   *Queen of the Golden Age: The Fabulous Story of Grace Wilson Vanderbilt.* New York: McGraw Hill, 1956.

Vanity Fair.   Many issues.

Van Wyck, Frederick.   *Recollection of an Old New Yorker.* New York: Liveright, 1932.

Walker, Stanley.   *Mrs. Astor's Horse.* New York: Frederick A. Stokes, 1935.

The Night Club Era. New York: Stokes, 1933.

Wall, Joseph Frazier.   *Andrew Carnegie.* New York: Oxford University Press, 1970.

Wector, Dixon.   *The Saga of American Society: A Record of Social Aspiration.* New York: Scribner's, 1937.

Wharton, Edith Newbold.   *A Backward Glance.* New York: Scribner's, 1933, 1964.
House of Mirth. New York: Appleton, 1905.

White, Elwynn Brooks.   *Here is New York.* New York: Harper, 1949.

Winkler, John Kennedy.   *Incredible Carnegie; the Life of Andrew Carnegie.* New York: Vanguard Press, 1931.

Wallace, Irving.   *The Fabulous Showman: The Life and Times of P. T. Barnum.* New York: Knopf, 1959.